What Did Jesus Drive?

Crisis PR in Cars, Computers and Christianity

Jason H. Vines

Published by Waldorf Publishing
2140 Hall Johnson Road
#102-345
Grapevine, Texas 76051
www.WaldorfPublishing.com

What Did Jesus Drive: Crisis PR in Cars, Computers and Christianity
ISBN: 9781942748113

Library of Congress Control Number: 2014948136

Printed in the United States of America

Table of Contents

Introduction

Relax, this is not a book about Jesus. However, He does appear in two chapters: first as a Hispanic grandfather from Waterford, Michigan, and later as the real Prince of Peace. No, this is a book primarily about my life in the public relations blast furnace in the automotive industry, along with a quickly-derailed attempt to help a friend rebuild Detroit's tattered image and, finally, trying to avoid another crisis with the number-one selling book of all time. No, not Harry Potter; the Bible.

I share lessons learned and mistakes made on some of the biggest PR stages in the world. If I can impart anything in this book, it would be the numerous guiding principles I believe useful for any organization or individual to avoid, mitigate or survive the inevitable crisis. If you think you are immune, you've already failed an overarching guiding principle.

I start this book with a simple question: why is it so difficult to tell the truth? Sadly, spoiler alert, I end it with the same question.

But first, let me share with you how I got into this crazy business. As a child I should have known that someday I would make a career out of public relations and be front and center in the biggest crises ever to hit two industries – automobiles and Christian publishing – and one major American city: Detroit.

I grew up in the metropolis of Pella, Iowa: home of the famous windows and surrounded by farms. It was founded in the mid-1800s by very religious Dutch folks escaping persecution in their native land. Almost everybody was Dutch; enough Vans and Vanders and DeKocks to plug a dike. We were Irish mutts with roots in Arkansas; my dad born in Oil Trough (no shit) and my mom from a small town just a few miles from a little town called Hope. Yep, Bubba Clinton's home.

To celebrate its roots, Pella's 6,000 residents held a three-day event every May called Tulip Time. There were parades, a Tulip queen (my "first love" at age five, was a Tulip queen), Dutch dancing, Dutch food and millions of tulips all imported from the Netherlands. The friendly people of Pella had forgiven their ancestors' persecutors for past transgressions and demanded only the best bulbs from the motherland. Besides, The Netherlands had moved on from killing certain Christians and had embraced prostitution and heroin as modern and legal businesses.

In the parades were marching bands from public junior and senior high schools where I attended. The private Christian school was also represented. We referred to the Pella Christian kids as the "offies." It was Dutch for "the others." To be honest, it was akin to calling an Italian a dago or black kid by the N-word; not racial in this case, but offensive nonetheless. Along with bands were the classes of every grade marching through the downtown in hideous Dutch costumes and the world's second worst product idea: wooden shoes that I am certain caused crippling diseases later in life. (The worst product idea? Ron Popiel's Pocket Fisherman.)

In 1968, eight-year-old Jason Vines was given a rare opportunity: I could skip the march in those hideous shoes, replace them with sneakers, and help my classmate's grandpa in "parade maintenance." I jumped at the opportunity and made sure it was OK with my folks who seemed genuinely thrilled.

Day one of the festival I was joined by my friend Arlen DeHere and his grandpa. His name was Slick Boffman. That should have given away what was to come, but hell, I was only eight. Slick, who I am sure hadn't been laid since the 1920s, actually smelled like he hadn't bathed since that roaring time. He was "colorful" but I think it was four decades of grime. Ol' Slick handed a shovel to each of us and proceeded to grab his wheel barrel, urging us to fall in line. Stationed immediately behind several details of mounted police and other parade riders we traversed the entire parade route, cleaning up after the elephants, er, horses in the parade. As I

6

passed my parents, I saw my mom in utter horror and my dad laughing his ass off. He took as many shots as humanly possible with his Argus C3 camera.

From that moment forward I was destined to clean up other people's shit for a living. The good news; it ended paying a lot better than the $20 ol' Slick gave each of us for three days work staring at a horse's ass. Thankfully, only a few of the crises I would clean up later in life were indeed looking at the ass end of a horse.

Chapter One: A Thermal Event

I entered the public relations profession by accident. Sure, I had an undergraduate degree in communications, another in economics, and a master's degree in Labor and Industrial Relations. My plan was to work for a few years and then go to law school. When Chrysler's HR department was put in charge of Employee Communications, they asked me to work there for several weeks until the required plant assignment came along. The assignment they offered was in Personnel at a local Detroit facility. Immediately, an image of Clint Eastwood came to mind. In one of his Dirty Harry movies, Clint gets busted for some infraction and is demoted to Personnel. His response: "Personnel? That's for assholes!"

No thanks, I'll stay where I am.

I somehow caught the eye of Joe Cappy, the last CEO of American Motors before Lee Iacocca scooped it up in order to get his hands on the Jeep brand. Cappy was put in charge of the new Jeep-Eagle division. The Jeeps would soon turn into a gold mine; the Eagle division was an unmitigated disaster. I was soon writing speeches for Cappy and he wanted me to join his marketing organization. On the Friday before I was to start, Joe called and asked a favor: would I go into PR instead? The Eagle PR chief had just been shit-canned and he needed that spot filled. Marketing? PR? What's the difference?

I would soon learn.

Within a couple years I was out of Eagle and promoted to PR for the safety, regulatory and high tech issues Chrysler faced. My first week, one of Chrysler's lawyers came to my office and said we were going to issue a recall on our Dodge Dakota pickup for a wiring harness issue.

"I haven't done a press release for a recall yet," I admitted.

"Not to worry, we normally write the first draft," he arrogantly expressed - as only an attorney can - while handing over a copy.

The press release stated that a failure to fix the vehicle could lead to "a thermal event."

I was young, but not stupid.

I asked him, "What the hell is a thermal event?"

"Um," he paused, "The vehicle could catch on fire."

"Holy shit," I screamed, "Then say so!"

Right out of the gate, I knew that guiding an organization, group or individual through a crisis meant being straightforward – not bullshitting the troops. Customers must come first, well ahead of any legal maneuvering or mumbo-jumbo. A thermal event? Sweet Jesus.

Within a few years "The Thermal Event" would look like child's play as I stared down the barrel of a crisis in the 90's that threatened to put Chrysler out of business.

Shortly thereafter, I was in the middle of the largest crisis in the history of the auto industry; the fight between Ford Motor Company and Firestone. I have navigated multiple crises in between and afterward. I quickly and sometimes painfully learned guiding principles to avoid or survive a crisis.

Crisis Lesson Learned: Tell it like it is, clearly and succinctly. Natalie Wood did not die from "excessive hydration." She drowned. And Tupac Shakur didn't die from "lead poisoning." He was shot. The art of being clever or linguistically illusive will compromise the integrity of your organization.

Chapter Two: Guiding Principles

The key to avoid, mitigate or survive a crisis is to accept the fact that one will come sooner than later. That requires getting ready for it - making sure your team knows how they are to respond, the critical roles they play, and the most important work each must do. Establishing your guiding principles in the midst of a crisis is not just dangerous – it's foolish. This will foster animosity between rival factions within your organization – PR vs. legal, finance vs. operations, etc.

In almost every circumstance, the number one guiding principle must always be protecting the safety and or/satisfaction of your customers. If legal (as in avoiding or preparing against potential lawsuits) or financial matters trump this guiding principle, you are prone to make decisions that will eventually hurt or destroy your "brand."

The Tylenol poisonings of the 1980s are generally cited as the way to correctly handle a major crisis; but I think Johnson & Johnson received a little too much credit. Don't get me wrong; they did the right thing and did so quickly by putting their customers' safety at the forefront. Nobody was blaming Tylenol, just some nut who had tainted its product. All Tylenol had to do is tell its retailers to dump the jars in a box and send them back for reimbursement. The Tylenol comparison came up all the time during the Firestone tire crisis. More on that later.

The second most important guiding principle is communicating openly, honestly and only with facts. Speculating is a hand grenade and, of course, lying is suicide. In July 2013, a Montreal Maine & Atlantic train carrying 72 cars of crude oil crashed and exploded in a small Quebec town, killing more than 70 and leveling the town. Soon after the crash, CEO Edward Burkhardt began publicly speculating about the crash. He first blamed the local fire department for "tampering" with the brakes while in the process of putting out a small fire just before the train lost control. The fire chief went nuts. Burkhardt then changed his story; he blamed one of his engineers.

The most often used cliché in PR is that a crisis is not the mistake made or deed done, but how you handle the aftermath. Team Nixon got caught in a third-rate burglary when Nixon's re-election was certain. But it was the cover-up that doomed him to disgrace. President Reagan's arms-for-hostages deal with Iran was much more serious in terms of national security, yet he took the blame – sort of – and the country moved on. Think about it: Oliver North has a show on Fox when he should be, some would argue, vilified as a criminal. People will forgive human frailty – they won't forgive outright deception.

When it was discovered that workers in Chrysler's St. Louis plant were driving new vehicles home with disconnected odometers, Chrysler CEO Lee Iacocca took the hit and said it "went beyond dumb and all the way to stupid." It was a two day story and then gone.

PR in a crisis cannot be cleaning up after the elephants in the parade. The PR team needs a seat at the table before, during and after a crisis. They have to have the guts to say when the emperor has no clothes. PR people that are "yes" people are worthless and do a disservice to any organization.

We live in a 24-hour news cycle which rewards only getting it first and not necessarily correctly. Turn on the news and you'll see the updated news scroll across the bottom of the screen. The words coming out of the anchor's mouth are already old. Historically, journalists would get multiple sources and you wouldn't see the story "in print" until the next day. Back then, the lowest common denominator in news was television. Now you see news – again, not always factual – almost instantaneously thanks to Twitter and the like. Mark Twain once said: "A lie can travel halfway around the world while the truth is putting on its shoes." That was before the Internet and other social media.

Everything you say will be used against you and will never disappear. Just ask former BP CEO Tony Haywood.

In the aftermath of the Horizon Deepwater well disaster in which 33 people died and much the Gulf of Mexico was rendered useless for months, Haywood remarked that he wanted to "get my life back." Livelihoods and lives were lost and a fat cat CEO wanted his life back? Good grief. Ol' Tony reinserted his head up his ass, only to pull it out a few days later to state that he was taking his son to a yacht race as people along the Gulf mourned. BP's brand recovered; Haywood's did not.

I didn't think it was possible, but Choo-choo CEO Burkhardt actually out-Haywooded Haywood. In addition to his stupid speculation as to the cause of the deadly train wreck, he focused many of his public statements on the fact that he was working 20-hour days, his investment in the company had dwindled to almost nothing and people were "putting words in my mouth." Boo-hoo-hoo!

A critical guiding principle before, during and after a crisis is to is keep your employees informed. They, simply put, serve as your best ambassadors to knock down lies and innuendo against your company or organization. Most CEOs only talk a good game about the importance of employee communication. Unfortunately, employee communication is often an early casualty during the crisis; preservation should be sacrosanct. People assume the worst when information is withheld. Employees are no different.

The final guiding principle is most often neglected or abused. PR and legal must be teammates and not adversaries. This requires developing a solid working relationship prior to a crisis. Trying to join forces during a crisis is almost always too late. Don't think I am always pinning the blame on the lawyers. It's a two-way street. For one thing, schools are neglecting to teach PR students how to write. Typically, I have found lawyers to be some of the finest writers in any organization.

13

Now – the illustrations.

Chapter Three: The first big crisis: Chrysler's UltraDrive

What moron names a transmission? Well, actually throughout the history of the industry – especially the early years, everybody did. But in modern history, car buyers didn't come into dealerships saying "I don't care what vehicle it is, just give me that new-fangled tranny". In 1988, Chrysler introduced the first fully adaptive, electronic automatic transmission – codenamed A-604 and stupidly marketed as Ultradrive. It was considered a marvel of science within the industry.

So great it was, the U.S. Patent and Trademark Office gave it the "Best New Technology Award" at its annual banquet while also honoring Leonard Bernstein and Stevie Wonder with lifetime achievement awards. Talk about the blind leading the blind.

Only problem was: the UltraDrive wasn't ready for prime time. Chrysler Vice Chairman Bob Lutz, perhaps unfairly, got the blame for pushing it out early. To be honest, we didn't have squat in the product pipeline. Unfortunately, the groundbreaking Jeep Grand Cherokee, along with the coming second generation minivan, were still years from being introduced into the market. These two vehicles would save the company and bring in an insane amount of revenue. But between 1988 and 1992, the new product showroom was dryer than a popcorn fart. We needed something to market. Our cars sucked; our pickup truck was 20 years old.

By 1991, hundreds of thousands of vehicles with the UltraDrive transmission, including the minivan, were breaking down. The vehicles were rendered useless. The National Highway Traffic Safety Administration (NHTSA) began an investigation. If NHTSA were to conclude a safety recall was warranted, the cost would run into the billions and bankrupt Chrysler. Already dangerously close to another bankruptcy, top brass knew another government bailout was unlikely. A decade earlier, Chrysler was saved and famously paid back the government loan guarantees early. Lee Iacocca became a household name. Not this time. The stakes were higher than anyone would imagine.

Early discussions with NHTSA gave Chrysler executives some assurance; NHTSA would allow Chrysler's "fix" of the Ultradrive without a formal recall. Unfortunately, the shit hit the fan. Consumers Union, the folks behind Consumer Reports magazine, announced a campaign against Chrysler and its defective transmission. It was something Chrysler, of course, didn't need – and public pressure NHTSA didn't want. Consumers Union had on its board of directors two members of the Ralph Nader-created Public Citizen, the self-proclaimed "safety advocacy" group: top dog Joan Claybrook and her head pit bull, The Center for Auto Safety's Clarence Ditlow.

Early in the process, this PR debacle was handed to me. PR people covering safety, regulatory and legal issues in the auto industry have a tendency to burn out quickly. Think about it: the folks on the front lines get the arrows or bullets first. Not to sound like a martyr, but it is what it is. They're the funeral directors of PR. At the same time, one of Chrysler's brightest engineers was put in charge of the program to save the Ultradrive and steer us away from bankruptcy. Chris Theodore had come over to Chrysler when the company bought American Motors. While "bright" American Motors engineer seems like an oxymoron, Chris was indeed bright; but I soon learned he had the media relations skills of Kim Jong-Il.

With an unrelenting Consumers Union breathing down NHTSA's neck, we knew we had to explain how the supposed "defect" in the transmission was actually a "safety feature." Traditional transmissions, when they broke, left a motorist stranded on the side of the road to face all kinds of peril – roving gangs of thugs, wolves and roadside vagrants. The Chrysler engineers had developed a new feature called "limp home mode." In the event of sensing an impending problem, the UltraDrive transmission would magically go into an operating mode that allowed the driver to drive at least 50 miles to safety at considerably lower speeds.

So, this was a "good thing." Kind of like a rash on your arm is better than a rash on your ass.

The customers affected, in fact, were not getting stranded along the road. However, an abnormal number of the transmissions were failing. Repairing or replacing transmissions, one-by-one as they broke, Chrysler could absorb the cost. A forced recall of all vehicles equipped with the transmission would be cataclysmic for Chrysler – and yes, the customers. A Chrysler bankruptcy would leave everyone high and dry.

But Consumers Union's pressure continued. We developed a three-fold strategy: one for our customers, one for the media and one for Consumers Union. The first was easy: if your transmission breaks, Chrysler will repair or replace it for free for the life of the vehicle.

Check.

The second strategy was more difficult with an increasingly wary media. We decided we had to put the cards on the table and prove to the media – one by one if necessary—how the system worked. Particularly, we needed to explain how the "safety feature" of the limp home mode operated.

The first interview was an eye-opener for Chris Theodore. On the phone we had Paul Eisenstein, a Detroit automotive journalist famous for his pontificating 18-part questions. Paul wasn't completely buying what Chris Theodore was selling.

Five minutes into the interview, Paul made a pretty ridiculous statement: "I understand you can break this transmission just by stomping on the throttle."

Chris exploded, shouting "goddammit!" The interview went downhill from there. As it ended, I immediately left Chris' office and grabbed my phone and called Eisenstein.

"What the hell was that?" Paul asked.

"Paul, give him a break," I pleaded. "He's been brought in to fix the situation and the pressure is enormous. Why don't you come here tomorrow and we'll give you a demonstration."

"OK."

"Thanks Paul, I appreciate it."

After hanging up, I ran back down to Chris' office. He was still steaming. Although he would later become one of my best friends, at that moment he was a senior engineer – one step away from a VP job – and I was a middle manager PR guy.

"Don't ever fucking do that again!" I scolded him. "We need the media to present the facts or we are dead. Pissing in their face is not the way to get there."

"Dammit, I know," he answered and it never happened again, at least on this issue.

The third and final stage of the strategy we knew would be the most difficult: getting Consumers Union to end what seemed to be an unholy jihad. We gathered in a conference room on the top floor of headquarters, a former assembly plant in Highland Park, Michigan. The team was Chrysler's top brass, excluding Lee Iacocca and Bob Lutz, but including the heads of Engineering, Sales, Design, PR, and Chris Theodore...

And me.

The question on the table was whether to fight Consumers Union tooth-and-nail or try to win them over. The former seemed silly on its face. After all, Consumer Reports was the acknowledged bible of product reviews. Years prior, Iacocca had praised the magazine when it gave a few Chrysler vehicles some rare praise. The next year, when Chrysler's quality went into the crapper and Consumer Reports scolded the company, Iacocca took a very public shot at them, calling them the "pot pie and shower head people." It was like the old line: what's the difference between a slut and a bitch? A slut will sleep with everyone; a bitch will sleep with everyone…but you. I was certain the folks at Consumers Union had a memory. Now they had a cause.

A big wave of testosterone was about to come crashing down on the conference room table. You've got to understand the typical automotive engineer's mentality when staring at a potential recall: 1) prove it isn't defective after all; 2) when that fails, put as small a fence as possible around the products contaminated, and; 3) plead with NHTSA not to call it a safety recall.

In his semi-heavy French accent, Francois Castaing, the affable engineering genius from American Motors via Renault, (yes another oxymoron) became livid; he demanded we kick Consumers Union's ass.

"I sync we should clean their socks!" he exclaimed.

Others chimed in on the merits of a battle versus an appeasement strategy, when suddenly we all looked over to see Castaing laughing so hard that tears were rolling down his cheeks.

A bit peeved, Design guru Tom Gale asked, "Francois, what's so damned funny?"

Castaing gathered himself and explained, "I sync I meant 'clean their clocks', not clean their socks."

The room broke up. When the laughter subsided, the "boys" realized the folly of a scorched-earth strategy and decided to engage with, not against the product reviewers at Consumer Reports. Technical meetings and test drives, led by Chris Theodore, with Consumer Reports staff were booked. After the jihad was over, NHTSA accepted Chrysler's non-recall fix and Chrysler would have to wait a decade and a half to go bankrupt.

The PR turd I was handed was successfully flushed. And, I had learned a valuable lesson: in PR you can decide between "fight" and "flight." To fight is to stand up for what you believe is the right course of action, even if you may get your ass handed to you. Flight is playing it safe, spinelessly, and letting the elephants romp through the crowd and then spending your time with a shovel scooping up the shit, but without ruffling any feathers. The latter deserve the most-despised moniker for my craft: spin doctors.

Chrysler engineers eventually traced the trouble with the Ultradrive transmission (also known as the A604 and identified as such in news coverage) to contamination during manufacturing. Dust from the plant had purportedly infiltrated the transmissions, causing them to malfunction. As in so many other instances at Chrysler, engineers and designers were maddeningly close to creating a vehicle that could blow its competition away -- only to be undone by a defect or problem that eluded them or that they failed to notice until it was too late.

Ultradrive was a primary component of Chrysler's minivan models, its most profitable and popular vehicle. Fortunately, Lee Iacocca and the top executives understood that Chrysler's very survival hinged on continued strong minivan sales. Unless they moved swiftly to reassure customers that their A604 transmissions would be replaced without charge, minivan sales would grind to a halt. When I left Chrysler in 1998 to join the struggling Nissan Motor Company, some customers were on their third transmission, while engineers debated the root cause of the malfunction. As big a hassle as the balky transmissions were for customers, at least they were assured Chrysler was prepared to stand behind its vehicles, no matter the cost -- which in this case amounted to hundreds of millions if not billions of dollars. In the end, Chrysler did follow the primary guiding principle of taking care of its customers.

The engineer thrown in to "fix" the problem, Chris Theodore, was now my brother-in-law, marrying my wife's sister, whom he met at our annual Halloween party the day his divorced was finalized. Considering what we had gone through together, I thought it was appropriate he came as a samurai. His would-be bride was dressed as Madonna, sporting a pointy metal bra. It was lust at first sight – for him.

Crisis Lesson Learned: Put the safety and satisfaction of your customers first and don't let the crisis be protracted; if it lasts too long, you stand a good chance of permanently damaging your brand, your company or both.

Chapter Four: The Almost Fatal "Line in the Sand"

Unfortunately, Chrysler learned very little from its near brush with bankruptcy thanks to its awful transmission. That can happen when you get fat and sassy. By 1994, the company was becoming the darling of the industry. The Jeep Grand Cherokee was printing money, yet another version of the wonderful minivan was just a year away and the company's breakthrough LH sedans had reinvented the art of vehicle design; at least among the domestic automakers.

As it entered its second major crisis in less than three years, Chrysler's top brass – at least its CEO Bob Eaton – decided the legal and financial implications were paramount to the perceived safety of its customers, defying what I believe is a guiding principle of any crisis.

The issue was the safety of the latches on the rear lift gates of the company's phenomenally popular minivans. A few years earlier, Chrysler had "re-engineered" the latch to better secure the lift gate in the case of a rear-end accident. What they had done was basically install a secondary latch. Think of a pair of trousers with a clasp and a button – you can fail to secure one without your pants falling down.

NHTSA, and plaintiffs' attorneys, began noticing abnormally high incidents of Chrysler minivan accidents in which passengers – mostly children – were being ejected through the rear of the vehicle and more often than not, killed. By the time NHTSA was knee-deep in a formal investigation, the media surrounding the issue had become white hot. And, the alleged "safety advocates" – who some will argue are really nothing more than shills for plaintiffs' attorneys – were having a field day.

Why? The minivans experiencing the problem were the ones built prior to the re-engineering of the latch. They had their smoking gun;

Chrysler "knew" it had a problem. Chrysler, meanwhile, argued its lift gate failures were no different than those of its competitor minivans (which was true) and the accidents reported were horrific wrecks, often at high speeds. But they didn't stop there. In effect, they all but blamed the parents of the accident victims for not buckling up their kids.

NHTSA wasn't listening and formally demanded a recall. It is rare in the auto industry when NHTSA demands a recall. In fact, the vast majority of recalls are voluntary. You can count on your fingers the number of times NHTSA has forced a recall since the agency was created in 1966. But Chrysler wouldn't give. CEO Bob Eaton, who had been hired by Lee Iacocca as his replacement, believed the stakes were too high and the damage too great to the company if he had to admit the vaunted minivan was defective. He told his troops that the minivan was the bread and butter of the company and, therefore, "we must draw a line in the sand."

A new definition of tone-deafness had been established. Chrysler argued vehemently to anyone who would listen that the re-engineering of the lift gate latch was merely "continuous improvement" and by no means an admission of guilt.

NHTSA continued to pound the company in the media as the lawsuits started to pile up. Worse yet, if that was possible, Chrysler's ultra-loyal minivan owners were starting to become unhinged, flooding the company with angry calls and letters.

I was working in Washington D.C. at the time, on-loan to the lobbying group for the Big Three; the American Automobile Manufacturers Association (AAMA). It would be a two-year stint, designed to help bolster the PR efforts of the organization and bolster the industry's image, especially in Washington. General Motors had also loaned executives to the group. AAMA was run by Andy Card, the former short-term Secretary of Transportation under George H.W. Bush, who later became more famous as George W. Bush's Chief of Staff and the man who whispered into W's ear that "America is under attack" on September 11, 2001.

As the minivan issue continued to dominate the news, I joined Andy at a speech he was delivering in D.C. I usually took notes whenever Andy spoke or did an interview. But on this day, my mind was on the minivan and the man newly promoted to develop the next generation of minivans, Chris Theodore. As Andy spoke, I did not listen, as I was furiously outlining what I thought was the right strategy for Chrysler. It was simple: if you think you are right, then go to war with NHTSA, not your customers. Announce a free retro-fit for all minivans in question. Then tell NHTSA to stick it and let the U.S. Government take you to court.

When we got back to the office, I got on the phone with Steve Harris, the head of Chrysler PR, my boss in reality despite working for AAMA and one of the biggest influences in my PR career. Steve really ingrained the tenet of complete honesty as, perhaps, the singular pillar of our craft.

"What's up?" Steve asked, always cheerful, even when Rome was burning.

"This minivan latch crap is killing us," I blurted out. "We've got to take care of the customer and then fight NHTSA."

"You think we didn't suggest that, Spanky?" he calmly replied. "The big guy (Eaton) wants no part of it."

"We're getting our asses handed to us," I said.

PR had a seat at the table, which is a guiding principle in any crisis; only, it was a baby chair in this circumstance. Chrysler PR would soon be cleaning up after the elephants in the parade.

Two days later, our family flew back to Detroit, staying with my brother-in-law, Chris Theodore, and his family. The next morning, as usual, Chris was up before the crack of dawn. At 4:30 a.m., I joined him for coffee in his kitchen as he poured over paperwork. I pulled my scribbles out of my briefcase and handed them to him. "Here," I said, "This is what you should do. Go to war with NHTSA, not our customers."

"Dammit, it was continuous improvement," he shouted. "If we give in here, every time we make a change we are going to get crucified by the fucking trial lawyers."

"Shut up," came the voice of my wife from the guest bedroom. "You're waking up the kids, you assholes."

"Chris," I whispered, "If you were changing the latch for next year's all-new minivan that would be one thing. Hell, you didn't make the change. But the guys before you changed the latch a couple of years ago. Why?"

"I told you, continuous improvement."

"Bull shit!"

"It's not bull shit!"

The shouting had resumed.

"You can't win this," I said. "All you will do is kill the loyalty of our customers and we'll lose every lawsuit. Here's how it plays out Chris: we save a buck or two on a cheap-ass latch, while those assholes at Ford put a double latch on the Winturd (what we called Ford's Windstar minivan) from the get-go; and people get killed. It doesn't matter that they were too stupid to buckle in their kids. It doesn't matter that they were stupid enough to put 12 workers in an eight-passenger vehicle. It doesn't matter that the fatality rates in Chrysler minivans are no worse than Ford or GM. What matters is they'll say you guys changed the damned latch because you knew you had a problem. And, there is no way in hell you can disprove that."

From on-high came another admonition: "I said shut up you idiots, we're trying to sleep!"

What I didn't know is that while Theodore was being the brave warrior for the company, he and other top brass were pushing Eaton to recall the vehicles. But Eaton, stupidly, stuck to his line in the sand. The surprise pick as Iacocca's replacement, Eaton had gained notoriety at General Motors as the engineer who in the 1980s somehow single-handedly convinced NHTSA not to call for a recall of GM's X platform of cars, arguably some of the worst cars in automotive history. Apparently Eaton thought he could perform the magic again. Or maybe…he was the rabbit in the hat.

It proved to be the latter. After weeks of brutal press coverage and badgering from NHTSA, Chrysler relented, "recalled" the minivans and finally put its customers first – with a gun to its head. Luckily for Chrysler, the new minivans that would come out the next year, featuring an industry-first sliding doors on both sides of the vehicle, would again leap-frog the competition and be the must-have minivan in the industry. The line in the sand had been smoothed.

Crisis Lesson Learned: Put your customer first at the beginning of the crisis, not midway through it. And never draw a "line in the sand" when your beach is under water. If your "king" has no clothes, have the guts to tell him or her. As the great General George Marshall said: "Speak truth to power." He believed his boss, President Franklin Delano Roosevelt, should be told what he needed, not what he wanted.

Chapter Five: "Suddenly Accelerating" Toward a Crisis

So-called "sudden unintended acceleration" occurs when a vehicle seemingly races out of control no matter how hard the driver tries to stop it. The phenomenon was created in the 1980s. Please notice I didn't say discovered or found or unearthed. SUA was a fictitious creation, made up, pure and simple, by the $100 billion-a-year plaintiff's bar supported by their "special friends" masquerading as "safety advocates." These ambulance chasers and their advocate buddies have been and still are ignorantly embraced by an often lazy and sometimes "short staffed" liberal "news" media. Liberal journalists treat the plaintiff's bar with adoration normally assigned to "Keeping up with the Kardashians" teenage-girl fan base.

On November 23, 1986, CBS's award-winning 60 Minutes aired what would become the first of many bogus "investigations" by various "news" media organizations questioning the safety of an automobile. They interviewed six people who were suing German automaker Audi. Mysteriously, their Audi 5000 had become possessed by the dreaded sudden acceleration demon; perilously careening out of control. Naturally, this was due to no fault of the driver.

However, 60 Minutes wanted a better story to show its viewers, so it hired so-called safety expert William Rosenthal, often a "star witness" in lawsuits against Audi, to demonstrate (rig is more accurate) how the Audi tragedy unfolded mechanically. Factually, the Audi 5000 did have an abnormally high number of accidents (700) and deaths (6) associated with claims of sudden acceleration, and NHTSA was investigating the model years 1982-1987. But 60 Minutes needed a juicier story. After all, they were 60 Minutes, the blockbuster ratings show created by Don Hewitt.

Audi was in a bind. As one of the premier engineering firms in the world, they knew exactly why their cars were racing out of control – the drivers, thinking they were putting their foot on the brakes, were actually smashing on the accelerator pedal. Witness after witness claimed "the harder I pushed on the brakes, the faster I went." Duh. But as a manufacturer, that guiding principle of protecting your customers first and foremost goes over like a pregnant pole-vaulter when you blame them for making a mistake. Audi tried, initially in vain, to spin what they already knew, by calling the driver error that lead to sudden acceleration, the kinder, gentler "pedal misapplication." Sort of like calling a vehicle fire a "thermal event." Remember?

The CBS "news mag" didn't care that the National Highway Safety Administration (NHTSA) had performed its own "demo" of the Audi 5000. The agency had let reporters get in the car, put a foot on the brake and then put the (accelerator) pedal to the metal; the Audi did not move forward. 60 Minutes producer Alan Maraynes "obviously" didn't care about this demonstration by the U.S. government's safety agency. No. 60 Minutes was determined to "prove" that Audi, the "obvious" German corporate whores they were, was selling possessed cars in need of a media exorcism. To show the world just how the vehicle went out of control, they had the consumer integrity "experts", er, "safety advocates" dishonestly rig the vehicle to necessarily speed out of control. 60 Minutes would later, begrudgingly admit to this phony demonstration but the damage was done.

Audi issued a series of recalls to make it more difficult for its customers to make a deadly mistake. Nevertheless, sales plummeted. Audi had sold more than 74,000 units in the United States during 1985. After the quake of media coverage, initiated by the sloppy handiwork of 60 Minutes, sales fell to only 12,000 in 1991. Audi did not reach its 1985 sales total until 2000, 14 long years after the slanderous exploits of 60 Minutes and the "creative" artists they hired as experts.

Sadly, a career was sidelined. Tom McDonald, the affable head of Audi PR, wrongly was assigned the blame for Audi's "PR disaster" and was shit-canned in a classic "blame the messenger" move. He eventually landed as the PR voice for the Association of International Automobile Manufacturers, where I got to know him, love him, and fight like a brother against him. In the mid-90s, the American automakers trade association, led by Andy Card (I was on loan) battled Tom and the automobile importers against Japan and Korea's blatantly unfair trade practices.

When the trade fighting was over (hell, I still don't know who really won), I left Washington D.C. and returned to Detroit and Chrysler. In 1996, I became the chief safety spokesperson. In no time, I was in the hot seat again battling the second major crisis involving sudden unintended acceleration. This time, the unsuspecting vehicles were the hugely profitable Jeep Grand Cherokee and older Cherokee.

The Grand Cherokee, first conceived by engineers at American Motors prior to Chrysler's purchase, had been launched in 1992 with great fanfare. At its debut during the Detroit Auto Show (orchestrated by now-General Motors' PR chief Tony Cervone), with Chrysler big wig Bob Lutz driving and Detroit Mayor Coleman Young riding shot gun, the Grand Cherokee literally crashed through the glass wall of Cobo Hall and into the display. The press cameras flashed away. It would be the start of an unprecedented string of show-stopping reveals Chrysler would pull off (much to the chagrin of our competitors). Little did I know the crash would be symbolic of Grand Cherokees as they made their way into the hands of customers around the world.

By the mid-90s, NHTSA was discovering an abnormally high number of sudden acceleration claims involving accidents with Jeep Grand Cherokees and Cherokees. They opened a formal investigation. The trial lawyers smelled blood and unleashed their peeps in the "safety" community to chum the water and arouse the population. Public Citizen, the "safety group" created by Ralph Nader and the Center for Auto Safety, were all too happy to help. Led by Joan Claybrook and Clarence Ditlow

respectively, the Jeep Grand Cherokee became Public Citizen Enemy
Number One. Demands were made for a massive recall and a slew of
lawsuits followed.

I answered my phone at work.

"Jason, its Tom McDonald."

"Hey Tom, what's up my friend?"

"I don't want to tell you how to do your job, but I want to give you
some advice I wish I had been given in my Audi days."

"I'm all ears, Tom. This is a shit-storm."

"It's simple: whatever you do, don't blame the customer."

This was advice I tried in vain to later share with a friend at Toyota,
the most recent benefactor of phony sudden acceleration claims. Toyota
probably could not have handled their experience in the PR oven any
worse, but then again, they were Toyota, with a huge bank account of
good-will that allowed them to survive pretty much intact.

"But that is exactly what is happening Tom! Almost every accident is
identical: the driver says the harder they pushed on the brakes, the faster
they went. And, it's usually someone unfamiliar with the vehicle, like a
car wash jockey with big, wet boots or a relative moving the Jeep."

"I know, I know. But you can't go to war with your customers and
win!"

Ah, that guiding principle of putting the safety and satisfaction of
your customer first. But how to get the facts out to convince the media,
NHTSA and the courts that it was truly, as Audi coined it, "pedal
misapplication?"

By now, the Grand Cherokee sudden acceleration crisis was the
biggest story in the auto industry and its waves were crashing on us daily
in both print and electronic media. So much so that Chrysler had put its
top Jeep engineer on it full time. I met with Craig Winn at his office in
Jeep's engineering headquarters in Detroit on Plymouth Road. If you

didn't know better, you would have thought the facility had been hit by a bomb. Falling apart and depressing, still it housed some of the brightest engineering minds in the company.

"Craig, how can we defend ourselves without blaming the customers?"

"We can't. The facts are the facts."

We argued back and forth for several minutes when we hit pay dirt.

"Listen Jason, I can take you outside, put you in the vehicle, have you put your foot on the brake and then put the accelerator to the floor, shift into drive, and the Jeep won't move a fucking inch."

"No shit?"

"No shit. Unless they're defective, the brakes will always overcome the throttle."

"The brakes always win?"

"Always."

Finally! We had something the media could get their arms around. If the gloves don't fit, you must acquit!

The brakes always win. We went to the back lot where Winn demonstrated the power of the brakes over throttle. He was right. Within days, we had arranged for the business reporter who had been covering the crisis for the local NBC affiliate, WDIV, to come out to the Jeep engineering center. When Rod Meloni arrived, we told him what we wanted do: Rod would stand in front of the Grand Cherokee on live TV. Craig Winn would start the vehicle, firmly apply the brake, then push the accelerator pedal fully to the floor and shift into drive.

Rod's eyes bugged out with that "you've got to be shitting me" look. But, his brain was churning: the potential for certain death versus an exclusive story he knew would travel around the country, perhaps the entire world.

"Mr. Winn, are you sure about this?" He asked with a nervous giggle in his voice.

"Let's put it this way: if I'm wrong, you're dead; but Vines and I are fired!"

As WDIV opened its six o' clock news, the shot immediately went to Meloni and he set up the piece before the station went to commercial. Back on the air, it was show time. I think Meloni's sphincter was on maximum tightness. Winn started the Jeep, stomped on the brake, hit the accelerator, revved to a constant 5,000 rpms and then shifted into drive.

It was an ugly scene.

As if possessed, the vehicle thrashed around like a bucking bronco on steroids, but moved not an inch toward the reporter. After 10 seconds, Winn shifted into park and turned off the beast. The air filled with the smell of pissed-off brakes. The brakes had won. A few minutes later, Meloni was back on live TV. This time, he was in the Grand Cherokee as a passenger. One more demonstration was prepared to prove that brakes always win. Despite the claims of accident victims, if a customer was actually "on the brakes" the vehicle would stop, not go faster. On a lonely back street behind the complex, Winn hit the gas, accelerating to 30 miles per hour. Then, he floored the accelerator with his right foot as he slammed his left foot on the brake, bringing the vehicle to a grinding halt after 100 yards, where it bucked and snorted, still at full throttle, one last time, in perhaps an even more impressive demonstration. Meloni's story found its way far beyond the Detroit city limits.

We had finally broken through with facts in a crisis defined by horrible stories of accidents and deaths. We thought we had survived the bullshit claims and bogus charges by lawyers and their "safety advocates".

But facts were not good enough for a reporter at the Fox affiliate in Chicago. He was convinced there was no way all of these victims could be wrong. His stories continued until he was sure he had hit pay dirt. He called me.

"I witnessed it myself, Jason."

"You witnessed what?

"Sudden acceleration in a Jeep."

The reporter had received a call from a guy in the western suburbs of Chicago claiming he could prove the vehicle was demonized. With camera crew in tow, he visited the man. Sure enough, the vehicle accelerated "on its own" with no feet on either pedal. That night he shared the story with his Chicago audience.

"Holy shit."

It was all I could say when the video arrived in my office. (Back then, there was no Internet to instantly watch news from other parts of the country.) I got in my car and raced out to see Craig Winn.

"Holy shit."

It was all he could say when I played the tape. Two hours later, I was on a plane to Chicago, along with one of Winn's top lieutenants, Jimmy Bielinda. We met the Fox reporter the next morning and drove out to the Jeep owner's house to inspect the vehicle.

Before the possessed Jeep sinisterly jumped into action, Bielinda attached an electronic diagnostic tool to the engine's main computer. While the test was running, I chatted with the reporter. Jimmy opened the driver's door and stuck his head under the steering wheel. One minute later he walked over to us with a smile.

"I know what it is."

"Hold on," the reporter quickly said. "I want to get this on camera."

As the camera rolled, Bielinda directed the reporter and the owner to the driver's side. Sticking his head in the vehicle again, he pushed down the accelerator pedal and it stuck behind the floor mat; a mat caked with road salt and frozen in place on this cold February day in the frosty Midwest.

"Holy shit," said the surprised and embarrassed owner.

With that, I suggested the reporter keep his camera rolling while we took a little ride. He took the shot gun seat and I got behind the wheel. With the camera over my right shoulder, we jumped on a local highway and over the course of our 15 minute ride, I floored the throttle several times causing the pedal to stick every time, sending the vehicle flying away even when I completely removed my foot. By simply tapping the throttle, the pedal became free and we quickly slowed. Case closed.

Maybe.

When we arrived back at the owner's house, he apologized for creating this stir.

"No problem," Bielinda said. "We're just glad we know what it is and how to fix it. A lot of people don't take care of their mats in the winter or they use the wrong mats for their vehicle. But, I've got one question: did you buy this vehicle new?"

"Nope, I bought it used from Village Ford a few months ago."

"Well, then you need to go back to the dealer and get some money back. When I hooked up my diagnostic tool to your engine it told me this vehicle has about 70,000 engine miles on it, but your odometer reads 25,000 miles. Somebody rolled back the odometer and that's against the law."

Fox ran the story that night and immediately the reporter was on a new story – at Village Ford.

Case closed? Not quite. We had not completely followed the premier guiding principle of a crisis – the safety and satisfaction of the customer is paramount. We had basically proven that sudden acceleration was pedal misapplication. But why was it happening so often on Jeep vehicles?

When Audi was in their crisis, NHTSA was also investigating more than 20 other vehicles after receiving claims of sudden acceleration. In our case, the Jeep vehicles weren't the only vehicles being investigated, but we had all the noise.

There was, after all, a "fix." The Grand Cherokee (and the older Cherokee) were among a small handful of vehicles that did not have, by then, a common technology called brake-shift interlock. This technology requires your foot on the brake before shifting out of park. In fact, other Chrysler vehicles in production at the time had the feature. In truth, this technology could easily be retrofitted onto an older vehicle. Most importantly, it was a feature that would absolutely stop people from putting their foot on the wrong pedal before shifting out of park. Unfortunately, implementation would be costly. Providing this for the consumer would become fodder for the trial lawyers who would claim the Jeep vehicles without it were "defective" and that providing this "fix" was an admission of guilt.

Craig Winn and I were adamant about what we needed to do: if we knew how to fix a problem (even if it was technically driver error), we had to do it. The debate within Chrysler was not protracted. The heat and volume were turned up in several meetings and I was probably a bit too vocal considering my middle management status. In the end, the decision was made to offer a free retrofit to all owners.

Minutes after we made the announcement, Ron Boltz, the Vice President of Regulatory Affairs and indirectly my boss, called me. Ron was a hard-ass from time-to-time, but a fair man and one of the smartest guys I had ever worked with. There was no hello, no hi, no how-you-doing.

"Do you realize you just cost this company $120 million?" he shouted.

I didn't have a clue as how to respond. A few silent seconds passed, until he added "good job" and hung up. NHTSA closed its investigation and we moved on, leaving it to ambulance chasers to keep the issue alive in the court system already burdened with frivolous lawsuits.

Crisis Lesson Learned: If your customers are "misusing" your product or are being unintentionally harmed by it, do something about it. Quickly. Think Tylenol. That tampering scare of the 1980s led to improved tamper-proof pill jars now utilized by the entire pharmaceutical and other industries.

Chapter Six: Killing Kids with a lot of Hot Air

Chrysler, in 1992, became the first major automaker to equip its cars with dual front seat air bags as standard equipment. It was a huge PR coup that quickly evaporated when – as predicted years earlier (most robustly by General Motors' engineers and scientists) – air bags would kill little kids and old folks.

Air bags had been pushed with a passion by then-NHTSA Administrator Joan Claybrook. She believed air bags would replace seat belts as the primary safety device. Automotive engineers, again most adamant at GM, believed Claybrook was wrong. Claybrook believed, thanks to her "research," seat belts didn't work for kids (true in some cases; flat wrong in most) and the elderly whom may be injured in a vicious crash due to their brittle bones. The "soft" pillow of an air bag was the panacea for both kiddies and old folks.

Claybrook ignored the evidence provided by scientists studying the cause. While auto companies and air bag enthusiasts talked about air bag "deployments" in the event of a crash, what really triggered the air bag was a detonation, powered by – no kidding – solid rocket propellant fuel. This type of explosion was necessary to inflate the air bag in milliseconds to save the passenger.

Don't get me wrong: air bags are one of the greatest safety devices ever invented, and not just merely for automobiles. Between 30,000 and 40,000 people die each year on our nation's roads, but it would be far worse without air bags.

In the 1990s we were not ready for air bags on both sides of the front seats, considering how we Americans drove and transported our passengers; especially our little ones. Worse yet, Americans stupidly still hadn't fully embraced seat belts despite pleas from government regulators and a push for more state laws to require folks to buckle up; think "Click it or Ticket." Automakers were accomplices as well, running advertisements showing air bags deploying in super-slow motion. These ads made it appear as though a huge, puffy marshmallow was going to save you from death if you bought their car.

In the fall of 1996, USA Today reported that kids were dying at an alarming rate due to the deployment of air bags in the front passenger seat. Led by reporter Jayne O'Donnell, a friend of mine then and now, USA Today predicted, according to those loveable "safety advocates"– one or two kids would die per week going forward. USA Today took on the issue as a crusade.

But what would Joan (Claybrook) do? As the leader of Public Citizen she was torn: continue her new role as "safety advocate" for plaintiffs' attorneys, suing automakers for air bag deaths of children riding in the front seat, or come to grips with her push for air bags as the ultimate safety advance despite the warnings from safety engineers? A conflicted Claybrook was lost. It wasn't the first time.

At Chrysler, while we solidly led the industry in incorporating air bags as a standard feature throughout our product line (Chrysler had typically been a fast-follower of GM, Ford, Japanese or German innovation), we didn't have a leg to stand on when it came to safety research. We didn't have any real scientists at Chrysler. The only doctors, for the most part, were in the company health department taking employee temperatures and giving sick-leave slips.

Case in point: when PETA, those wackos that treat mosquito life more important than humans, went on a jihad against the auto industry's use of live pigs in crash testing, I asked our safety experts if we "animal tested." Some in the media were siding with PETA and polling the automakers to create a hit list of evil animal killers. I asked our leading crash test expert if we conducted tests with animals.

"We don't have the scientists to do animal testing," he responded. "We could put a pig in a car and crash it, but all we could tell you is that the pig is dead."

Chrysler relied on data shared from GM's and Ford's pig-killing scientific analysis through the Society of Automotive Engineers (SAE). We were, by association, "dirty" if you have a problem with killing pigs to save human lives. Think about that on your next trip to Famous Dave's or Chili's (I want my baby back, baby back, baby back ribs or consider that some ice cream shops are putting bacon with the creamy goodness).

As the issue of kids potentially dying created a rage on the pages of USA Today, Public Citizen's Joan Claybrook began to feel the squeeze. Increasingly, the media was calling her to task for ignoring the warnings from actual safety engineers trying to perfect air bags decades before when she was the head of the government's highway safety agency. This wasn't a he said/she said argument: GM had shared with Claybrook's NHTSA literally thousands of pages of test data warning repeatedly that children and old folks would be subject to air bag injuries at the air bag deployment strength and speed Claybrook's NHTSA had demanded.

It was a rare moment. We had a plaintiffs' attorney ally, a former NHTSA Administrator, on the mat. Public Citizen's spokesperson was on life support. It was a magical opportunity for all automakers: the ability to finally squelch a blow-hard who played loose and fast with the facts to support her lawyer buddies. The automakers (me for Chrysler) and the media were pummeling her and Public Citizen on a near-daily basis.

And then the call came. It was from Ron Boltz, my quasi-boss that had semi-scolded me for fighting for the Jeep Grand Cherokee retro-fit a year earlier.

"You gotta stop the fight on Claybrook," he said.

"Come on Ron, she's almost dead," I figuratively cried. "Why?"

"Ford. They have no spine for this," Boltz said, confirming that an industry often under attack, from time-to-time, worked in concert. Not in collusion; but in concert for strength against the "little guys" like the $100 billion plaintiff's bar.

With Claybrook saved, the issue was still alive and not well: the prospect of killing kids.

While simultaneously bashing Claybrook, we were trying to figure out the best way to educate Americans about the life-saving power of air bags and the potential deadly power when used improperly. For adults, it was simple: buckle up dammit! Air bags were already-proven life savers when they were the secondary safety device, working like a tag team with safety belts. For children, the issue was trickier. For the average teenager and older, air bags were useful, but for younger kids, 13 years old and younger, the potential for injury or death was evident.

While the issue was tricky, the solution was amazingly simple, in theory: put the kids in the backseat where there were no air bags. The industry, and NHTSA, had reams of data showing rear seat passengers almost always fared better than front seat passengers. Hell, it followed that old adage: always be the last to arrive at the scene of an accident. How could we convince adults to put their little snots in the backseat?

I hired Stratacomm, a Washington D.C.-based boutique PR firm founded by another former NHTSA Administrator, Diane Steed, who had followed Claybrook in the post. Unlike Claybrook, Steed actually listened to the automakers concerns about rushing into air bags before they were ready for prime time. The Stratacomm team also included Ron DeFore, a former NHTSA spokesman and Jeff Conley, a brilliant strategist who had served as a consultant to Andy Card and myself when we were at AAMA. We brainstormed ideas that would get out the message.

But how do you convince adults who continued to let their kids ride in the front seat despite extensive press coverage about the growing threat?

We figured we could try, but that our best shot was convincing kids themselves.

It had worked before. The greenies smartly got into the schools to promote "Give a Hoot, Don't Pollute" and the anti-smoking crowd were most successful getting to kids at a very early age.

But how do you get it in the head of a 13-year-old, just one year from high school, that he or she belonged in the back seat with their 4-year-old sibling? It had to be pervasive. More importantly, it had to be fun.

We hired Learning Works, a firm famous for developing curricula schools actually used. Schools are constantly flooded with curriculum suggestions from outside sources. Often, the message had broad application but time constraints (No Child Left Behind) which leave these messages unused or under-utilized. The program became known as "The Back is Where It's At!" Ironically, we were preparing to reach out to every public and private school in the country with an educational program that was grammatically incorrect!

To make it fun, Stratacomm's Jeff Conley suggested we reach out to someone hip that pre-teens identified with who could tell the safety story: Bill Nye the Science Guy. Nye jumped on board for all the right reasons: saving kids' lives…and getting paid. During a lull in the press days at the 1997 Detroit Auto Show, our team joined a conference call with Nye and his writers. Over an hour, we mapped out what the message had to be and then let Team Nye go to work. Within two weeks, a script was delivered. It was strong and it was typical Bill Nye – goofy, funny and smart.

The filming took place at several locations in metro Detroit. By early February, a rough cut was delivered to my hotel room in Chicago. I was in town for the Chicago Auto Show. With the air-bags-killing-kids mania still white hot, it was great to be at another car show where everybody was happy. Michelle Tinson, who worked with me on safety issues, joined me in my room. I put the tape in the VCR and we sat back and watched Nye's handiwork. It was brilliant. At the end, I looked over to Michelle, who had tears rolling down her cheeks. I was crying too. If this didn't work, nothing would.

But, we knew we would need help. A Chrysler-only program, no matter how good the curriculum, no matter how brilliant the Bill Nye video, would stand little chance to make it into the schools and be used. We needed a coalition. Stratacomm went to work. We soon had the endorsement of the nation's pediatricians, AAA and its affiliates, cops, nurses and emergency medical physicians. Critically, we had NHTSA on board. We were ready to launch.

At a May press conference in the gymnasium of an elementary school in Washington, D.C., Chrysler CEO Bob Eaton, AAA CEO Robert Dalbernet, NHTSA Administrator Dr. Ricardo Martinez and Bill Nye kicked off the nationwide program. They were appropriately playing for the television cameras in hopes that adults, especially school administrators in charge of curriculum, would hear the message. I was nervous about the Bill Nye video, the cornerstone of the program. Kids in attendance, hundreds of them, would determine if we had hit the mark.

Genuine laughter and rich applause were the only reviews we needed. I knew it was not only a home run, but a grand slam.

"The Back is Where It's At!" curricula, bad grammar and all, was used in its full form in an amazing 95 percent of the public and private schools in the country. Newspapers across the country ran photos of the executives in suddenly-hip black-rimmed sunglasses sending the message "It's cool to sit in the back seat."

To complement the program among the general public and reinforce the danger of air bags, we turned to the media by conducting a series of live air bag deployments, demonstrating the explosive nature of the event. On one occasion, while running a press preview outside of San Diego for the Plymouth Prowler hot rod, I broke away to a safety conference in San

Francisco to meet with NHTSA Administrator Ricardo Martinez. I put my bag through the X-ray machine in the airport and was quickly surrounded by half a dozen cops. Stupidly, I had put the equipment I needed to detonate an air bag – a pint-sized battery and some wires – in my luggage. Holy shit! A frickin' bomb – or so it seemed.

The cops escorted me and my bag to a room off of the security zone. As we walked, all I could think about was the impending full body cavity search. Inside the room, they asked what exactly was in my bag and what it was for. I explained the event I was attending and the reason for the equipment. They weren't completely buying what I was selling. I had screwed up and had left my business cards at the resort. Finally, the light went on. I had the press release I would be handing out at the event in the bag. I told the cops exactly where it was and within a few seconds a screener retrieved the package of paper. The cops read the release and then told the screener to grab the battery and wires for inspection.

I explained why we were trying to get the word out about the danger of air bags for kids. The cops shook their heads and said they were fully aware of the situation. Within minutes, I was on the plane headed for Frisco, my sphincter intact.

With cameras rolling, a local dealer mechanic wired the Chrysler LeBaron Convertible and detonated the front-seat air bags. It was a blast. Literally. Some in attendance almost jumped out of their skin and I think a few Depends were soiled. The detonation was so great, in fact, the windshield of the vehicle literally cracked. So much for the image of soft, puffy marshmallows that guaranteed safety.

"Oh, that's not good," Martinez whispered in my ear.

"Actually, it is," I answered. "It's good TV."

I then cautioned all the media in attendance not to slow down the video of the demonstration when showing it on air.

"We need your help in getting out the message."

Importantly, the issue of air bags potentially killing kids dissipated quickly. The one-to-two dead kids per week thankfully never materialized. America's kids and parents were listening. NHTSA would later call "The Back is Where It's At!" one of the most successful passenger safety programs in history. I was proud we were along for the ride.

Crisis Lesson Learned: In a crisis, use every communication avenue to get out your factual message. Get creative when necessary. Reach out to your natural allies and ask them to amplify your voice.

Chapter Seven: Thank you Anthony Weiner!

I had the honor of holding the worst press conference in the history of mankind until former New York Congressman, Anthony "Show Me Your Weiner", wrestled the title away from me., It was at the 1998 North American International Auto Show in Detroit and we were launching a concept "mild hybrid" version of the fabulous Dodge Intrepid and an abundant use of plastic.

In reality, it was what the new non-hybrid Intrepid would look like. Chrysler had become the envy of the industry in auto show unveilings, always with a large dollop of show business; but we never imagined we could take it too far. Yes, we and I were cocky. Too cocky.

In a brainstorm session between the Chrysler PR staff and our agency that pulled off our show business, Ross Roy, someone came up with the idea to play a mock version of Jeopardy. The game would incorporate famous innovators from the past linked with Chrysler's innovation today. On stage were Leonardo di Vinci, Madam Curie and Albert Einstein as the "contestants." The script was hilarious...for an American audience. However, this was an international audience including hundreds if not thousands of French, Japanese and those wacky, laugh-a-minute Germans.

Despite arrogantly priding myself on my sense of humor, I foolishly assumed our comedy would translate. The script called for the game to be played with much frivolity, and finish with the unveiling of the car by design guru Tom Gale and an 8-year-old actress driving a small, plastic car.

See, this design was all about building cars greener and more efficient for the "next" generation of buyers. Get it? Doh! As Tom Gale spoke to the virtues of the Intrepid concept, the little shit – ahem, the little sweetheart – decided it was below her to be merely a stage prop, so she hopped out of her vehicle and started to do some improvisational ballet. Gale didn't know what to do. No one heard a word about the car.

I was later told the press conference lasted 22 minutes. I swear it lasted two or three years. Meanwhile, while running the most heinous presser, two men – Daimler's Juergen Schrempp and Chrysler's Bob Eaton, were at Chrysler's HQ in Auburn Hills discussing what would become the most controversial deal in automotive history – the soon to become, laughable "merger of equals." Maybe, my nonsensical press conference had given them "cover."

Depressed, I called my friend at Nissan. Tim McCarthy was head of Government Affairs for Nissan and had been a friend for about five years despite battles over U.S.–Japan trade agreements. We were like the wolf and sheep dog in the Loony Tunes cartoons that fight all day and then punch out with the salute "Goodnight Ralph, Goodnight Sam." Nissan almost hired me in 1992 but instead chose Debra Sanchez Fair. Tim had put feelers out the previous December. I told him "thanks - but no thanks."

Despite the disastrous press conference (with that bitch I swear someday I will run over and enjoy the prison term), my job wasn't in jeopardy as I was on a fast track up the Chrysler career ladder along with now-GM PR chief Tony Cervone. But times weren't fun at Chrysler. Give me a break; I know work is work and doesn't have to be always "fun." But, you spend more time at work than with your family, so it should be at least enjoyable – rewarding. If nothing else, hell, less painful. I would soon begin learning that in addition to enjoying work, in the toughest times, not balancing your life between work, family and friends can impede your ability to think clearly, make you lose touch with reality and perhaps impact your sanity.

CEO Bob Eaton had destroyed the camaraderie of the place by announcing that one of the five executive VPs would follow him in the top job. Friends overnight became foes and the departmental silos that had been successfully destroyed over the prior few years were instantly rebuilt; designers fought with the engineers, manufacturing fought with engineers, and everybody hated sales and marketing.

On the phone with Tim McCarthy, I told him I was ready to make a move. He was thrilled.

"I'll call California and tell them the good news," he said.

Tim and I met a few weeks later on the sly during the Chicago Motor Show.

"Can you get out to California next week to meet with Mr. Nakamura?" he asked.

"Sure, I'll make something up. But Tim, this has got to move quickly."

The next week I was in Gardena and looking up at Nissan's rather stark North American headquarters. Nissan had been in the news of late and the news wasn't good: Nissan was hemorrhaging cash both in America and in Japan, its home, and had sustained a massive drop in market share. I met with North American CEO Minoru Nakamura and his number two, Koji, both native Japanese. Both men were sent in by the parent company to clean up the mess laid at the feet of one of the last American leaders, Bob Thomas.

Koji was an affable little guy who seemed genuinely thrilled that I was considering coming on board. Nakamura was more stoic. He asked me about my style and what I thought of Nissan.

"Great company that lost its way," I said. "You need to do two things: stop wrapping yourself in the American flag and restore your DNA – the Japanese car company with an attitude."

He smiled. "You mind if I have a smoke?" Nakamura asked.

"Why are you asking me, you're the boss? Can I join you?" I said as I pulled out a box of cancer sticks.

His eyes bugged out. "We go outside. No smoking in building in California."

Outside, we smoked and smoked and smoked. He asked me about my family; I about his. I could see Nakamura was happy. If nothing else, he had a smoking buddy in P.C. California. Back in his office, he got all serious on me.

"We have a number of problems. We need to move fast. If we offer you the job, we will not negotiate."

Two days later, Tim McCarthy was on the phone again.

"Hey, they loved you. Now I know this is going to piss you off, but you've got to do one more interview. The head of manufacturing in Smyrna, Tennessee, Jerry Benefield, is a big swinging dick in the company and he wants to check you out. The fact is he put his HR guy, Bucky Kahl, up for the PR job. While he knows his guy isn't a PR guy per say, he wants to kick your tires. The guys in California promised him that courtesy."

Another excuse for my bosses at Chrysler and another plane ride. I sat down with the good-ol' boy manufacturing chief.

"How do I know if yer just using this job as a stepping stone to a bigger job?" he said.

"You don't," I shot back, "I'm not; and as we sit here today, and from everything I have read and heard, the Nissan PR job is a pretty big job considering the state of the company."

From Smyrna, I was back on a plane to Phoenix for a Chrysler ride-and-drive. No one was the wiser.

Back home in Detroit two days later, the call came from Nissan HR in Gardena. They wanted to make me an offer. I gave them a fax number in the Chrysler PR office and nervously stood by the machine until it spit out the offer. While a good increase from my Chrysler salary, it didn't seem like enough, considering my potential at Chrysler.

That night my wife put it succinctly around the dinner table: "I'm not moving these kids to expensive California for that."

After dinner, we played our usual basketball game with our boys, aged 10 and 8, and our daughter, aged 5. Five minutes in, my wife grabbed the ball, came over to me and gave me a kiss.

"We'll go where you go honey."

Around noon the next day, I called Nissan and told them the offer needed to be better. They said they would get back to me. An hour later, they were back on the phone with a substantially better offer.

"That's more like it. Send me something to sign."

Again, I waited nervously by the office fax machine. The offer came through, I signed it and faxed it back and then waited for the confirmation note to print. I called Nissan HR 15 minutes later.

"You get it?" I asked.

"Yes."

"Am I officially on-board?"

"As we speak."

I went back to my office and drafted a resignation letter, printed it and then walked into Steve Harris' office.

"Can we close the door?"

"Oh boy," Steve said.

"I'm the new head of Nissan North America PR."

"Nissan? Bob Lutz (Chrysler vice-chairman) and I were just talking the other day and he said Nissan is going down," Harris blurted out before realizing his words were a bit harsh.

"Sorry about that. What I meant to say is congratulations, they can use you."

"I know they're in bad shape, but I don't think it's that bad," I said, sad to leave my friends but thrilled about the opportunity.

We shook hands until Steve gave me a hug. He had been a huge force in my communications career; a brilliant manager who was not afraid to surround himself with smart people. An ego-less teacher.

"You're Yoda, Steve," I said as I left his office. He had selflessly been teaching the future Jedi-masters of automotive PR.

"Hmmmm, teach you I will."

At the end of the day, as I packed up my office, suddenly one of the security guards, John Teholis, who was a close friend, was standing in my door with a cop. Alongside him was Mike Morrison, the walrus-mustached speechwriting chief (he wrote almost all of Lee Iacocca's great speeches) and second in command of Chrysler PR. Morrison stood there just shaking his bald head. Mike liked me because I had given him a lot of laugh lines for Iacocca over the years. But he wasn't happy, and Mike was not a guy you wanted to piss off.

The security guard, John, gave me the bad news: they had been monitoring my expense reports and I was being charged with embezzlement.

"Sorry, Jason," he said. "The Sergeant is here to arrest you and escort you out."

Morrison continued to shake his head.

"What the hell are you talking about?" I squealed. "Let me see your badge."

The officer showed his badge. It was real – O'Brien with some numbers. It was heavy.

"Come on, this has to be a joke."

Morrison finally spoke. "We've been looking for a long time. Dammit Jason."

I was in a fog, half-smiling as the officer led me out to the hallway, cuff-less thank God. As we exited the office suddenly a chorus of "surprise" hit me. It was the entire department wishing me well and pulling a massively dandy prank on someone who was known for pulling all sorts of practical jokes. It was magical actually. John couldn't contain his laughter and Morrison was literally busting a gut.

I looked at the officer and said "Who the hell is this?"

It was one of John's security buddies. And he was clearly of Mexican descent. They pulled it off with a Mexican cop named O'Brien. Geez.

Chapter Eight: Hit by a "Stupid Stick" at Nissan

The next Monday I was in Gardena to fill out some forms and get acclimated. I wouldn't officially start for two weeks, but we wanted to get some things out of the way. Chrysler had treated me graciously on the way out, although I couldn't stay for the typical "two-week notice." I was going to a competitor.

I was whisked into Mr. Nakamura's office. I was his new PR guy. Traditionally Japanese, he was stern.

"I thought I said we would not negotiate?"

Wow, I'm going to get fired on day one of my employment, I thought.

"I thought you agreed to make your best offer first?" I answered.

My mind was racing – do the Japanese get sarcasm, am I being a smartass with the CEO; have I shit the bed?

"Touché," Nakamura responded. "Let's go have a cigarette."

I think Phillip Morris stock went up that day. I later flew back to Detroit a happy camper. I felt wanted, very wanted.

The challenge was enthralling. But, the shit was about ready hit the fan or, the uchiwa (oo-cheewah). That's Japanese, in which I quickly became fluent.

Not!

Nissan's North American arm had been funding a music project in Greater Los Angeles for young African-American people via Thelonias Monk, the jazz guru. They had funded Monk foolishly, providing 90 percent of his organization's funding. No good 501c3 relies on one donor for that much revenue; it is too risky, especially when your funder is driving itself into bankruptcy.

Hours after arriving back in Detroit, Nissan's legal team was calling: "Can you come out early? We have a problem."

Days before, Nissan had informed Monk's group it could no longer fund their efforts. Nissan was within its contractual rights to end the relationship, but that was inconsequential. Monk's existence was on the ropes and his people didn't give a damn about contractual rights. They had called in "Mr. Shakedown" to help them out; The Reverend Jesse Jackson.

As we gathered in a conference room on the floor that housed Nissan PR, one of the lawyers described the battlefield. Nissan had every right to discontinue the contract with Monk's group, but The Reverend Jesse Jackson was threatening a nationwide boycott of the company. With the company losing money at an alarming rate, anything that negatively impacted sales would be disastrous. Worse yet, it would be an alienation of a whole set of Nissan customers. Nissan had an overall market share of about four percent in the U.S., but its market share among African Americans was a whopping 8 percent.

"I don't know what you folks did to deserve that large of a market share among African Americans, but it's clear a boycott could be killer," I said.

Bucky Kahl, the good 'ol boy from Tennessee who had just been installed as head of Nissan HR quietly sat by and listened to the lawyers and the Nissan PR people, including me. He had had enough.

"We've provided funding for these poor, inner city black kids for years and now we are racists?" he drawled. "This is nothing more than pure extortion."

"No shit," I deadpanned. "But here's the reality Bucky: we put ourselves in a position to be extorted. Being in effect the sole funder of a charity is crazy. Jesse Jackson will have a field day with this one. I doubt he'll even break a sweat. It's poor black kids and music for crying out loud! I've experienced Jackson's shakedowns in the past. He's really good at what he does, despite the fact it's usually a load of crap. Cut a deal, wean them off our teat and let's move on. We've got much bigger issues."

Move on we did... to the greater crisis. Nissan wasn't going bankrupt, it was beyond bankrupt. With the exception of 1996, Nissan had been losing money since 1991. Its global market share had fallen over that time from 6.6 to 4.9 percent. One point of market share in the auto industry amounted to roughly $3 billion in revenue, so we were talking about a decline of about $5 billion annually. Making matters worse - the pipeline of new vehicles was barren, Nissan's product development system was badly broken. Critically, there were too many people and too many plants to support constantly deteriorating sales globally.

Nissan's North American operations were particularly screwed up. You would think the collective goal of all Nissan managers would be to sell cars and trucks in the U.S. at a profit. But no. Nissan Manufacturing, based in Smyrna, Tennessee, considered itself a "profit center" and spread its fixed costs over as many vehicles as it could spit out despite a lack of real customer orders.

Nissan Financial, whose job it was to finance new car sales, was hell-bent on being profitable on its own even if it meant bad news for Nissan as a whole. And Nissan sales and marketing? A disaster. Under the former CEO Bob Thomas, these folks had devised a quirky ad campaign that featured a squirrelly little "Oriental" dude saying "Dogs love trucks" and offering $75 a month leases to people who didn't have a pot to piss in and routinely defaulted on their lease. Nissan North America had become Repo Central.

Thankfully, Nissan was getting serious. Despite its overall state of disaster, Nissan had been incredibly successful in the northeast part of the country – New York, Massachusetts and New Jersey in particular. They snatched the top sales guy from the region and put him in charge of Nissan sales for the entire country. His name was Mike Seergy. Seergy's sales team was outselling Toyota and Honda in the New York area. He was a smash-mouth Jersey guy straight out of central casting, with an MBA and a highly refined analytical mind. Profane and blunt, we were instant friends. I mean instant.

"How did this company get so screwed up?" I asked him during our first meeting.

"Dogs love trucks," he laughed. "Only problem is, dogs don't buy any fucking trucks. We sold cars to people who couldn't afford a cup of coffee and after three months of non-payment, we got their shitty truck back worth less than half the original price. It was like rotting produce in your grocery store. Our residual values are shit. No, less than shit. We gotta shake this place up."

I was on-board and knew I had a brother-in-arms who knew a hell of lot more than me about the nuts and bolts of selling cars. But we needed much more.

I had been at Nissan a little more than two weeks when one of my PR teammates, Tim Gallagher, drove me down to Nissan's North American design center in LaJolla, California. Tim was the classic auto PR guy – affable, out-spoken and a complete bullshitter, who could wine and dine any automotive journalist on the planet.

In LaJolla we met design Chief Jerry Hirshberg. Hirshberg was short, yet stocky and in amazing shape for a 50-plus guy. He was a ball of energy. Jerry gave us a tour, showed me some old concept vehicles and then took us into the main studio where a small staff of designers tried their magic when they weren't playing basketball outside in the courtyard. Only problem was, there hadn't been a lot of magic of late or, perhaps fairer, Nissan HQ in Japan had stymied them.

In the center of the studio was a large table with a ¼ scale clay model of a concept they were exploring.

"What's that?" I asked Hirshberg.

"We call it an SUT. Part SUV, part pick-up truck," he answered. "We found the typical pickup owner only uses about one-third of their bed at any given time, so why not allocate the wasted space to the cabin and upgrade it to mimic the interior of an SUV."

"Is this a go?" I asked.

Hirshberg's smile turned to a frown. "We can't get squat to move ahead."

I looked around the studio. "Where's the Z?"

The Nissan Z took America by storm in the 1970s as a hip, great looking and fast sports car. It had debuted as the Nissan Fairlady Z in 1969 in Japan. Nissan would soon export it to the U.S. as the Datsun 240 Z. But most important, it was supremely affordable. It immediately changed Nissan's image from a Japanese maker of small cars to the Japanese car company with an attitude. Not a cocky Maserati attitude and not an American muscle car over-the-top attitude. It was smart and sexy. However, after a couple of decades, the Z engaged in a super car battle with Toyota and Mitsubishi and went high-end, losing its affordability charm. It was doomed.

"The Z," Hirshberg said grinning as he pointed to his head, "It's in here."

"Well," I said putting my arm around his shoulders, "Get it the hell out."

"I'd love to, but we just don't have the money," Hirshberg lamented.

"I'll get it for you," I said cockily, "How much do you need?"

"For both?" Hirshberg said referring to both a new Z and the SUT. "Full scale clay models, probably a couple million. But I'll get real numbers by tomorrow if you are serious."

"Hey, if we don't show the world this company gets it, we're toast," I said as we left the studio and headed back to Gardena.

The next morning I made a bee-line for Seergy's office.

"Hirshberg has two killer concepts we need to build to show we have some life left in us, but he has no money," I began. "One is an SUT. It's a —"

Seergy cut me off. "I saw it two weeks ago," he said. "It's fucking killer. What's the other one?"

"It's still in his head," I said. "A new Z that goes back to the car's roots as a hot, affordable sports car."

"How much money does he need?" Seergy asked. You could see he was getting ginned up.

"Couple a million," I answered.

"Holy shit," Seergy cried. "I can find you a million, but let's talk with Minilou."

Minilou was our boss, CEO Minoru Nakamura, my smoking buddy. When he took over as CEO, he was introduced by then-marketing chief Jerry Florence in a town hall as "Minilou," not Minoru, Nakamura. Florence was shown the door soon after my arrival; later to become a high-ranking executive at AARP before he died too young. I almost pissed myself when Seergy told me the story. Minilou. Hilarious.

"Let me handle Minilou, I have a secret weapon," I told Seergy. "I'll tell him you support it and that it's your money."

My secret weapon had become obvious two days earlier. Every day since joining the company, I would meet Minilou in the courtyard for smokes – morning, noon and after work. I didn't need to go to his office to get approval for this or that. We conducted business in the fog of Marlboros.

Then it happened.

Minilou came down to the PR floor and walked into my office unannounced. My secretary remained seated at her desk in awe. He walked over to my desk, extended his hand and revealed what looked like a "dad's coin purse". He snapped it open to expose its lined, fire-proof interior. It was a portable ash tray.

"I got you one of these," he said and walked away.

Bonnie came in. "What was that all about?" she asked. "He gave me this," I said, holding out my gift from the CEO.

"Oh my God, do you realize how important that is?" she said.

"Yeah, I really needed one of these portable, Japanese ash trays."

"No, you dope," she said. "It means he likes you. In all the time he's been here, he's never, I mean never, ever come down to our floor."

And they say smoking kills. Ha!

I called Minilou's secretary, Judy.

"Let me know when he's headed down for a smoke, I have something important to share with him," I said coyly.

"But, he's right here and can talk with you now Jason."

"Oh no," I barked, "This has to wait for a smoke."

Hours later it was me, Minilou and Mr. Morris (Phil to those familiar). I told him of the plan to build the concepts and that Mike Seergy was on-board in spirit and financially.

"I say go ahead," Minilou said as he finished his third cigarette in the span of 10 minutes. "But, keep it quiet for now. We cannot let Japan know yet."

Chapter Nine: Rediscovering the lost, good DNA

Jerry Hirshberg was on the phone the next morning. Metal Crafters, the concept car builders for many auto companies, wanted $2 million to build two full scale clay models. I told Jerry we had only (Ha! Only!) $1 million. He came back a day later with a compromise. One full scale Nissan Z and one ¼ scale SUT.

"That'll look like a kid's toy Jerry," I said. "These have to be real."

Hours later, Hirshberg had cut a weird deal with Metal Crafters. Both vehicles would be full-size, but they could only complete them on three sides. The fourth side would be rough clay.

That was completely wacky.

"We can sell it like it is a work in progress," I said, pulling an idea directly out of my ass.

"Works for me," said Hirshberg.

We had no choice and no other money. The SUT design was done and delivered to Metal Crafters, but the Z was still in Hirshberg's head. We all knew what we wanted – an update of the original, affordable Datsun 240Z – but getting there would be tough.

Hirshberg transformed the studio back to the 1970s and brought in an original for inspiration. It proved a distraction. It was like making love to your new wife while your ex was reading the National Enquirer in a chair next to your bed. The old Datsun 240 Z was removed.

While Hirshberg was busy making hopeful magic, Seergy, Minilou and I were trying to get people excited about Nissan again. Remember that guiding principle of putting your customer first? Well, Nissan had done a completely shitty job.

Shock alert: Nissan's customers, like Ford's, Chrysler's and Toyota's, were and are not the buying public. Nissan's customers were its dealers.

Period. And they had been shat upon as Nissan's product pipeline dried up. We had to, yes, convince the public that Nissan could come back. More importantly, we had to convince the dealer body to stick with us.

"We need a Road Show, Seerg (as I came to call Mike Seergy)," I said. "We need to give our dealers, analysts and media a peek under the kimono."

It wasn't a new idea; Chrysler PR head Steve Harris had employed the same strategy when Chrysler was swirling around the toilet bowl in the early 1990s.

"Show the all-new Xterra (awesome), show the new Maxima (a punt), but show the concept cars – the SUT and, more importantly, the Z, our DNA," I begged Seergy.

"Let's go talk to Minilou," he said.

I didn't want to use my "secret weapon smoking ploy" for this. We needed Seerg, his energy, and his marketing money.

"Let me map this out before we meet with Minilou, including costs."

I worked through the night and by morning I had a plan. Show the new Xterra SUV, Maxima and new Frontier small pickup already in the works, plus the concept cars – the SUT and the kicker, the Z. Start in New York, for our dealers first and then the analysts and media. The tour would then go to Detroit, then to Smyrna, Tennessee, to try and excite our production workers who were on a company-mandated summer hiatus to try and reduce inventory, and end in L.A.

Within a week, Seergy and I were in front of Nakamura with a plan to roll-out the "new" Nissan in a Road Show. He liked it, but wondered why it didn't include Nissan's luxury division, Infiniti.

Infiniti had been a basket case since its inception. Infamously, this rival to Toyota's Lexus division had launched itself earlier in the decade with a series of commercials; amazingly refusing to show a single image of their products. Instead, the ads showed nature and landscape and would be mocked by the auto industry as the "rocks and trees" ads. Infiniti had some pretty decent cars; but as a brand - it was stillborn.

Regardless, we asked Infiniti's leader Tom Orbe to join us on the Road Show to declare that Nissan – and Infiniti – were alive and kicking. He declined. We told Nakamura as much. We also told Minilou we needed to act with urgency. Our dealers were losing faith, our market share was still on the decline and the media was up our ass.

"You are not telling me anything I do not already know," he said.

Nakamura had to get an okay from corporate headquarters in Tokyo; a headquarters that was melting down. As the folks in Firestone's U.S. and Toyota's U.S. operations would learn, all major decisions would come from Japanese headquarters. Frustratingly, this meant delay upon delay while they tried to pull their heads out of the sand and, ahem, other places.

Nissan wasn't merely bleeding cash; they were a corporate hemophiliac. Rumors swirled within the U.S. executive team that the company was on life support. Later, rumors percolated that the Japanese government had given its number three automaker an under-the-table-no-repayment-necessary loan of $500 million dollars to keep it afloat. To their credit, the Japanese government appreciated their manufacturers and job creators. Unlike the U.S. government, which about a decade later would chastise U.S. auto industry leaders in a kangaroo court (Congress) before agreeing to bail out GM and Chrysler. Conversely, Japan, like Korea and Germany, appreciated the impact of a strong auto industry on their economies.

A week later, Minilou called me and Seergy into his office.

"You can do the Road Show. Try and keep costs down," he said, breaking into a smile.

Start spreading the news!

A month later we were in the Big Apple at the Sheraton Hotel on 53rd and 7th. We owed it to our dealers to let them peek under the kimono first. They loved it all. Mike Seergy and Jerry Hirshberg served as the Vegas showmen. Seergy had ripped open his hand the week before fishing for tuna in the Atlantic. He used his wrapped hand as a prop. He told the dealers, "Remember those stupid ads with the dog? Well, I got attacked by a dog. A now unemployed dog." The dealers went nuts.

As we unveiled the "New Nissan," the applause altered between so-so to pretty good. And then we unveiled the new Nissan Z concept. The place exploded. The standing ovation was sustained. I could see several dealers wiping away tears of joy. No shit. Nissan was getting its mojo back. Maybe, just maybe, the millions of dollars these dealers had invested in their businesses would pay off.

The presentations to analysts and media that immediately followed were positive, but far less over-the-top. They remained skeptical. The future of Nissan was the here-and-now. Desperately on the brink of bankruptcy, Nissan seemingly had no way out. Most believed they needed a lifeline from a stronger automaker willing to buy on-the-cheap.

The Road Show continued to Detroit and then finished in L.A. At the end of the L.A. show, I felt I had moved the needle for the company. In my own mind, I was living large and basking in the glory of my accomplishment.

Until I got a call from Infiniti's head of product planning.

He was an insufferable prick. I was driving home back to Newport Beach when he called my cell.

"Nice job on the Road Show," he said. "But, you offended everyone at Infiniti for not including us and I want you to know it."

My bubble burst, and dead tired from too long on the road, I pulled no punches. "I begged you guys to be a part of this from the get-go. And you assholes declined. You had a better idea which turned out to be no idea. Fuck you and shame on you for this call!"

Strong memo to follow. I pulled up in the driveway and there was my wife and kids drawing with chalk on the driveway.

"Hi honey, how'd it go?" she said, planting a beauty on me.

"Swell," I said, deflated.

Chapter Ten: Jumping the Shark

The Road Show had been an unmitigated home run, but the questions concerning Nissan's actual future were almost a daily media occurrence. Bob Simison, working out of the Detroit bureau of the Wall Street Journal, came to L.A. for a feature story on Nissan's potential "revitalization" – at least in the United States. Bob and I had become friends during my stint in Chrysler PR. He appreciated my candor and brutal frankness.

When Nissan announced that I was joining the company after years of fighting the Japanese on trade issues, both with Chrysler and the Big Three's lobbying association in Washington, D.C., Simison wrote an incredibly clever and smart-assed story in the Journal titled, "Legendary PR flack takes flak for jumping to Japanese rival." He interviewed Mike Seergy, Minilou and then me.

Bob asked, "What happened here to get this company in such dire straits?"

"Well," I said, "we sold cars and trucks to people that couldn't afford them, lost money on every vehicle and had a ridiculous ad campaign that tried to sell vehicles to dogs."

Simison laughed out loud, scribbling as I spewed.

"Basically," I continued, seemingly on a roll, "we got hit with a big stupid stick."

Out of my mouth and into God's ears. And into paragraph one of his feature story two days later.

"I laughed my ass off," Mike Seergy said with the Wall Street Journal in tow.

"Stupid stick; fucking classic!" he said.

Of course, Seergy liked the article because it contained the line "Seergy and Vines are willing the company to success."

But, what would Minilou think? The article was mostly ass-kicking, but there was that ever-present cloud over the future of Nissan as a whole, despite a new feeling of inspiration in the United States. It was time for a smoke.

"So, Jason, tell me: what is the meaning of 'stupid stick'?" Nakamura asked.

I took a drag on my 'Boro' and thought.

"Well, it's a reference to the past regime," I answered.

Then I thought, did Nakamura know the English term "regime?"

"By regime I mean –."

He cut me off. "Of course I know what that means. I was not hit with a stupid stick. For the most part, great article. But I am not sure Tokyo is completely pleased. But, I've got your back, as they say. Keep it up my friend."

Weeks later, Newsweek ran a story based on my "stupid stick" line. It led with the notion that most corporations would have fired their head of PR for such a comment. They opined the fact the company had embraced their situation with brutal honesty was probably a good sign in the midst of the horrible situation at Nissan. I would survive that quote and later recycle it for our benefit. Whew!

Meanwhile, Jerry Hirshberg was working on the new Nissan Z and our coming out party was just a few months away – the North American International Auto Show; or as I prefer, the Detroit Motor Show.

We almost jumped the shark. (Program note: "Jumping the shark" is a clever term coined years ago indicating you have completely lost your being or mission. When the hit show Happy Days was running out of steam, in one episode, the former thug Fonzie had become a softy and literally jumped on water skis over a man-eating shark. It was beyond stupid. The show would soon die.)

Mike Seergy came into my office and was practically bouncing off the walls.

"I've got an idea to cut through the clutta and I need your help," he said in his heavy New Jersey accent.

"What?" I answered.

"We go out and get the mutha of all pitchmen to do ads for us!" he spewed.

"Who?"

"Lee Iacocca!"

"Lee Iacocca?" I said, my jaw dropping.

"You bet your ass, Lee-fucking-Iacocca. And you're going to help me get him!"

I had to admit; it was ballsy and so far over the top that I thought oxygen masks were going to fall from the ceiling of my office. Sure, I knew Lee and he knew me. At the time he was nudged out of his CEO role and into retirement I was merely a mid-management PR guy who had written an occasional joke for his speeches.

There were other issues, the trickiest being the fact Iacocca had been labeled a "Japan basher" for his past tough stances on Japan's unfair trade practices. But that was a double-edged sword. What better way to stand up for a Japanese automaker than with someone with a history for taking on the Japanese. We shared the idea with our PR agency, Edelman. They loved it. One of their top dogs, Ronald Reagan's former chief strategist Mike Deaver, said he could at the very least set up a meeting with Iacocca.

A week later it was breakfast at the Peninsula Hotel in Beverly Hills; Seergy, Deaver, Lee and me.

"Are you out of your mind?" Iacocca said as we shook hands.

No "good morning" or "hello" or "good to see you again." No "why the hell you working for the Japanese." Nope.

"Are you out of your mind?"

Iacocca had kept himself busy by selling electric bicycles. Seergy suggested perhaps we could cut a deal and help him market his bikes alongside our cars and trucks if he would serve as our pitchman. The irony would be wicked.

Lee seemed intrigued, perhaps for the mere opportunity to pay back the folks at Chrysler who had kicked him to curb after he had famously saved the company from the trash heap in the early 1980s. Seergy then added the kicker: in addition to paying Lee for his ads, Nissan would give $1 million to Iacocca's pet Statue of Liberty project. A Japanese car company giving money to help preserve America's symbol of freedom; how's that for delicious? Iacocca agreed to consider the proposal and Seergy promised story-boards in a week for him to examine.

Iacocca would be in his New York apartment the next week. He would give us an hour. But, he added, this wasn't going to be easy. He would have to check with his daughters, Kathy and Lia.

On the ride back to Gardena, Seergy was quickly on the phone with the folks at ChiatDay, Nissan's ad agency. It was a Friday. Seergy told them they needed to work over the weekend and "give me a shitload of ideas" to share with Iacocca. To their credit, with little time at hand, they delivered a slew of ideas by Tuesday. The next day Seergy and I were on our way to New York.

That night we had dinner with Deaver.

"Lee's almost there, but his daughters are afraid he'll be ridiculed," he cautioned. "They're worried people will call him a whore. They're ultra-protective of their old man."

We had a chance, but a very small one. Inside Iacocca's spacious Waldorf Astoria apartment, we sat down with the legend.

"My daughters think I'm crazy to even consider this," he said. Seergy tried as hard as he could to keep Lee focused on the story boards.

Iacocca was in a different place; detached from our pitch. The meeting ended cordially with Lee promising to consider our offer when he joined his family for a get-away.

Monday the call came in from Deaver: "Close, but no cigar." Lee Iacocca had toyed with the idea of being Nissan's "face" in America; a face previously occupied by that weird little Oriental dude with the dog.

We soon would find that face just down the road in LaJolla.

ChiatDay had actually considered using me as that face and one of their account execs floated the idea in front of me.

"No way," I said. "I'm a PR guy, the soft-side of the business."

I later wanted to take myself to task for spewing those words. PR may be the alleged "soft side" of the business, but helping navigate Nissan through this shit-storm was anything but "soft" or easy; especially for a company whose Japanese PR staff couldn't grab their ass with both hands. If they could suddenly improve their game by ten-fold, they would jump to the level of "completely worthless."

ChiatDay had an alternative: design Chief Jerry Hirshberg. The same Jerry who had wowed the audiences as the face of Nissan while on the Road Show.

"Perfect," I said. "He's a good designer. More importantly, he has hutzpah," I said, not caring if using a Yiddish phrase to describe the Jewish Jerry was politically incorrect.

As Hirshberg traded the design studio for a sound studio, news about Nissan's future viability – or lack thereof – increased and got ever-the-more ugly as we were limping out of 1998. But we had hope. Hell, it was all we had. However, I would learn time and time again: hope is not a strategy.

The Detroit Motor Show would be, perhaps, Nissan's most important in it's up-again, down-again history. Nissan was the roller coaster auto company and I wasn't sure where we were on the tracks. We had a stellar line-up to show the automotive press. As Monty Python would say, "We're not dead yet."

Burl Ives described it brilliantly in Rudolph the Red-Nosed Reindeer: "And then it hit."

I could handle a head-in-the-sand mentality in Japan. I could handle a media piling on and piling on about our impending doom. But, I couldn't manage Mother Nature. The storm of the century was hitting Detroit the weekend before the Detroit Motor Show. Two feet of white shit (yes, there is such a thing) and sub-zero temperatures. Northwest Airlines would famously trap its passengers on the tarmac of Detroit Metro Airport for eight hours. Airplane bathrooms went out of order. Babies on board had no formula. It was chaos. The city had been crippled.

Detroit Mayor Dennis Archer infamously went on the Today Show with Katie Couric and said the city had never experienced a storm like this. It was a crock. Detroit got hit by a storm like this once or twice a year. Streets would remain unplowed for weeks as the city had become inept at handling basic services. Detroit's biggest show, the Motor Show, was in danger of being cancelled.

I was supposed to leave on Saturday afternoon from LAX. I called Northwest Airlines; they told me the bad news. I couldn't possibly get out until Tuesday at the earliest. I wanted to cry. Check that; I started to cry in my kitchen. Every ounce of sweat that I, Seergy, Hirshberg and Minilou had put into Nissan's coming-out party was about to evaporate; actually freeze.

Franticly, I called Nissan's travel counselor – Michael something (Sorry Mike, early-onset-kinda-Alzheimer's has crippled my memory) – and he said he was on the case but we were basically screwed, except...

"Except what," I asked.

"I could try to find a private jet," he said.

"Go!" I screamed.

69

Within 15 minutes, God's gift-to-me Michael, was back on the line.

"Okay, here's the deal. There is one, one jet left. It's 35 thousand dollars and we have to commit in the next 15 minutes."

"Give me a second and stay by the phone," I said. I searched for Minilou's cell phone in my briefcase. (For you Millenials and GenXers, we didn't store all these numbers in our cell phones, which were, at the time, still closer to The Flintstones than Google Glass.)

"Mr. Nakamura, it's Jason. I can get us a plane to Detroit, but it will cost us 35 thousand dollars."

The phone went silent. Nissan, as a global entity, didn't have 35 thousand dollars. Shit, they didn't have 35 dollars. Nakamura ended his silence.

"Is there room on the plane for me?" he asked.

At that very moment I realized just how much I loved my smoking buddy.

"You bet. I will call you back with the details but start heading to LAX now."

With the plane booked, it was wheels up a few hours later for a four-hour flight to Detroit Metro Airport.

We landed, stayed on the tarmac for two hours, and finally picked up an Infiniti Q45 left for us at Airport Parking. Stupidly, I had no gloves and the car was buried under Mother Nature's "Fuck You Jason" snowfall. It took me an hour to dig us out. We pulled out of the space. My hands were numb.

The drive to downtown Detroit and our hotel – normally a 30 minute drive – would take an additional two hours. But, we had arrived.

Although only half of the 5,000 journalists had made it by the opening of press days for the Detroit Show, it didn't really matter. Those not there in time would read the news.

First up, for us, was a surprising, affordable and rugged new entry into the exploding SUV market – the Xterra. When I first heard the name I winced, until I heard the leading alternative: the Tamarack.

"Wow, that is totally gay," I told Hirshberg.

Perhaps I was un-PC before my time. Whatever. The Xterra was designed for those that didn't need creature comforts but wanted a vehicle to take them everywhere and with the ability to wash out the whole damn vehicle, inside and out, with a garden hose. Its rear tailgate featured a "bump out" where, from the inside, you could stow your back pack.

It was cool.

Our thought for a press conference? The world's biggest backpack. As the show began, the Xterra was hidden in a 25-foot tall backpack from which it would emerge. The press release and photos were delivered in normal-sized backpacks handed out to the greedy press. If it was for free, the media gobbled it up. I had learned the gig from Steve Harris while at Chrysler.

Give the media meaningful 'tsotske' that they can use time and time again and never discard. Here was something supremely useful. Press event after press event, the media would discard the bags and other crap offered by other manufacturers and store all their goods in our backpacks with Nissan Xterra splashed all over.

As the show ended and the media were checking out of the downtown Detroit hotels, bell captains' carts were loaded with literally thousands of Nissan Xterra back packs for the trips back to England, Germany, Japan and wherever.

Day Two of the Detroit Show had to be the money day for us. The Nissan Xterra would be a profitable vehicle for us, but only a Band-Aid to stop our hemorrhaging of money. We had to show that Nissan was regaining its mojo beyond a single new entry in the SUV market dominated by Ford, Jeep, Chevy and others. It was a 'Come-to-Jesus' moment for our company. This press conference would feature the SUV-slash-pickup truck Nissan SUT. More importantly, the new Z was to be unveiled.

Of course we started with the SUT. I didn't give two shits about the vehicle. However, the Z was Jerry Hirshberg's, Mike Seergy's and my baby. Hirshberg had created a decent re-creation. Not bad. Not great. It didn't matter at this point: the car just needed to be there.

The media reaction: perhaps Nissan was rediscovering its DNA. We represented 4.4 percent of all U.S. sales, but we received more than a third of the total media coverage coming out of the Detroit Show.

It was a slam dunk! We were able to celebrate for all of a month, until the third wheel fell off of Nissan's wagon and the "For Sale" sign was fully exposed in Tokyo.

Just prior to the annual February Chicago Auto Show, DaimlerChrysler announced their interest to purchase an 'on-its-deathbed' Nissan Motor Corporation.

This was particularly depressing.

"What happens to us?" my wife queried.

We were in god-awful expensive California with 10, 8 and 5-year-old kids.

"Hell, honey. I have no clue. But, I think somebody has to buy us."

"Did you know how bad off this company was Jase?"

"Kinda, sorta, not really. It was a chance to become a VP. Maybe my little head was thinking for the big one," I answered.

"We'll be okay; we always are," she cooed.

What a woman. What a partner.

But Nissan did not want to sell itself to the Germans. Yes, the two countries had been joined at the hip in the Axis of World War II, but effectively Japan had kept German auto companies out of its market and vice-versa.

DaimlerChrysler Chairman, Juergen Schrempp, was seeking to create a new world order in the auto biz: a German-led European, American and Asian "global motors" that Lee Iacocca had sought and failed when he tried to combine his Chrysler with Mitsubishi and Fiat a few years earlier.

But Nissan Motor's CEO, Yoshikazu Hanawa, wanted to get in bed with the folks in Dearborn, Michigan – the Ford Motor Company. Hanawa was smart enough to know that GM was a Titanic waiting for the next iceberg and Chrysler was on the brink every day of the week.

Hanawa had secretly flown to Detroit to meet with Ford CEO Alex Trotman. Hanawa would literally beg the Ford CEO to take over Nissan and protect the company.

Ford was the only American company he trusted - knowing its roots as a family business. Hanawa, was rumored to have cried in front of Trotman. He begged Ford to buy Nissan and save the company.

Despite Hanawa's tears, Trotman passed. He had quickly peeked under the kimono and saw a big, saggy sack of shit. Nothing more. His own company was on the brink of disaster, although it was presently experiencing record profits. For now.

We arrived in the Windy City with nothing new to show. We had shot our wad in Detroit the prior month. Sure, Chicagoans got to see their first glimpse of the Z concept car, but the news media was transfixed on our impending doom should the DaimlerChrysler deal fall apart.

And then my buddy weighed in.

Bob Lutz, the former Marine fighter pilot, Chrysler co-chairman, Lee Iacocca's public enemy number one, product guru and by then-CEO of a large car battery company, decided the media needed to hear from him concerning the proposed deal. He tossed out a gem: discussing the merits of investing in near-dead Nissan by his former (Daimler) Chrysler colleagues.

Lutz said perhaps the best way to do it was to "put $5 billion or $6 billion of gold bullion into a huge container, spray paint the word 'Nissan' on the side, tow it out to into the middle of the Pacific, and dump it overboard. That way only $5 or $6 billion will be wasted."

Ugh.

Thanks Bob! Thank you sir, may I have another?

When asked in an interview on the floor of the Chicago show about Lutz's comments, Mike Seergy could hardly contain himself.

"Tell Bob Lutz to stick to making batteries and play a little more shuffleboard," the New Jerseyian spewed, thankfully leaving the F-bombs out of his rant he had practiced prior to the interview.

The courtship with DaimlerChrysler – our survival perhaps resting on its outcome – lasted little more than a month. DaimlerChrysler officials were given unlimited access to Nissan's books. It was a corporate version of a full cavity search with all sorts of probing devices. Nissan's dignity had been cast aside.

Juergen Schrempp desperately wanted the deal as a symbol that he was the king of one of the most powerful industries in the world. But even he couldn't stomach the carnage uncovered in Daimler's due diligence of Nissan's operations and prospects.

Nissan's debt load was massive, with seemingly no way out. At the same time, Daimler was getting whiffs of the giant fart it had purchased in Chrysler the previous November that up to this point was silent (but would become deadly).

Schrempp couldn't take the risk. If Nissan was un-saveable and Chrysler's real troubles were unmasked, Schrempp would be the laughing stock of the industry.

By Wednesday, March 10, 1999, the deal was kaput.

"We discussed our options of a potential partnership very openly, and in a very friendly atmosphere, but finally decided not to pursue a participation," Schrempp told the media, after letting Hanawa know he was leaving Nissan at the altar, pregnant with a bankruptcy baby due any day.

Hanawa tried to save face saying, "We will continue to look into the possibility of cooperation projects, which will not involve capital transactions with DaimlerChrysler and we will actively pursue a possible linkup with other companies."

Allow me to translate Hanawa's gobbledy-goop: "HELP! I've fallen and I can't get up!"

Chapter Eleven: "Les Francois" to the Rescue

Enter the French. Think about it: when was the last time anyone counted on the French to come to the rescue? Okay, the French helped us big-time in the American Revolution, which we paid back with tons of interest in the early-to-mid 20th Century. And then some.

One of my favorite jokes was a supposed classified ad in a newspaper: "French World War II rifle: Shot once. Dropped once." Har!

French automaker Renault was serious and realized that Daimler's pass meant Nissan could be seized at a rock-bottom price. Renault was sitting on $2 billion in cash and indicated it was willing to invest in Nissan without taking a controlling stake.

Not losing control of their company was important to Nissan management and Board of Directors. They were proud. And stupid. They were convinced their current troubles were a cold, not pneumonia.

The fact was, and Renault would soon find out, a cancer had metastasized inside the company. On March 27th, the alliance between Renault and Nissan was announced. Renault held a veto-holding 33.4 percent of the Japanese automaker. The heavy lifting was about to begin and I got to go along for the ride. Japan Inc. would be changed forever.

As Renault continued to assess its potential alliance with Nissan, we knew we had to put our best face on the company. Our efforts at revamping Nissan's image – at least in the U.S. – had been somewhat successful. Earlier, I had arranged for Road and Track magazine writer Sam Mitani to become (almost) embedded in the Nissan Z concept project. And it paid off.

In a massive article in the April edition of the magazine, he told the story of the rebirth of the signature car and how it represented the company finally "getting it." The last line of his story was stolen from the movie Field of Dreams: "If you build it, they will come."

76

Yeah, that's the ticket. We stole Mitani's stolen line and ran with it in short order. Working with George P. Johnson, the exhibit company, we concocted an unveiling for the New York Auto Show just a month away based on the theme.

We arrived in New York on March 31st. The plan was simple: we would announce that the Nissan Z concept was a go! The real thing would soon be arriving at a showroom near you.

Only one problem: Nissan Japan had not given us approval. The call to my hotel room came at 11 p.m. It was Minilou.

"Mr. Hanawa has not given his approval for the Z."

I was dumbfounded and deflated. "Well, you tell Mr. Hanawa he gives us the okay or I go on a hunger strike."

Crickets.

"Jason, no one care if you go on hunger strike."

I could hear his smile over the phone. Minilou had become as big a smart-ass as his smoking buddy.

"Don't worry, I will handle it," he said as he hung up.

Three hours later, I was still up. Anxious and pissed. I had reached out to my team and told them perhaps it was all for naught.

The phone rang. Minilou again. "We are okay, but Mr. Hanawa is upset that we pushed this without his blessing."

Minilou must have gotten the living shit beat out of him. But, he prevailed.

"Hey, I am sorry if I painted you into a corner," I told him.

"Jason, we both painted ourselves into this corner. Meet you in front of the hotel for a cigarette."

If you got 'em, smoke 'em. And later that day, it was exactly what we would be doing: Sssssmmmoking!

Having earned the crown of worst press conference of all-time in my last days at Chrysler a little more than a year earlier, it was time to make amends. I prepped Minilou behind stage and then moved into the audience to watch the press reaction. All the seats were taken, but no worry. Being insanely ADHD, few chairs ever had the pleasure of my butt.

The stage went dark as the classical music began. Soon the curtains opened and exposed a field of fake rows of corn that George P. Johnson's team had created. I was back home in Iowa. This was MY field of dreams. It's what I, my PR team, Seergy, Hirshberg and Minilou, had sweat for.

Minutes before, GM PR chief Steve Harris, my mentor and the Yoda of PR, had told his team, "Come with me to the Nissan press conference and learn."

The field of dreams was breathtaking. I started to cry. I was so damned tired. And so incredibly happy. Then the spotlight hit Minilou, sitting stage left, on the front of the stage on a bench. He had a cartoonish, oversized copy of Road and Track – the one with the article about the Nissan Z.

"Build it and they will come."

Here was a Japanese CEO performing in front of an American and international crowd of jaundiced journalists. It wasn't Kabuki Theatre. It was the life and death of our company. God, I loved this man.

As the music faded away, Minilou read the last two paragraphs of Mitani's prose, ending with the line, "If you build it, they will come."

He put down the ginormous magazine replica and stood up.

"We will build it!" he shouted, pumping his fist in the air as the corn field parted and exposed the Nissan Z.

The cameras clicked frenetically. Think Justin Bieber coming out of a court house. We were back!

Maybe.

After all, it was April 1, 1999. April Fools' Day. I thought about Nissan's old tagline: 'Life is a Journey. Enjoy the Ride.' What a ride it had been.

About two months later, on May 28th, the marriage of Renault and Nissan was complete. We had a new lease on life, perhaps. Nissan remained a mess so bad that even Renault in its quick due diligence could not comprehend the turmoil.

A new board of directors would be established later the next month. Most importantly, a new management team was put in place on July 1st, led by Renault's Carlos Ghosn. Ghosn had cut this teeth restructuring and bringing Michelin, the tire giant, back from the brink of disaster. He was so brutal in his cost-cutting prowess that he had been donned with the nickname "le Cost Killer."

As the French takeover took hold, Mr. Nakamura – Minilou – was out. He had broken too many eggs in making our comeback omelet in the U.S. He was reassigned back to Japan to lead one of Nissan's supplier companies. Japanese companies were famous for their keiritsu – an integrated system of company-owned supplier firms that controlled costs and prices. They made real competition non-existent.

His successor as head of North America, Yuki – assigned by the Japanese as temporary head – was such an ass that Mike Seergy soon quit. Just days before he left I asked Seergy about our new leader. Seergy told me that Yuki had already served a stint at Nissan North American where he had cheered the "Dogs Love Trucks" nonsense. "He's a manipulative bastard right out of central casting for 'The Bridge over the River Kwai', Seergy said, quitting the next day to join Priceline.com. Woof!

In a gallant effort prior to his departure, Seergy begged Yuki to allow him to appear before the Nissan board to make a case for Minilou staying on as CEO. Yuki told Seergy, "I will not help you."

I was without backup and the new guy was "le Cost Killer." Enjoy the ride? Buckle up.

Our family had left California and returned to Michigan. It was simple: the schools in California were crap. The waiting line into private school was years. No one in our haute Newport Beach community, man or woman, had any original equipment on their bodies. I wanted to go home and Nissan made it possible.

They were going to get rid of Tim McCarthy (my buddy - the guy that got me to Nissan) and replace him with HR chief Bucky Kahl to oversee government affairs.

"Give me government affairs and I will fly to L.A. once every other week and Washington, D.C. the next; I can do it out of Detroit as a central location," I argued. "Give me an office at the technical center in Farmington Hills (just outside Motown)."

I was lucky; they didn't want to lose me and I got to reunite our family and with my wife's family. Nissan would treat me better than I would soon treat them. To this day, I am ashamed of that.

The day before the announcement was made that I was moving back to Detroit and taking over government affairs, I got call from McCarthy.

"Are you in favor of replacing me?" he asked.

I gulped, feeling like a shit. "Tim, they are replacing you, and it's either me or Bucky. I'll protect your team. He'll fold like a cheap lawn chair from Kmart."

The phone went silent for a few seconds. "You know one thing I have learned over my years on this planet?" he asked me.

"Life sucks?" I responded.

"No," he quickly countered. "Bitterness is a poison you take yourself."

My friend had been cast out, not classed out. His words impact me today.

Chapter Twelve: "le Cost Killer" kills

Carlos Ghosn left his new home in Tokyo and flew to America. He had just installed a new management team intended to save Nissan. He stopped in L.A. and then traveled eastward to metro Detroit. The troops in both locations were nervous, but hopeful. Technically, he wasn't in the No. 1 spot; that position "still" belonged to CEO Hanawa who had started to develop health issues from the stress he had been under. But there was no question among the U.S. troops who was in charge of Nissan moving forward if it could survive.

Ghosn took up shop in one of the main conference rooms at the Detroit-area tech center. The tech center was run by Yoshi-something. A nice-enough Japanese manager, he had little sense of cultural nuance. He was pure Japanese.

Less than a year later, he would peek his head in my office and say, "Jason-san, my wife and I are looking forward to your surprise birthday party."

Cripes! My wife was planning a 40-year-birthday-bash, and Yoshi had just let the sea urchin out of the bag. The night before the soiree, he returned to my office.

"Jason-san, see you tomorrow night at your surprise birthday party."

Come on! I mean really; the Japanese, of all people, knew the art of the "surprise" as they had perfected it about 60 years prior at Pearl Harbor.

I sat down with Ghosn. I wasn't nervous. Nervousness reigned for days after DaimlerChrysler had abandoned us; this felt hopeful.

"I have heard a lot of good things about you," Ghosn said. "I need your help. We have so little time, so I will cut to the chase. Tell me who is good and who we should get rid of in your opinion."

Wow. This guy was everything everybody had said about him. No B.S. Matter-of-fact, cut to the quick. I spewed for 15 minutes, identifying the keepers and the hanger-ons. One keeper was Jed Connelly, the top sales guy.

"Not the smartest guy I ever met, but bright, supremely solid, loyal, honest and being tapped at about 50 percent capacity. Most importantly," I told Carlos. "He's not an asshole. As we try and fix this train wreck, we need some folks that people want to work for. These people have had the shit kicked out of them."

Ghosn was a genius and wanted to mine every resource at his disposal. "Anything else?" he said as I was ready to head back to my office.

"Yeah, don't trust the PR team in Tokyo. They suck."

He stopped me. "You willing to come and spend a few weeks there as we roll out the plan?" he asked.

"I'll be there."

It was a good meeting.

Back in my office, Fred Standish flew to my desk. We were the only Nissan PR guys in Detroit. A former reporter for the Associated Press, Fred had gone to the "dark side" of PR years before to finally earn a decent living. I had grabbed Fred months earlier by the scruffs.

"You are the laziest PR guy I have ever seen," I had said bluntly, assessing his tenure at Nissan. "And, I think this position is underpaid. Here's the deal: you step up your game and I will increase your salary 50 percent. Or, I fire you. Your choice."

Fred paused. "I'll take door number one."

We laughed and he became one of the finest, hardest working and smartest PR guys in the industry. So, here he was, eagerly wondering what had transpired with Ghosn.

"Swimmingly," I said. "He's looking for our support. This is one smart sonofabitch. Trust me."

As October rolled in, I was on a plane to Tokyo to help with the communications effort that would become known as the Nissan Revival Plan or NRP. It was grandiose sounding, but that was Carlos Ghosn. Almost single-handily, he was trying to right a ship that had more holes in it than the U.S.S. Arizona, lying in its surreal grave in Pearl Harbor.

Joining me was Daniel Ward, Nissan's European PR chief. Daniel was a classy, tall Brit who made me look like the country-bumpkin from Iowa, turned smash-mouth Detroiter, I had become. It was Tiffany and Target. But, we would make a good team. And Nissan, with its weak Japanese PR team, needed that. Ghosn needed that. I soon learned that I could be as frank and blunt with Ghosn as he was with me.

Ghosn had assembled a team of super smart French and American finance and product development guys, including the supremely arrogant Patrick Pelata, whom he had put in charge of fixing Nissan's broken product development system.

Within our PR team, Pelata would soon be known as "AllottaPelata." Why? We were notorious Austin Powers fans. My second all-staff off-site meeting was followed by the entire team attending the opening of Austin Powers 2: The Spy That Shagged Me. Oh, behave! Powers had Allotta Fagina in his first "moooovie." We had AllottaPelata.

He, Allotta, had found that Nissan had a track record of launching new vehicles in Japan and then, mind-bogglingly, waited 12 to 18 months to launch the same vehicles in Europe and the United States. By then, they were like old produce and flailed in the market. Toyota did not do this. Hell, even Ford didn't do this. But the clowns at Nissan did. He directed his Japanese product planners to come up with a fix and gave them a week to figure it out.

It was early evening in Ghosn's office. The clock was ticking and we were working from 7 in the morning until 10 at night. We had no wives and kids to go home to; we were living out of a suitcase in a hotel three blocks away in the Ginza. The showers sucked; built for 5 foot 2 Japanese dudes. I was – am – almost six feet tall. My belly button got most of the shower spray.

I would work throughout the day, run back to my room, have a Sapporo, send emails to my staff in California and then crash with silly Japanese game shows on the TV running in the background. I think Ghosn was working on zero sleep and I hit him at a weakened moment in his office.

Ghosn was being vilified in the Japanese press; he was a man sent in to destroy the Japanese way of doing business. There were daily death threats. There were rumors Ghosn had closed down the near-by house of prostitution that had been a "service center" for Nissan's Japanese executives. A Frenchman closing down a hooker joint? Breathtaking!

Rumors were rampant that Ghosn was threatening to close plants and rip up the corrupt keiritsu system that permeated the Japanese auto industry. Parts suppliers, owned by the big automakers, fixed prices and corrupted the "free" market.

"You need more security," I said. "I run back to my hotel every night across the street."

"Why across the street?" Ghosn asked.

"I'm afraid one of these bastards is going to jump out the window and I don't want them using me to break their fall."

Ghosn laughed, although he realized the seriousness of the situation. Lots of folks were hoping he would fail in his attempt to transform the Japanese auto model. Check that: the Japanese business model.

And then he focused on himself; or as my other French friend, former Chrysler chief engineer Francois Castaing would say – he "fuckused" on himself.

"How do I change my nickname?"

I paused and then laughed. I laughed at one of the most powerful executives on the planet. "Are you kidding me?" I said. "You don't give yourself a nickname! What d'ya want: 'Stud?' Will that work for you?"

Ghosn sat silent. Had I gone too far? I continued: "You get a nickname for your image or what you do. You just can't go out and say, from here on out, my nickname is such-in-such."

Still crickets. Finally, Ghosn started laughing. He got it.

His nickname would soon change to: 7-11 (the convenience store). Ghosn would be working around the clock to save Nissan from the graveyard and would become, no shit, a comic book hero. That's the way it works. Your actions and your deeds.

As we laughed about his nickname concerns, AllottaPelata burst into the office. He was pissed. His Japanese product development team had come back to him with their "fix" for the delay in launching Nissan vehicles in Europe and the USA.

"Can you believe this?" he said, spitting like an ostrich, "Their answer to the problem is to delay the launch of our vehicles in Japan by 12 to 18 months in order to fix the problem. They are idiots."

Allotta then spewed something in French. I reached for my Blackberry to provide the translation, but then realized it hadn't been invented yet; or, at least I couldn't afford one.

Whatever; it was Greek to me.

Ghosn sat measured. He had studied the Japanese culture in depth prior to his arrival. He knew he could not save the company by being, for lack of better words, an "ugly American" even though he was French.

"What did you tell your team once you heard them?" he queried Pelata.

Pelata continued, completely razed up. "I told them shame on you, shame on you, get out of my office!"

Ghosn shook his head. "You need to go back to your team and apologize before they jump out of the building. You don't tell our Japanese colleagues 'shame on you'. Never."

AllottaPelata left the office with this tail tucked in. While he was right that his team was negligent, he had been schooled by Ghosn in dealing with the Japanese, a proud people. I took note, thankfully, and it would serve me well.

Ghosn put his team under extreme pressure and urgency. He immediately realized he was against a recalcitrant group of Nissan executives and board members who thought this was a momentary glitch, a frickin' speed bump.

"They think that this will all be better in a few months and they will get their company back," he told me, shaking his head. "This is permanent, if we survive."

I was watching a French Peter Townsend at work, orchestrating the biggest comeback in business history since Lee Iacocca had saved Chrysler. This was "Tommy" in my midst; a rock-and-roll masterpiece. And I was playing drums.

As we got close to the planned announcement of the Nissan Revival Plan, Ghosn had become extremely cautious.

"Do not share any details of the plan with the Japanese PR staff, they will simply leak it to curry favor with the media," he admonished.

Daniel Ward, my European counterpart, and I had formed a bond. Side-by-side in a conference room down the hall from Ghosn's office we had been writing the press releases announcing the plan. A proper Brit next to a profane "Detroiter", we would write and re-write Ghosn's remarks and the press release announcing the Nissan Revival Plan.

Draft after draft, Ward would continually remove my "Zs." Analyzing transformed into the proper British form "analysing." With a frickin' "S". What did these damn Limies have with the letter "Z"? Finally, I won the day. We had developed separate press releases for the U.S. and European press. In both, we announced the two regions of the world would soon be getting the all-new Nissan Z sports car. The resurrected vehicle was promised months earlier in the Field of Dreams press conference by Nissan North American CEO Minilou, my friend Nakamura-san.

"So, Daniel, are you Brits going to call it the Nissan Z or the Nissan S?" I said with the heaviest dose of sarcasm I could muster.

"You win," the affable Brit muttered. An American, a Brit and a bunch of French dudes trying to save the Japanese from themselves. Go figure.

Two days before the press conference we assembled in the hotel ball room in which the announcement would be made. Nissan's Japanese PR team was in charge of the logistics. We walked into the gigantic room and looked at the platform from which Ghosn would announce the most sweeping change in the history of Japanese business.

"Are you shitting me?" I said, not caring if that all-American phrase translated. "There will be a boatload of media pressing the stage and our new leader (Ghosn) isn't exactly tall."

The Nissan PR staff said nothing could be done. They were trying to exert their "power." I argued for 15 minutes. I was getting absolutely nowhere. I walked outside and lit a smoke, hoping to channel Minilou to get my way. On my last drag, a limo pulled up; it was Carlos Ghosn.

I laid it out: "You have to be seen full metal jacket – not a head peering over a crowd of reporters."

"I will handle this," Ghosn said, entering the hotel. He walked into the room and approached the Nissan Japanese PR staff.

"The stage needs to be two feet taller. Please make it happen," he said pleasantly.

Done deal, without breaking a single egg.

Back at headquarters later that afternoon, we were suddenly thrown a curve ball: Chairman and CEO Hanawa had unexpectedly decided to speak at the Nissan Revival Plan press event. Hanawa had recently developed an eye twitch reminiscent of Chief Inspector Dreyfus in the Pink Panther movies. He was not in good health. The cratering of Nissan had taken its toll. He had promised he was going to stay in the background as Ghosn rolled out the plan to save the company.

Something had changed. Carlos Ghosn handed me Hanawa's proposed remarks. I read the five-minute speech. It was an unmitigated disaster. Hanawa was prepared to say that Ghosn's Nissan Revival Plan was nothing more than a continuation of the reforms he had already initiated. It was like saying Ronald Reagan was working off of Jimmy Carter's script.

"I need you to fix this," Ghosn said.

Holy mother of pearl!

I marched over to the conference room we had been working out of and snared Daniel Ward. I shared Hanawa's proposed remarks and side-by-side we rewrote his speech. Happy with our effort, I headed to Nissan PR and found the number two guy who was also Hanawa's handler.

I cannot for the life of me remember his name for a variety of reasons; number one that he was a despicable shit. He had tried to thwart Daniel Ward and me at every intersection as we tried to move the company forward.

"I need to talk to Mr. Hanawa about his speech. Mr. Ghosn has asked me to assist you," I said.

Within ten minutes I was in the chairman's office.

"Mr. Hanawa, Mr. Ghosn and I feel that your speech will undermine the efforts of the Nissan Revival Plan," I spoke respectfully.

My Japanese PR counterpart quickly translated. I wasn't sure if he was saying "this American shithead should be shot."

I continued my argument in front of the Chairman hoping to convince him to change his words, waiting for my associates' translation of my plea. Nothing was happening. Hanawa seemed stunned.

Finally, with my ADHD kicking in, I said, "Mr. Hanawa, if you give this speech, you will look like a dick head."

Had I gone too far? Was I too much American cowboy? I waited for the translation. As my Japanese cohort started to speak, Hanawa interrupted.

"I don't need translation. I know what dick head is," he said in broken English but with incredible clarity. "What should I say?"

I pulled out the speech that Daniel Ward and I had crafted. The paper was still warm from the printer. Hanawa took five minutes to read it.

"This is good," he said.

Mission accomplished.

A day to go, I called my parents in Iowa. I had created incredible "challenges" for them in my "youth." But they felt subsequent pride as I (slowly) matured.

I was being driven by a chauffeur in Tokyo, living large. Before I had accepted the Nissan job, I had asked my dad if he was okay with me working for a Japanese company. He was a World War II Pacific Theater vet. He walked off his ship and into Nagasaki two weeks after The Bomb.

"We saw you on the news last night," my mom beamed.

"How's dad?" I asked.

I was, at that moment in the spotlight of the PR world. But, my dad was slowly dying. I was on top of the world and completely miserable. But, and it's a big but, I had made my old man proud.

Back at headquarters, Ghosn was preparing to meet that evening with the Nissan board of directors to lay out the plan. He brought Nissan's Japanese PR leaders into a conference room to explain what would happen the next day. Daniel Ward and I already knew the plan, but he wanted to put the fear of God into these folks.

"We are going to close five plants," he said. "If this leaks out before tomorrow, I will close six or more."

Ghosn was sick and tired of the leaks coming out of Nissan PR and its Japanese board of directors. Daniel Ward and I had developed an extensive Q&A to share with the board as Ghosn prepared to lay out the plan at 10 p.m. the night before the announcement of the Nissan Revival Plan. He wanted to share his plan with the board at the very last minute fearing leaks to the media.

I cautioned him: "The Japanese are famous for removing the 'Qs' when they don't like the 'answers'. Don't let them do it."

After his board meeting, I was back in his office.

"Remove these questions and answers," he said.

"I warned you about this Carlos," I said, incredulously.

"Jason, just remove them. I know the questions and the answers. I don't need them on paper. Make these people happy. OK?"

While I was being frustrated, he was just being smarter. The guy had the Japanese culture down to a T. I was leaving his office at midnight when he stopped me.

"What headline do you want to come out of our announcement tomorrow?" Ghosn asked me.

"We're changing Japan Inc. Period," I replied.

I raced to the hotel and collapsed on the bed fully clothed.

The press conference was, well, breathtaking. I cannot tell you the number of cameras. But what I CAN tell you is the swarm of media that attacked the stage as Ghosn began to speak. And they were all standing. Had the stage height not been increased, Ghosn would have looked like a midget as he offered up his plan for Nissan's survival. A Napoleon. However, he reigned supreme.

The next day I was at the Tokyo Motor Show. Spent. In the morning, I found myself at Narita Airport buying my kids toys. I had been an absent father. I was trying to make amends. I spent a fortune and then slid into my seat on Northwest Airlines. Ken Zino, former Road and Track Detroit bureau chief and newly–minted Ford PR pit bull, tapped me on the shoulder.

"You're not paid enough," he said.

He didn't know the first of it. Although, he soon would know.

Crisis Lesson Learned: If you are on the verge of or in a crisis, do not stick your head in the sand hoping it will soon go away. To steal the old cliché: hope is not a strategy. And if you work for a global company or organization, make sure you fully understand the cultural nuances of various parts of the organization.

Chapter Thirteen:
The Mother of All Crises –
The Ford/Firestone Tire Debacle

I was forced to join Ford Motor Company.

Months before, at the 1999 Tokyo Motor Show, I ran into Pulitzer Prize-winning Wall Street Journal reporter Joe White, who was talking with Ford Motor Company PR chief Vaughn Koshkarian. Vaughn, an affable gent, was not a PR guy by trade, but rather an expert on business in Asia. He had been thrown into the PR job and was obviously not thrilled about it. Luckily for Ford, Koshkarian was a Ford lifer and would do whatever he could for the company. Vaughn knew of me and my high-profile work at Nissan – especially the Nissan Revival Plan announced a day earlier in Tokyo.

This is how our introduction went:

"Jason, this is Vaughn Koshkarian, the head of Ford PR," said White.

"You want my job?" Koshkarian pleaded as we all laughed.

"Nice to meet you too, Vaughn," I said.

But why wouldn't you want to be the head of Ford PR? The company had become the darling of the industry by late 1999. Profits were huge and CEO Jacques Nasser, with the support of Ford scion and Executive Chairman Bill Ford Jr., was personally changing the stodgy, rust-belt image of the industry. The company had the audacity to give all employees free home computers and internet access. They wanted workers and their families to become more web savvy. Other automakers were jealous as hell they had not thought of the idea. Nasser and Ford were looking more like Microsoft than Studebaker. The media took note.

The opportunity didn't arrive for a few months. After accumulating an assortment of Japanese cutlery in my back as Y2K rolled our world into a

new century, I was ready for a change, and my brother-in-law Chris
Theodore, now the product chief at Ford, knew it.

After church services, he pulled me aside: "You have dinner with
Jacques Nasser Friday night. Be at the Glass House (Ford's HQ in
Dearborn, Michigan) at 6 o'clock."

That night I sat on my patio contemplating my future and a near
disaster. Just a month earlier I had been out in Gardena, California hosting
my PR team at a Christmas lunch. At my table was Kurt von Zumwalt, a
PR veteran loved by the media. A former hippie back in his formative
years – not surprisingly the subject turned to pot.

"Shit, I loved pot in college," I admitted. "But, I seriously don't have
a clue where to buy it."

At 39 years old, I hadn't smoked pot in 16 or 17 years. Two weeks
later I was back at my house in the suburbs hosting dinner for my
California team. It was the night before the first press day of the 2000
Detroit Motor Show. We were in great spirits despite the uncertainty of the
proposed Renault takeover and our continuous plunge toward bankruptcy.
We had become "the most interesting automotive PR team in the world."
The company was relying on us.

The dinner was a blast! Afterward, I escorted everyone out of the
house through the entrance to my garage; Kurt von Zumwalt was the last
to leave. As he walked toward his car, he suddenly stopped and turned
around. Reaching into his pants pocket, he pulled out a Kodak film
canister and tossed it to me. "What's this?" I asked as I opened the lid.
"Oh my," I said as I ogled at two joints inside the canister.

"You said you didn't know how to find it."

Yowza.

That night, on the eve of the Detroit Show, our future on the line and a
new alliance with no guarantees, I needed a respite. At least in my mind.

After midnight, with my wife and kids fast asleep and Ted Koppel signing off of Nightline, I snuck into the garage and secured my quarry. I pulled out a joint and grabbed a lighter. Just as I flicked my Bic, the door suddenly opened.

"Daddy, what are you doing?" said my seven-year-old daughter, peeking into the garage. I quickly stuck the unlit-joint back into the canister and into my pocket.

"Nothing honey, let's go to bed."

A month later I would be in Ford Medical taking a drug test. Holy cow, Batman! Saved!

Or, maybe not.

I arrived 30 minutes early to the visitor's lot at Ford headquarters – The Glass House in Dearborn. 1 American Road. I was nervous as hell and smoked about a half a pack of Marlboros before dousing my throat with Listerine to "cover" the smell of tobacco. I checked in at the executive desk and was escorted to David Murphy's office on the 12th (top) floor. David was Nasser's closest ally and global head of human resources. Both Aussies, they had grown up through Ford Motor Company, starting at the bottom – Grade One managers. The interview, which I wasn't told was necessary, was a bit prickly to say the least.

"How many people report to you at Nissan?" Murphy asked.

"About 30," I answered, although truth be told I had become somewhat head of PR for Nissan globally in a de facto manner.

"Well, do you think you can handle a global PR staff of more than 300?" Murphy continued to probe.

"Sounds like you've got too many PR people," I countered as my mind raced as to whether I was being too ballsy with an executive I just met.

The interview lasted only a few minutes when Murphy told me we were meeting Nasser at the Ritz Carlton about a half mile up the freeway from the Glass House.

We entered a special private dining room; there was Nasser and Koshkarian. They welcomed me wholeheartedly; we started to talk as we ordered food and drinks. Nasser asked me about my PR philosophy and what, if anything, Ford was doing wrong. The latter was a bit of a shitty question considering the guy they wanted me to replace was sitting across the table. I stayed as positive as possible, but told Nasser if I had one piece of advice, from my experience with Ford, it was simple:

"Be less mean. If GM announces a press conference tomorrow at 10 a.m., don't let your PR people announce a press conference at 9 a.m. It only pisses off the press as they have to pick which to attend. Your people do that."

Koshkarian nodded in agreement. It was clear he wanted to get back to being an Asian auto expert and not in the PR hot seat. Instantly, we were friends. Dinner, two glasses of wine, six glasses of water, two cups of espresso and three hours of talk, I felt as if I was being worn down. Worse yet, my bladder was bursting and I cried uncle:

"Excuse me gentlemen, but I have to pee."

Returning from the can where I believe I had flooded the Rouge River when I flushed, the mood had changed. Nasser was all business.

"I am convinced you'd be great for our team, but... (Oh shit, here comes the BUT!), you'll have to meet with (Chairman) Bill Ford on Monday morning to get his buy-in."

I had won over Nasser, but to this day I still don't know why I decided to possibly snatch defeat from the jaws of victory when I said:

"I guess you forgot that I publicly called Ford stupid a couple of times?"

"Didn't forget, Jason," he deadpanned, "Just need to keep my enemies closer."

Nasser laughed loudly.

We parted ways as I drove to Chris Theodore's house to meet my wife, her sister and Christo. The interview had gone well, but the weekend of anticipation would prove excruciating. If it worked out, I would have the premium PR job in the auto industry – hell, perhaps the best PR job in the world. Ford, one of the largest companies on the planet, had effectively shed the "rust belt" image with which the U.S. automakers were constantly pummeled. However, I would be leaving some wonderful friends at Nissan.

Monday morning I was escorted to Bill Ford Jr.'s office.

"Welcome on board," were Bill's first words.

So much for an interview, thank God. My promise to him: I would never blow smoke up his ass and would only give him my best counsel.

His response: "You'll be a breath of fresh air around here."

Signed, sealed and...deliverance: The Ford/Firestone tire crisis – still considered the greatest crisis in automotive history, unless General Motors bungles its way to top it with their ignition switch disaster -- would begin in earnest in just two short weeks. This crisis would become the fodder for university ethics in business classes for the next decade.

Crikee.

Chapter Fourteen: Fan: Meet the Shit

I immediately befriended the Chief Counsel of Ford, John Rintamaki. John was not the Ford I had witnessed from afar. He was soft-spoken, enthusiastic and likeable. Who woulda thunk it?

Susan Krusel was in charge of Safety/Regulatory PR; like in my stint at Chrysler during my early years -- a stint you must complete to climb the corporate PR ladder. I had established an open door policy for my office: you didn't need to be a direct report to come and see me.

Krusel told my assistant, Lynn Quigley, she needed to show me something: a news series from Anna Werner at KHOU in Houston involving Firestone tires on Ford and other vehicles experiencing tread separation. The results were nothing short of horrific; devastating and deadly crashes.

"Let me show you the news clip," Susan said as she entered my office.

"Nope," I countered without knowing much about the content, "Let's go to Rintamaki's office to watch."

My assistant called Rintamaki's assistant and said we were on the way up – one floor.

When we arrived, Rintamaki said "What you got?"

"Not sure," I said, "Susan has a concern."

Ford's media monitoring folks had compiled KHOU's three-part series on one video tape. (For those not understanding this antiquated terminology, a "video tape" is about the size of half an IPad, only thicker. It has film that you "play" in this thing called a VCR. Sorry, just wanted everyone to be on the same page.)

As the news reports began, we saw a horrible tale of multiple accidents, some fatal, where Firestone tires on two Ford Explorers and a GM Suburban had experienced tread separation and the vehicles rolled-over. Passengers were killed or injured. Krusel had been working on this issue for several weeks with the Ford lawyers. As we watched the video, suddenly a statement from Ford appeared in the newscast denying any knowledge of a problem based on information they had received from its tire supplier. They were, in some way, actually "blaming" the customer for improper maintenance.

"We're blaming the customer?" I asked, remembering the debacle of the Jeep sudden acceleration saga.

Then, it got silly. Ford had supplied KHOU with a Ford-produced demonstration using a Ford test driver piloting a Ford Explorer, as engineers methodically blew out a tire to show it was simple to bring the vehicle to a stop with little effort and (of course) accident-free. My jaw dropped. The "test" vehicle had outriggers attached, specifically designed to prevent a roll over.

"What the hell? The vehicle has outriggers on it and the driver knows what's coming," I shouted at the TV as the video played.

Seconds later, a safety "expert" – aka a plaintiff's bar "friend" – was on camera saying "the vehicle has outriggers on it and the driver knows what is about to happen." He was right about one thing: the Ford test driver knew what to expect. Those regular customers traveling on what would be determined as defective and deadly Firestone tires, did not. Sadly, some would never know what hit them as 271 would die and even more would be injured.

Rintamaki saw the danger and within a week or two; (Spoiler alert! Sorry, Ford captured all of my files when they fired Nasser, Murphy and me 20 months later. My dates may be a bit fuzzy - but not directionally wrong) John convinced Nasser to create a "tire team" he would lead. It would include Nasser as well as the heads of manufacturing, engineering, procurement and supply, advertising and me. Initially, we would meet every few days. As the crisis escalated it became necessary to meet daily to share updates, respond to new information, and plan strategy. To this day I am proud of Ford Motor Company's response to the crisis. Our strategy was a testament to a company that cared more about customers than its own ass – (I mean bottom line).

Long before the historic fight between Ford and Firestone would develop – Okay, weeks – we had determined the "tire team" would base ALL of its decisions on a short list of Guiding Principles; no decision would be made that violated any of those principles. Period. The 3M Company would have been proud; we had listed those Guiding Principles on one of its enormous chart thingees and taped them to the wall of our tire team meeting room. The principles were simple. I know; the magic marker was in my hand while we debated them.

Number One: The safety and satisfaction of our customers was paramount.

Number Two: We would work tirelessly to identify ways to find replacement tires for our customers. In fact, we would scour the global tire industry 24/7 to do so.

Number Three: We would communicate honestly and openly at all times. We would base our responses on facts and facts only; never on conjecture or a guess.

Number Four: We, Ford, would protect Firestone.

Those that followed the crisis may find the last Guiding Principle a bit far-fetched. But, hear me out.

Early on, Firestone was in a far more financially tenuous position than Ford Motor Company. Ford was (literally) sitting on billions of dollars Firestone simply did not have. Early signs indicated this was a significant tire problem just twenty years removed from the Firestone 500 tire debacle of the 1970s. That crisis eventually sent a great American corporation to the auction block only to be purchased by Japan's vaunted Bridgestone Tire Company.

But we knew. We knew that if the plaintiff's bar and their happy "safety advocate" buddies like Public Citizen's Joan Claybrook and Clarence Ditlow and Safety Research and Strategies' Sean Kane could convince the media and the public ALL Firestone tires were faulty, it would create panic in the public and intentionally disrupt the auto industry. Ford's future, at least short term, as well as General Motors' and Toyota's, was at stake being big customers of Firestone. I was repeatedly quoted in the press. For people (see…agitators-for-money) like Claybrook and Kane, their narrative was "every tire that was round and black was defective and deadly." Their plaintiff attorney buddies were lapping up their rhetoric. I needed to clarify and change the message.

Ford had to protect Firestone in order to calm customers driving on good Firestone tires. We desperately needed time to get the bad Firestone tires off the road.

Around May of 2000, the crisis started to escalate, and not just in America. In fact, America was late to the party. Ford officials first started seeing problems with Firestone tires on Explorers in the Middle East and in Venezuela – two regions that had two things in common; namely, hotter-than hell climates and lots of Ford Explorers, the number one selling SUV in the world. In the late 1990s, Ford Middle East officials starting getting lots of complaints regarding tread separation of Firestone tires on Explorers. Inquiries were made countless times to Firestone officials. Each and every time, the formal response from Firestone HQ was a "lack of proper customer maintenance".

True, many owners in the Middle East would lower tire pressure in order to get more grip while crossing the desert and then not re-inflating the tires' air once back on the highway, thus causing great heat in the tire (the enemy of tire safety). However, the constant reply of "no problem here" from Firestone simply kept Ford people in the dark.

The incidences were equally severe and even more deadly in Venezuela, which had become a huge market for Ford Explorer because of its incredibly shitty roads. Heat and crappy roads are bad news for a tire; especially a poorly-made Firestone tire. The National Highway Traffic Safety Administration (NHTSA) was now breathing down the neck of Ford and Firestone, and the media had taken up coverage of the crisis full time. Ford engineers grabbed a boatload of Venezuelan Firestone tires and tore them apart. They were not only not up to spec; they were total crap.

The relationship between Ford and Firestone was tearing apart at the seams despite their 100-year history. Consider: Bill Ford's mother, by birth, was a Firestone. Bill's great-grandfather Henry was Harvey Firestone's smoking buddy. The pictures of Henry, Harvey and Thomas Edison with smokes and guns filled the executive floor walls of HQ.

Nasser and I agreed that we were on the verge of a "Tylenol moment" – the signature corporate crisis beautifully contained by Johnson & Johnson during the 1980s that occurred when their product was criminally contaminated by a single actor. The act of pharmacological terrorism spread fear and panic throughout the entire nation – even though the event was contained to the criminal footprint around Chicago. Johnson & Johnson forfeited hundreds of millions of dollars in favor of public safety and public trust.

Now, Ford was prepared to do the same.

The dreaded call came. Nicole Solomon, head of public affairs in Ford's D.C. office, had bad news. (I had hired Nicole away from General Motors after working side-by-side with her years earlier at the American Automobile Manufacturers Association – the Big Three automakers lobbying arm in D.C.)

"There's been an Explorer rollover on the Beltway and all the local TV stations are headed to the accident. I'll keep you up to speed."

NHTSA and the national media are breathing down our neck and they'll get Exhibit A in their back yard? Shit!

I sprinted up to Nasser's office to find he was in a meeting in the executive conference room. I burst into the room and interrupted the presentation – whatever it was – in front of Ford's top execs.

I went over to Nasser and whispered in his ear, "Sorry for interrupting but I think we just hit Tylenol. Explorer rollover on the Beltway."

"Keep me informed Jason."

Back in my office, Nicole Solomon was back on the line.

"False alarm; it was a Suburban and didn't involve any tire issue."

I walked back to the meeting, slowly, and reentered the room. Jacques stopped the meeting.

"Guys (yes they were all guys), an Explorer rolled over on the Beltway a little while ago and I think we've hit that Tylenol moment we've talked about," Nasser told the group before I could say anything.

"Actually Jacques, I gave you bad information. It was a Suburban. Sorry about that," I said.

I felt like Chicken Little.

"Jason, it doesn't matter. There will be a rollover any day now and the media will be all over it. Our Tylenol moment has arrived."

On May 6, Jacques Nasser called me up to his office. Just three months or so into my tenure, the two of us were trusted friends. I didn't blow smoke up his ass (OK, maybe a little) and he kept nothing from his PR chief.

"I'm going to talk with Ono in a few minutes and I want you to hear what he says. It's important as we go forward."

Nasser wasn't talking about Yoko Ono, although I would love to ask her why SHE BROKE UP THE BEATLES!

No, Ono was the CEO of BridgestoneFirestone North America and to date, had been stonewalling us. The two companies had discussed potential responses in Venezuela; but it was quickly apparent Firestone was not on the same page. The phone was on speaker; Ono was obviously speaking from a prepared script. His voice was quivering. Nasser looked at me and rolled his eyes. When Ono was done, Nasser got firm.

"We are going to replace these tires with or without you," he said.

The line seemed to go dead until Ono said, "Good bye."

I looked at Jacques. "Holy shit," I said.

"This is going to get ugly, Jason."

The next day Ford recalled the Venezuelan Firestones and NHTSA opened a formal inquiry into the Firestone tire crisis in the United States. Sadly, game on. Good-bye family; see ya when the smoke clears in 18 months. The NHTSA action made a big story even bigger, which I thought was impossible considering the media attention my team was handling. And not just in Dearborn. Remember the Guiding Principle of "protecting Firestone." We were walking the talk. We had deployed several Ford PR people to Nashville to help Firestone PR handle the media onslaught. They were somewhat appreciated at first, and then loathed.

At one point, the late Mike Vaughn called me and said, "We don't feel safe down here."

It was getting ugly. Firestone, on a daily (even hourly) basis, was telling journalists there was nothing to these reports of tread separation deaths in Ford Explorers that were beginning to stack up across the country, usually in the hot south – 12, 24, 80, 120, etc. As we had promised in our Guiding Principles, we communicated only with the facts in hand and said we were continuing to investigate as we begged Firestone for more data.

But, they refused. They controlled the data up to that time; tires had a separate warranty from all other components of a vehicle. Ford engineers and the data experts wanted the "claims data" from Firestone.

Unfortunately, the company was giving Ford the cold shoulder. Contentiousness between the companies grew by the day.

I always tried to bring some levity to those on the tire team as we dealt with a growing crisis and an even more growing fissure with our supplier. At one point, I asked the head of safety and environment at Ford, Helen Petrauskas – a tough old gal with a gentle heart – whom she wanted to play her in the inevitable movie about this crisis.

"Hell, I don't know," she answered.

I suggested Susan Sarandon. She just laughed, as did Tom Baughman, the lead Explorer engineer and a prince of a human being.

"You?" I asked him.

"I'll get back to you on that," he countered.

A few weeks later, after a particularly cantankerous meeting with Firestone officials over recall efforts in Venezuela, Baughman stormed out of the meeting and made a bee-line for my office.

He charged in. "Johnny Wadd Holmes!" he shouted.

"What?" I asked.

"You asked me who I want to play me in the movie, remember?"

"Yeah," I said not knowing what the hell he was getting at.

"I want (pornographic actor) Johnny Wadd Holmes to play me so that at least in the movies, I have a big Johnson."

Fuck. We were all getting stressed.

My stress was then tinged with enormous sadness with the loss of my father on June 3rd. A World War II vet, baseball star, teacher, feed salesman and a fabulous dad, Cecil Vines could no longer fight the "something" that doctors were struggling to diagnose. I flew to Iowa and watched him die from congestive heart failure after a stroke and heart attack had felled him. Watching your old man drown in his own blood is horrific. The funeral was about to begin when through the front door of the First Baptist Church walked Jacques Nasser and John Rintamaki. In little

Pella, Iowa. I had only known them for four months. At that point I knew we were blood brothers in one of the biggest crises in U.S. corporate history.

Chapter Fifteen: The worm turns: temporarily

By mid-July 2000, NHTSA demanded Firestone turn over all "claims" against their tires. Days later, those same documents were finally shared with Ford's experts. Why were they suddenly working together with Ford?

Knowing that NHTSA is one of the biggest "CYA" agencies on the planet, perhaps Firestone finally realized that Ford really was their ally – the biggest frickin' customer they had had for 100 years.

Regardless of the why, Ford data and engineering experts went to work on the "data." It was a dog's breakfast. Nothing was consistent. Spread sheets, computer files, and seemingly endless data on the back of napkins was provided by Firestone for the only part of a car that actually makes contact with the road.

"It's a complete cluster-fuck," said Ernie Grush, the mild-mannered, self-proclaimed "geek" running all the numbers behind the crisis. "We've got shit, and shit and more shit. I'm going to need a frickin' supercomputer."

Within days, Grush and his team (I think three other people) had cracked the code of Firestone's data. The problem was with the tires made in their Decatur, Illinois plant. During the early 1990s, the plant had experienced incredible labor strife. This manufacturing site clearly stood out in their defect record compared to other Firestone facilities making the exact same tire. The bottom line: although they were the "exact same tire," they weren't. The Decatur tires were failing on Ford Explorers at alarming rates. Other vehicles, including Chevy Suburbans and Jeep Cherokees, using the defective Firestone tire as replacement tires, were similarly failing.

Had we been adversarial with our key supplier – who had treated us with total disdain – we would have leaked this information to the media to bury them. But, remember our Guiding Principle – Protect Firestone – for what it could do to the industry and ultimately our customers. People, real people just like those in your family, were now scared and were going into Ford dealerships, sometimes in tears, demanding new tires despite the relative safety of what was on their vehicle. Fortunately, the majority of Explorer owners didn't have Decatur Firestone tires.

Days later, in late July, our team met with the Firestone team on a Saturday. Firestone presented its case which could only be described in one word: Complete Bullshit. (Sorry, took the Joe Biden course on word counting.)

Then, the Ford team did a scientific dance on "Firestone's" data. It was beyond compelling. This is your Explorer on good tires. This is your Explorer on bad tires. Any questions? As Ernie Grush would tell me, it smelled like shit in the room as the Firestone guys literally crapped themselves. There was a break in the meeting.

Moments later the Firestone guys returned and said "We need to recall the tires."

Ding, ding, ding. We have a winner Johnny!

The real shit-storm was just days ahead.

NHTSA was alerted to the need for a recall and there was close coordination between the government agency, Firestone and Ford. Ford, for its part, did not have to participate AT ALL. It was a tire issue covered by a separate warranty. But we at Ford wanted none of that. Considering Firestone's stonewalling tactics – and the bigger fact that it was OUR vehicle – we wanted to get over this as fast as possible. Remember the first Guiding Principle: the safety and satisfaction of our customers is paramount. We began to discuss with Firestone officials how to handle the announcement, while Firestone kept telling a rabid media contingent that they saw no problems with their tires.

We shook our heads in disbelief.

The announcement was scheduled for August 9th at Washington D.C.'s National Press Club. In the days leading up to the announcement, I was assigned as the point person working with Firestone to develop the final wording on the recall. By now, the issue was white-hot. Sitting in my office watching the evening news with my chief lieutenant, former Road and Track journalist Ken Zino, our eyes rolled when ABC's World News Tonight started the broadcast with a line something like "topping our stories tonight as usual; Tires and Fires." Fires were raging in California and, hell, we were the tires.

Firestone's PR chief, Christine Karbowiak, sent me an initial draft of the recall announcement and it contained something very troubling for Ford, particularly considering this was Firestone's recall and Ford was participating to help pay for it in the hope that customers would be served as quickly as possible. The trouble: Firestone was implying the problem was not the tire itself, but the tire pressure specification set by Ford – 26 psi. Firestone was implying that had Ford set a higher tire pressure spec, their tires would not be as susceptible to danger when the actual tire pressure fell below that level.

They had a point. Kind of. The driving public had become extremely casual with the maintenance of their vehicle's tires for lots of reasons. Tires were better than in "dad's days" (my Dad rotated his tires and replaced them on strict intervals); more and more people were leasing automobiles, thus not keeping them long enough for real tire problems. And as Service Stations went the way of the VHS video tape, there was no longer the gas station attendant filling your tank, checking your oil and making sure your tires were fully pressurized.

One thing that Firestone and Ford engineers agreed on was that lower than specified tire pressure created unnecessary heat in the tire, and as Tom Baughman told me, "Heat is the enemy of the tire." What we would discover was heat, for a lousy tire, could prove to be deadly; and not all tires had been created equal.

We had a silver bullet should Firestone continue their insistence that tire pressure was the bad actor here and not a defective tire; but we didn't want to use it. We knew we were on the brink of a nasty pissing match that the media and plaintiff attorneys would cheer on. If Firestone and Ford escalated an already ugly corporate battle, it would make the story bigger by the day, it would piss off Explorer customers and juries would want to punish these corporate "fat cats." That silver bullet came courtesy of Goodyear, the other major tire supplier for the Ford Explorer.

Over a two-year period, Goodyear had supplied roughly the same number of tires as Firestone for installation on Explorers. Goodyear's PR chief Chuck Sinclair had become a friend through the process and I asked him if Goodyear had noticed anything abnormal, even scary, in their claims' data regarding their tires on our Explorers. After a thorough search of their data, Sinclair provided a Goodyear statement indicating zero tread separations. And the tire pressure specification requested by Ford for Goodyear to meet?

26 p.s.i.

The silver bullet was even stronger. The Explorer was built in two assembly plants; one in Louisville, Kentucky and the other in St. Louis, Missouri. By pure serendipity, during one year Ford manufacturing officials had Firestone tires delivered to the St. Louis plant, and Goodyear tires to Louisville. They fortuitously flip-flopped the respective tire deliveries the next. Had the culprit been tire pressure, the Goodyears would have been failing as well. Had it been a plant issue, the flipping of the tire deliveries would have borne it out. Had it been an Explorer issue, Goodyear tires couldn't have made the difference. It was crystal clear that the issue was defective Firestone tires.

Defiantly, Firestone, in correspondence after correspondence, was putting all its chips on tire pressure. Perhaps it was an act of desperation as the alleged "safety advocates" were calling for all Firestone tires to be removed from the road and sales of Firestone tires for the after-market were plummeting. Two days before the recall announcement, I had had enough of Firestone and their PR chief. We had tried our best to work with them and protect them.

"Are you kidding me?" I asked Karbowiak. "We are standing by you and helping to pay for this despite the fact that it is your recall, and you want to throw us under the bus? Stop it with the tire pressure crap. Here is what WE need to do. We need to do a Harry Pearce!"

Harry Pearce was General Motor's general counsel who personally destroyed Dateline NBC, Jane Pauley and other charlatans at the network who allowed a couple of plaintiff attorney's "safety experts" – Byron Block and Ralph Hoar – to concoct a bogus "test" showing GM's pickup truck side-saddle tanks were defective and deadly.

In perhaps the greatest press conference in automotive history, Pearce systematically took the media through an hour-long defense of its product, exposing the criminally fraudulent means that NBC had employed.

I was a young PR guy at Chrysler, listening to the news conference on the radio on the way back to HQ, glued to the radio for more than an hour in the parking structure. Detail after detail, fact after fact, Pearce was magnificent. Pauley would later that night be forced to apologize on the air over her semi-dead body. The NBC president was gone in days. This, I told Karbowiak, is what we had to do:

"Stick to the facts in order to determine which tires are bad and which tires are good, based solely on the science, so that the plaintiff attorney shills don't convince the public that all tires black and round are bad, and create a panic. If we get into a pissing match, everyone loses; you, us and our customers."

She said she got it, but that it was Firestone's press conference. However, she didn't know the information I had at my disposal.

On August 8th, around midnight, as I tried to get some sleep in my room at the Mayflower Hotel on Connecticut Avenue in Washington D.C., a knock came on my door with a delivery. It was the final press release for the next morning's press conference announcing the recall. Prominent in the announcement was the claim that Ford had ordered an unsafe tire pressure for the Explorer tires made by Firestone (and Goodyear).

I grabbed a beer, chugged it, got dressed and walked the three blocks over to Firestone's PR agency, FleishmanHillard. A security guard met me at the door and ushered me up. Inside the agency, I noticed the PR people and lawyers still hard at work around the main conference room table. I asked for Karbowiak and they took me to a temporary executive office they had provided her. The exchange was short and not-so-sweet.

I slammed down the press release and a copy of Goodyear's statement on her temporary desk and said sternly: "Take out the reference to p.s.i. or I will drop the fucking Goodyear Blimp on you."

While the Nissan Revival Plan announcement in Tokyo was the biggest press event I had ever been a part of, the Firestone tire recall presser was the most intense. Leading the charge for Firestone was their sales leader Gary Crigger, while Helen Petrauskas from Ford joined him on the stage. Karbowiak served as the M.C. There were 20 TV cameras, every big network as well as foreign news correspondents. The room was packed.

I stood in the back alongside Diane Steed, the former NHTSA Administrator under President Reagan who had started a communications firm with friends Ron DeFore and Jeff Conley, two Washington PR geniuses. I had been working with them for years, as they were smart, connected and, most important, ethical beyond reproach. There would be no scientific, systematic approach to this press conference. No Harry

Pearce-style dissection of the data and the science to determine what Firestone tires were bad and which ones were good. Nope. Only a short statement read announcing the recall. And then right out of a 1950s Hollywood movie a young lady entered the room and handed a piece of paper to Karbowiak.

"I have just received a statement from General Motors," she said and then went on to read the missive that indicated GM had had absolutely no problem with Firestone tires. I looked at Diane Steed, my eyes bugging out.

She rolled hers and then whispered in my ear, "This is going to be war."

The rest of the press conference was a brutal Q&A session for which Firestone had no answers. Firestone's Crigger was incoherent. Much to her credit, Ford's Petrauskas did not take the bait to throw Firestone under the bus. The first shot in an automotive world war had been fired; by Firestone.

Chapter Sixteen:
Corporate "War in our Time"

Moments after the press conference announcing the recall of millions of Firestone tires, the shit officially hit the fan. Firestone had bungled the announcement so badly that the media, and more importantly, the public didn't know which Firestone tires were good and which were bad. Ford dealers had Explorer customers flooding their stores demanding that their Firestone tires be switched even if they weren't the recalled tires manufactured at the Decatur plant. Some customers were in tears.

Dealers typically acquiesced, creating another problem: customers with tires included in the recall would have to wait longer to get replacement tires. Simply put, there weren't enough tires in the world to replace the number of vehicles involved. Tires are "tuned" for each particular vehicle line.

The "safety experts" like Joan Claybrook, Clarence Ditlow, Ralph Nader and Sean Kane were particularly unhelpful. Check that: they helped create a public panic among Explorer owners that made the situation worse and potentially more deadly. By condemning all Firestone tires, they helped create what was effectively a "run on the bank" – of tires. It was shameful; but this is what these folks do for a living in order to create a toxic atmosphere for their trial attorney buddies.

Two days after the disastrous recall announcement, our tire team chief John Rintamaki sat down with me and my evolving go-to guy in the crisis, Ken Zino. Zino was the smartest guy on our PR team. A former journalist, he had been hired away from Road and Track magazine several years earlier and came into the staid Ford Motor Company like a bull in a china closet. He had pissed off everyone he came in contact with; his former colleagues in the media, Ford insiders and I think, even God.

When I met with my top team after it was announced I was the new head of Ford PR, I openly told him: "People are telling me I should fire you Ken." My ego had overcome me. Just 40 years old and the PR chief of one of the world's largest and most renowned companies, I was acting like a dick. I later apologized to Ken for my rudeness. He became a rock solid performer for Ford, me and Ford's customers.

Ken and I told Rintamaki we had to take the upper hand in the debacle and Rintamaki agreed. But how? It was a Friday.

I had never held a press conference on a Saturday. We called most of the media covering the tire crisis and said we would have a conference call to lay out the data regarding the recall. We could not call ALL the media as there was not enough time as the media list was in the hundreds.

Each journalist on the call was faxed a copy of a presentation we had begged Firestone to share – the "Harry Pearce-style" dissection of the data in order to clearly define a "good" Firestone tire versus the "bad" tires in the recall. I led the call, supported by Ken Zino, Ernie Grush the technical analyst, Explorer chief Tom Baughman and assistant general counsel Dennis Ross. We sat around a table in my office and talked for about an hour, taking every question the reporters threw at us.

I left the Glass House and made my way home where my wife Betsy met me at the door.

"Christine Karbowiak from Firestone called a few minutes ago and she sounds pissed," she told me.

I called Christine and we had yet another "professional" call.

"That conference call you just did was the most unethical thing I have ever seen," she shouted on the phone.

I gathered myself – something my friends know I rarely do – and in a calm voice responded: "What are you talking about? You idiots have created so much confusion out there that people with good tires are demanding new tires while people with your shitty tires are forced to wait.

You want to give me a lecture on ethics? More people are going to die because you've tried to cover your ass. We have to stop the hysteria now. There are not enough replacement tires to waste, dammit."

The phone went silent for a good 15 seconds until Christine seemingly "got it."

"We need to have a conference call together with the media tomorrow and go over the material you covered today," she said.

Repeat a call we had already had? Weird. A Sunday press conference? Nothing seemed to be too weird in this crisis. The call took place with Ford and Firestone arm-in-arm to the media, yet increasingly at arm's length in reality. And everybody would soon see it.

Later, a couple of journalists called me and said the repeat press conference was the weirdest thing they had ever experienced covering the auto industry. I didn't care. We didn't need an escalation in a war with Firestone. Perhaps this was a hopeful sign. Or perhaps, I was thinking that monkeys would fly out of my butt.

A week later, I was with Nasser, other Ford executives and my family at the most opulent car show in the world, the Pebble Beach Concours d'Elegance. People with more money than God strolled around the property looking at classic cars worth more than some countries. It was not to be enjoyed. I was on the phone constantly, answering media calls. My wife was pissed.

"Honey, this was our chance to get away."

It had gotten so bad that my eight-year-old daughter, Lane, would cry whenever my cell phone rang. At one point, Betsy grabbed my phone and threatened to flush it down the toilet.

Pebble Beach has some of the greatest golf courses in the world and on Hole three of the signature course, my cell phone rang; it was Jacques Nasser.

"Jason, I want to shut down our Ranger (pickup truck) plant and divert the tires there toward the recall. What do you think?"

The Ranger, Ford's small pickup truck, was equipped with the same Firestone tires as the Explorer; it made sense as the Explorer was born from the Ranger.

"It's a bold move," I said. "And it's what we said we would do when this whole shit-storm started – work around the clock to find replacement tires."

The plant was shut down; workers were still paid. Amazingly, many of the UAW production workers volunteered to load the tires on trucks to be distributed to Ford dealers.

We were starting to make some headway, but we knew much more was needed. The Firestone tire crisis remained the biggest story in the auto industry on a daily basis and often times the biggest news story period. The "safety experts" continued their mischief, spreading B.S., fear and hysteria.

Congress announced upcoming hearings into the issue and Ford customers continued to demand replacement tires even if not included in the recall. During one of our tire-team meetings, a procurement and supply executive mentioned that she had been approached at her kid's soccer game by an Explorer owner and asked whether she knew if the tires were good or bad.

"I walked over to her vehicle and told her she had 16-inch Firestones, not the 15-inch Firestones in the recall. And then I thought, how many people are confused about this?"

Within a few days, every Ford employee in the United States had a laminated card identifying the recalled tires and information on where to go if the customer's tires were defective. We realized we had an army of ambassadors we needed to engage to help us navigate the crisis.

My assistant Lynn poked her head in my office. "Don Hewitt from 60 Minutes is on the line."

Shit. Hewitt was the creator of the kick-your-ass television news magazine. All PR people knew you didn't want to be a subject of 60 Minutes, especially when people had died in your product.

Hewitt didn't mince words. "Jason, we think your company is doing the right thing and we'd like to imbed a crew into your company to follow Ford as it navigates this crisis." I told him we were doing all that we could, but that we were facing a whole lot of B.S. and lies on a daily basis. This misinformation was supplied by various plaintiff attorneys, alleged "safety advocates" and, sadly, Firestone.

"I'm in favor of doing this but it may be tough to convince my bosses. Bill Ford will be the toughest, as he was indoctrinated by his old man to hate the media. Who would do the story?"

"Lesley Stahl," he responded.

Gulp. Lesley had a reputation as a sweetheart off-camera and a pit bull once the klieg lights were lit.

I made a beeline up to Nasser's office and told him of the call.

"What's your advice, Jason?"

"Jacques, they're going to do the story with or without us. We are doing the right thing so I think we should take our best shot and use up as much time in the broadcast telling our story. We promised to be open and honest."

"Let me think about it and I'll let you know tomorrow, Jason."

Tomorrow came and I was back in Nasser's office. "I called Jack Welch last night and asked his opinion," Nasser said. "He said the same thing you did: that they would do the show regardless if we cooperate. He said if it was Dateline NBC, he'd say 'no way' because they can't be trusted. But he said, 60 Minutes is tough, but fair. Here's what I want to do. Get Lesley Stahl out here for a lunch and we'll decide after."

I said Okay, and then added, "If this blows up on us, you won't have to fire me; I'll resign. But I know it's the right thing to do."

Chapter Seventeen: Enter the Tiger

Stahl and her producer Rich Bonin arrived two days later. Without the favorable camera tricks, Stahl looked much older in person, but she was still a babe. Bonin and I had talked often leading up to the meeting, and our exchanges were always friendly – he needed me as a friend to get the most out of this story.

In my office we talked about what they wanted to do: basically be a fly on the wall as we went about the business of scouring the world for replacement tires and gathering evidence.

When it was time for lunch with Nasser, I walked Lesley up one floor to Jacques' office. Nasser's assistant Terri Behrik ushered us into his office where lunch was waiting, and then I quickly turned around to leave.

"Where are you going?" asked Stahl.

"Jacques' a big boy, you don't need me."

She would later confide that she'd never seen that before – a PR guy leave his boss to the media wolves – she was impressed.

After the lunch, I walked Lesley and Rich to their rental car in the visitors' lot and told them I would let them know Nasser's decision as soon as I knew. I walked back to my office and Lynn met me at the door.

"Call Jacques."

Shit, I thought, that's too quick.

"Jason, did you know the average 60 Minutes piece lasts 14 minutes?" Jacques asked when I got him on the phone.

"That sounds about right."

"So do you realize your career has come down to 14 minutes?"

For once, I was speechless. Nasser hadn't forgotten my pledge to quit if the 60 Minutes piece turned out to be a disaster.

"Yeah, right," I responded.

There was a moment of silence until Jacques started laughing. "Don't worry. It's the right thing to do. But, I gotta tell you, Bill (Ford) is nervous as hell about it, so we better limit his exposure."

I called Rich Bonin at CBS; Game On! But, we had to agree to ground rules if we were to go forward. I told him we would have our own camera during every interview (so portions of an interview could not be cut and pasted and taken out of context) and no surprise documents – if they wanted us to respond to a document they would let us see it in advance, off-camera, so that we could determine the veracity of the information. He agreed to the ground rules; within days, 60 Minutes began its month-long stay in our bedroom.

By late August, the crisis was white hot. I would have 100 media calls by 9:00 a.m. every morning from all over the country and around the world. Ford and Firestone were on the verge of an all-out war; something we did not want. We had not launched any attacks on Firestone as we were putting out the facts as we knew them, usually in response to an unsubstantiated charge.

Then came the call that caused me to lose it.

ABC's Lisa Stark, one of the lead reporters on the crisis – and a fair one by the way – was on the line.

"Jason, I think I have the smoking gun."

It was a 25-page document created by an independent tire testing company in California from 1988. Inside was evidence that the 15-inch Firestone tires used on the Explorer had fallen apart prior to the Explorer's introduction. I asked her to fax me the document.

I called up my right-hand man, Ken Zino.

"Holy shit," was all Zino could say.

We "knew" they were defective...apparently. With "smoking gun" in tow and a lump in my throat, I made a bee-line for the war room. There, as usual, was Ernie Grush, our research guru.

"Holy shit. Give me a few minutes Jason."

Within 30 minutes Ernie, along with Explorer chief Tom Baughman, were in my office.

"You're missing two pages Jason," Ernie said as Baughman smiled.

The missing pages were the two cover pages in which the lead test engineer explained that the faulty 15-inch tires noted in the report were actually 16-inch tires they were doing additional testing on. When the tests began, a similar set of 16-inch tires had fallen apart and the tire testers wanted to replicate that failure. That was, after all, what they did for a living.

"Those 16-inch tires never went into production," said Baughman. "And, the assholes who gave this document to Lisa Stark knew it."

Again, the same game of phony information from those that wanted the crisis to boil over, give the media fodder and enrich law firms around the country as it was apparent the "deep pockets" were not at Firestone, but with Ford Motor Company. By this time, one leading "marketing guru" had deemed Firestone "dead brand walking."

"Lisa, Jason Vines. About that smoking gun, you're missing two pretty important pages."

I faxed her the cover letter and took her through the details. She had almost been duped.

"I think you need to go back to your source and tell them what they are: liars, complete liars. Perhaps criminal liars."

Two weeks later the call would come from the Wall Street Journal's Pulitzer Prize-winning journalist Joe White – one of the smartest and most ethical journalists on the planet.

"I've got what I think is a smoking gun that is going to give you real heartburn," Joe said.

"Let me guess Joe, is it a 25-page tire testing document showing the 15- inch tires failed back in 1988?"

"How'd you know?" he shot back.

I faxed Joe the cover letter and took him through the hoax. He was pissed; not at me, but at his source who had tried twice to deceive ethical journalists and lay a turd in our punch bowl.

By late August, Congress had investigators climbing up our shorts and demanding a slew of data while they grilled our engineers, procurement folks and me. Our communications troops on the ground in Nashville, sent to support Firestone, were called home to Dearborn. The food fight between Ford and Firestone was becoming too intense. Mike Vaughn, who had earlier warned me about the tension in Nashville, told me "they're yelling at us and some of our team have been reduced to tears."

So much for our Guiding Principle of "protecting Firestone." It was clear that in Firestone's mind, if they were going down - they would take us down with them.

Forbes was writing a major story on the crisis under the headline "Nasser's Toughest Test." They wanted a photo of Jacques in the "war room."

Before the Forbes photographer arrived, Ken Zino and I checked out the war room to make sure nothing sensitive or proprietary could be captured on film. On the back wall was the original list of Guiding Principles. We had written them with a red marker. We knew red wouldn't show up well in a photo.

"Ken, redo the list with a black elMarko. Oh, and get rid of the last guiding principle (Protect Firestone). Not gonna do it," I said mimicking Dana Carvey's impersonation of George H.W. Bush.

As Ford and Firestone continued their brawl in the media, the public was understandably confused, thanks to the wonderful work of the "safety advocates." We knew it was time to put a "face" on Ford. Zino and I agreed that whoever that face was would most likely face the music in front of the recently announced Congressional hearings. We both agreed that we could not offer up the family scion, Bill Ford Jr., as some were arguing.

Congress would consider it sport to chew up Bill and spit him out; especially the Republicans on the committee as rumors were swirling that Bill was on the verge of endorsing Al Gore for President. (Gore and Gore's people were calling Bill's office non-stop, pleading for his endorsement.)

Jacques Nasser had to be the spokesman. The Ford Board agreed. Zino and I wrote the initial script on Thursday and gave it to marketing for the agency to refine. By Saturday, Nasser was in front of the cameras shooting the commercial that would tell Americans with Firestone tires on their Explorer or Ranger pickup what the company was doing to help them. It was not a defense of the Explorer.

Nasser shot the commercial in bare feet. No, I don't know why. Really.

Ford had no time to test our message prior to running the spot on Monday Night Football; Ford's agency actually "focus-grouped" the commercial live. The results were solid. People wanted to see a human being in charge of things at Ford talking directly to them, although there were a few criticisms.

"I wasn't looking at the TV when the commercial came on," said the late Detroit Free Press publisher Neal Shine. "At first I thought it was an Outback Steakhouse ad and then I looked at the screen and see this little Arab guy with an Australian accent. It was surreal."

Between the initial commercial and its follow-up, the ground shifted yet again. We were now forced to defend the Explorer thanks to Firestone and the "safety advocates" who were intentionally misleading the public we were trying to protect.

Their continued strategy of misinformation caused a blunder on our part – not a major one, but a blunder nonetheless. The agency's next commercial script had Nasser defending the Explorer saying "my family has three of them." The ad blew up in focus groups when first aired.

Respondents almost universally concluded: "Sure, you have three Explorers and I bet they have great tires on them."

Shish. That commercial was dead on arrival.

The Congressional hearings were looming as we entered September of 2000. Both houses of Congress wanted a piece of flesh out of both Firestone and Ford. The House Committee was led by Louisiana's Billy Tauzin, a Democrat-turned-Republican (for the purpose of getting elected: think Specter in Pennsylvania and Crist in Florida, i.e. going the other way from Tauzin, from GOP to the Democratic Party). Billy Tauzin wanted to make a name for himself nationally. Tauzin employed as his attack dog a pit bull named Ken Johnson, who knew "everything" about cars thanks to his poly-sci degree from Southern Illinois University.

The first Senate committee, led by John McCain and Arlen Specter, would lead the assault on Ford and Firestone. The Senate had agreed to accept Ford's favored witnesses: safety leader Helen Petrauskas and Explorer chief Tom Baughman. But Billy Tauzin and his lapdog, Ken Johnson, were playing hardball. They wanted Nasser or nothing. Billy was the forerunner of opportunist Rahm Emanuel; "Don't waste a good crisis." These "concerned public servants" wanted a spectacle. When Billy T. and Kenny J. were offered up Ford's "lowly" Helen and Tom - they were pissed.

"We've got a deal," said Janet Mullins. Janet was Ford's allegedly-connected Republican "mover and shaker" - and head of Ford's Washington D.C. office. Mullins jumped on a conference call with John Rintamaki (the leader of the whole "war" effort for Ford), myself and Ken Zino. Ken and I had been advocating that Nasser had to be the witness. Conversely, Mullins was relying on her Washington "savvy" and connections. Rintamaki asked Mullins for her opinion.

"We have offered up Helen and Tom (instead of Nasser); Tauzin will complain (about not getting Nasser) and beat us up for a few minutes (minutes are 60 seconds each) and then accept our witnesses," Mullins said.

This was the moment when I was most proud of my friend and colleague Ken Zino. The blood rushed to his head; he got indignant.

"This isn't about what plays inside the Beltway. It's not about the kangaroo court in Washington, D.C.; it's about the court of public opinion. We're gonna get creamed."

"Ken's right," I said. "If Jacques can do a commercial as the face of Ford, he should face the music in D.C. Besides, he's the best one to handle this shit-storm. He'll be the smartest guy in the room."

We argued back and forth for half an hour. At times, the passion of Zino and myself almost got the best of us. Finally, Rintamaki said the discussion was over and that he would decide which way to go. It was 7:30 at night and I was pooped. I had only been at Ford HQ for 14 hours that day.

I got in my Range Rover (yes, tough having a free corporate car) and headed home. On the way I called Rintamaki's office and left a message: "Whatever decision you make I will support." To her credit, Mullins had left a similar message for John. That night, Rintamaki had to defer to his Washington experts. The next morning Tauzin was informed of the decision: no Nasser. Jacques was busy working to find replacement tires around the world. The shit hit a windmill farm.

"Nasser too busy to testify." How do you like that headline?

Congressman Tauzin had betrayed the supposed promise to Ford's D.C. office. The Congressional committee didn't take just a few minutes to blast Nasser for refusing to testify; it was an all-out assault on Nasser's manliness. The attack was led by Tauzin's pit bull Ken Johnson.

125

"If he has time to do commercials, he has time to appear before the American people!" was the cry.

By noon, the assault on Ford by Johnson and the media was at a fever pitch; Nasser called his top lieutenants into his office. These were all executive vice presidents and me, the lowly PR vice president, 10 to 20 years their younger. We sat around Nasser's contemporary glass table.

"Jason, what's the mood out there?" Nasser asked me.

I think my entire blood supply flowed into my left testicle – the gutsy one. (Trust me, there is science behind this.)

"The mood is that you're a fucking coward," I said.

It seemed I was in almost slow motion. Jacques had become my friend, but looking back it seems almost too brazen. Maybe it was Tourette's.

The next 1.5 seconds lasted a century. The other executives looked at me with shock, with the exception of sales chief Robert Rewey and general counsel Rintamaki.

"Dammit, Jason! I said I would testify," Nasser said as his arms dropped to his side.

Nasser, ethnically Lebanese, had been a fighter all of his life. He had given speeches that brought people to tears, talking about the prejudice he had faced as a youth going to school in Australia with a different lunch (hummus, taboulli and pita bread), and a different skin color and look than the local Aussie kids. As CEO of Ford, he was chastised for declaring "there are too many white faces in this company" at a senior management meeting when he was calling to diversify Ford management. A true renaissance man, smarter than hell, he'd risen from a Grade One Ford employee in Australia to the top of the heap. His company was broken – the product development side - and he was now steeped in the largest crisis in the history of the automobile industry.

"What do we do?" he asked.

"You agree to testify and we announce it in an hour," I said.

Several of the other executives hemmed and hawed about reacting too fast. Then Rewey, one of the deans of the industry, weighed in:

"We need to stop the bleeding. Jason's right. Let's get past this."

The press conference an hour later was a feeding frenzy. It included Bill Ford and Jacques. The bleeding stopped. For Congressman Tauzin and his pit bull, it was victory: bring an industrial power to its knees, shaming it along the way.

We arrived in D.C. two days before the scheduled hearings in a Senate committee and the bigger, meaner House hearing led by Tauzin. The Senate had no problem with Ford safety chief Petrauskas and Explorer head Baughman as witnesses. It was apparent that the Senate hearing was perfunctory. The upper chamber would let the junkyard dogs in the House piss on the carpet. After all, the Representatives (Ha! Sorry) needed to get elected every two years and needed an issue to polish their bone more than the Senators who only stand before the voters every six years.

We spent the time in Ford's D.C. office and at a law firm on 12th street around F Street where, in a mock hearing, we beat the crap out of Nasser to get him ready.

"Don't make up shit; use the book" was the command. The team had developed an in-depth book of all the facts regarding key correspondences from Ford execs in the Middle East who first brought the defective Firestone tire and subsequent deadly Explorer roll-over crashes issue to bear. We were not training a rookie; Nasser was better on his feet than anyone in the room.

For Helen Petrauskas, who would lead Ford's testimony out of the gate in front of a Senate committee, it was different. Despite her reputation as a tough-old-broad, I soon realized that Helen was a sensitive sweetheart. Helen had spent the last three months with me. She was droopy-eyed (probably due to our heavy smoking as we used tobacco to survive the lack of sleep). She was terrific in the prep work that we did with her two days before the hearing.

But then, I blew it.

I wanted her to meet with the media the day before the hearing to get our message out. I knew the results from a bogus Senate hearing would be a bunch of mush – nothing more than a "dog and pony" show. We gathered in the big conference room in Ford's D.C. office. Helen made a brief statement and then the onslaught began. Led by CBS's Sharyl Attkisson – the press conference devolved into a brutal series of "when did you stop beating your wife" questions for Helen (who was a woman, by the way). Helen had no time to sell our message. Five minutes into the briefing, Attkisson got up to leave. I pulled her aside.

"Where are you going? You haven't heard what we have to say," I said.

"I have to file," said Attkisson.

Shit. File what? We hadn't even laid out the facts. It was the Year 2000 and the media was becoming ADHD by the millisecond. The expansion of our digital media "get-it-first rather than get-it-right" mentality was merely in its infancy.

The media update (see debacle) ended. In the back of Ford's Washington office, Helen Petrauskas was literally shaking when the briefing concluded. She wasn't ready for the battering. That was my fault. The next day she would be on the national stage in front of a Senate committee with little regard for fairness and dignity.

"Go to your room. Read your notes. Then have an expensive dinner – I mean, a really expensive dinner – on the company, and order a really expensive bottle of wine," I told her.

"A bottle Susan Sarandon would order?" she said with a smile.

"You go girl, you'll be fine."

I realized at that point what a fabulous person I was working with. She gave a shit; yet was scared as hell. Her mission was making Ford vehicles the best – both in terms of safety and environmental friendliness. She had crashed the glass ceiling of the auto industry to get in her position to do just that. She didn't need this crap - but accepted it with dignity and grace.

Later that day, things got weirder – if that was possible. Stratacomm's Ron DeFore called my cell.

"Fleishman just quit," Ron said.

"What?" I asked.

"Fleishman resigned the Firestone account today."

In the PR world, it was a big deal. As an agency, especially one as big as FleishmanHillard, you just don't leave a client pregnant at the altar. The kangaroo court of Congressional hearings was less than 24 hours away. I called my friend Richard Kline, one of the top dogs at FleishmanHillard.

Earlier in the crisis, I had reached out to Richard when we seemingly couldn't get any cooperation from Firestone or the Fleishman PR folks. He connected me with Marianna Deal out of their St. Louis office who was one of the team leaders.

The phone conversation got a bit heated until Marianna shouted "Jason, can you just shut up for a minute and listen?"

"Go ahead," I answered.

"We're trying, but they (Firestone) just won't listen."

Channeling Bubba Clinton, still President at the time, I felt her pain. But today they no longer represented Firestone.

"What happened Richard?" I asked, back on the phone with Kline moments after the FleishmanHillard news hit the press.

"Jason, let's just say it was a question of ethics and leave it at that."

Ketchum PR, an Omnicom company as was FleishmanHillard, quickly picked up the scraps of the Firestone account.

Years later, sharing a smoke with Omnicom CEO John Wren at the Frankfurt Motor Show, I recounted this story and asked him, "So, do you have ethical and non-ethical divisions of your company? Just wondering."

He knew I was being a smart ass; we both laughed. But in September of 2000, in the midst of the crisis, it was far from funny.

The next day, September 6, was the double whammy for Ford and Firestone. Our first battle was with the Senate; and then the House, with Billy Tauzin, took over. The Senate was straight-forward. A Commerce committee led by Republicans John McCain and Arlen Specter was only for show. Chairman Ono represented BridgestoneFirestone's North American Division. He bowed more than a sorrowful Catholic after a bender, apologizing profusely the entire hearing.

Firestone's PR people would soon plead he was not apologizing for their tires, but merely the "situation." Please! Ono was like one of those plastic birds with the red fluid bobbing downward thanks to physics. Helen Petrauskas, representing Ford, was magnificent! I was not there - we were prepping Nasser for the later Congressional hearing with Tauzin. I watched the entire hearing on C-Span. I called Helen when the Senate hearing was done.

"You rocked it, Ms. Sarandon."

"Yeah, it was OK. Thanks for beating the shit out of me to get me ready."

I paused, thinking of the right words to say. Nothing. After what must have been an uncomfortable pause, I said, "Sorry I beat you up. And thanks for not screwing this up. You are awesome - you tough old gal. Let me know if I can rent your balls sometime."

She coughed and then laughed before saying, "You asshole."

"Thank you very much, Helen."

Onto the House of "Representatives." Ha! Nasser was prepared. A team of lawyers and myself had literally beat the crap out of him for two days prior to the hearing in a mock trial. Various Congressmen were depicted in a take-no-prisoners grilling of the Ford CEO. By the end, he had his facts and courage intact; but he was tired. The night before the hearing he went to bed early. He needed to be sharp.

Ford's D.C. chief Janet Mullins had supposedly cut a "deal" with Billy Tauzin's committee: the witnesses, including Nasser and Firestone's executive vice president John Lampe, would be sworn in in a back office next to the hearing room in order to avoid what the media lusts after – business big shots in a line-up with their right hands in the air. Remember the images of Big Tobacco execs portrayed as criminals?

As we took our seats, Tauzin called the hearing to order and immediately asked the witnesses to stand and be sworn in. I didn't roll my eyes or react aggressively (we were told to sit still and make no expressions), but I turned my head and glared at John Rintamaki who was glaring right back at me. What a crock of shit.

Those Congressional bastards, or maybe their aides, could not be trusted.

Nasser was ready. His answers were succinct. When he didn't know the answer - he said so - and promised to get the committee answers quickly. Importantly, he relied on his black binder to share key facts and relevant dates. He refused to make stuff up.

His bottom line: "This is a Firestone tire problem, not a vehicle issue."

Firestone, on the other hand, was squishy to the max, saying they were part of the problem, but not the whole problem.

Lampe testified, "The mistake we made is we never used claims data as a measure of tire performance."

But; big but: Only Firestone had the claims data; either they were deadly incompetent or lying. On the plane ride back, I asked Helen Petrauskas about Lampe's claim.

"That's a damn lie if I ever heard one," she said.

Another round of hearings would follow in both houses of Congress.

Back in Dearborn, the Ford researchers and lawyers had discovered a Firestone report called Q95. Firestone had discovered back in 1995 that its Wilderness ATX tires were in fact performing badly in the field (so much for Lampe's "never used claims data" testimony). But there was a problem; the report was under court seal. The only way to unearth it was for someone to ask Firestone about it under oath.

That person would be Michigan Congressman John Dingell, one of the deans of the House and an auto industry loyalist. Dingell met with Ford officials and was given a series of questions, all legal, that would smoke out the damning Q95 report.

At the September 21 House hearing, I sat on the edge of my chair as Dingell put the ball on the tee. Over the next excruciating five minutes, Dingell whiffed countless times and finally shanked it into the woods, as Firestone's Lampe successfully played dumb or gave non-answers. Dingell's time was up. The line of inquiry that would, finally, totally expose the fact that Firestone built a deadly tire, knew about it, provided a fix going forward but did absolutely nothing about the bad tires still in use - completely evaporated. Q95 was akin to the nuclear bomb that abruptly ended the war with Japan. However, this time the bomb was a dud, and the war between Ford and Firestone would not only continue, but get uglier by the day. And the media – and the plaintiff's bar – loved it.

Chapter Eighteen: I need a break

Finally, I took a reprieve from hell. My wife and I landed at DeGualle Airport in Paris as the press days were opening at the Paris Motor Show. However, the day before I had had a meltdown in front of my family while we were barbequing at my brother-in-law's house. Tragedy had struck in a way that affected me deeply.

We had learned a Ford dealer had scored replacement tires for a customer driving an Explorer. Unfortunately, when she got to the dealership she didn't like the lettering on the tires. The dealer informed her it would take at least two weeks to get her the tires she wanted. Tragically, she decided to wait. A few days later, one of her recalled Firestones blew apart and she rolled the vehicle. Her daughter was killed. All because of cosmetics.

I started to tell the story and I fell apart.

Thankfully, I had my family around to pick me up. I learned that a key principle to personally surviving a crisis when you are on the front lines is to not isolate your support system from the crisis. Your family can and will provide perspective, priorities and, if nothing else, comfort and love. The job was taking an emotional and physical toll on my health. The crisis required that I spend significantly less time with my family than usual. However, when they were around, my mind was on them and not the tires. They were and are my anchor, despite my momentary meltdown.

Ah, Paris. After checking into the hotel, my wife went shopping with a friend, Barb Gentile. I joined my right-hand man, Ken Zino, at a street bistro to talk about, well, Firestone, and the road ahead. We were both dead tired and realized the only cure was to drink an expensive bottle of French wine. Brilliant. I think I went to bed at 4 p.m. and slept through the night. My wife was pissed. The City of Love and great dining and I was in bed (alone).

The next day was the first for the motor show press. This was the fun part of being in the auto industry – talk cars during the day and party at night on a company expense account. But I didn't get to talk about cars; it was still all about the damn tires.

Csaba Csere (pronounced Chubba Chedda – ah, those crazy Hungarians) was editor of Car and Driver magazine and considered by many the most influential automotive journalist in the U.S. – and perhaps on the planet. He ran a magazine that couldn't be bought with marketing dollars – a trait not universally held in the automotive enthusiast press.

Csaba grabbed me as I walked the floor show with Zino and Nasser. He had a proposition: give him an Explorer to test. What he wanted to do was blow out the rear tire and show how easily the vehicle could be brought to a safe stop.

"No way," I said.

But Csaba was not giving up. He would put a cage and a roll bar in the vehicle at his expense.

"You don't understand Csaba," I countered. "Your driver is going to know something is coming. That's not how this whole disaster has happened in the real world. It was 'boom, what the hell,' and then out of control at 70 miles per hour. Regular people, not Car and Driver test drivers."

Csaba was undeterred, and within a couple of weeks had acquired a tire fiasco-era Explorer and track time. They rigged the vehicle with a shot gun aimed at the tire. The test driver got up to 70 and the tire was blown. The driver didn't know exactly when it would happen, but knew it WOULD happen. He safely and easily brought the vehicle to a stop without incident. The test was replicated with a new tire, only this time once blown, the driver safely brought the vehicle to a stop without having his hands on the steering wheel. A day later the entire episode was aired on NBC Nightly News with Tom Brokaw. It was a rare bit of good news for

Ford that involved anything to do with Firestone tires. However, it was bullshit.

The tread separations of Firestone tires on real world Explorers that had caused so many accidents, injuries and deaths were not explained by the Car and Driver test. Csaba's gang blew out the tire, but the tread stayed on the tire and being flat, actually had more grip on the road than normal.

In the real world, Firestone tires had their tread completely stripped off in seconds in very loud and unexpected events at high speed. The drivers were normal people, not test drivers who knew it was coming. Most importantly, what remained of the shredded tire was one of the steel belts in full contact with the road. It was as if the driver was suddenly – again without warning – driving on the equivalent of black ice. They would over-react and lose control, often times rolling-over in a vehicle with a higher center of gravity compared to a normal passenger car.

Despite the fact that the Explorer had one of the finest safety records on the planet, as verified by the federal government's FARS data (Fatality Analysis Reporting System), rolling an Explorer at high speed was a dance with death.

When asked to comment on the NBC report, I said I welcomed the test that shows the safety of the Explorer, but that the facts in the real world accidents were different from accident-to-accident; our customers driving on defective Firestone tires never knew what was coming. Embracing the Car and Driver test would be misleading. There were hosts of others that made sending misleading information and claims into the media an art form. Ford would not engage in the deception – they had too much integrity as a company.

Chapter Nineteen: 60 Minutes and a tightrope without a net

We left Paris for a short flight to San Tropez (I know, rough) for the press ride-and-drive of our new Ford Mondeo for the European market. Ride-and-drives are a hoot. Drive hard during the day and wine and dine at night. Everybody's happy. Except me.

I was in my room basically the whole time, taking media calls about Firestone tires and trying to calm the nerves of the tire team in Dearborn, none-to-happy that 60 Minutes was pressing to get, perhaps, too much access.

I called producer Rich Bonin at CBS and said "We've given you enough. We'll do the Nasser and Bill Ford interviews next week and then we are done."

Bonin didn't bitch; he knew I had put my job on the line to help make him a star.

The Ford video camera was set up in Nasser's conference room just as Bonin and his camera crew arrived. They took about 30 minutes to get everything right, especially the lighting. Then the Tiger entered and she was pissed.

"What the hell is that camera for," Lesley Stahl sniped.

"It was part of our deal from the get-go, right?" I said as I looked at Bonin.

"Yep."

Nasser entered the room after the necessary makeup application. We didn't want Stahl all decked out looking great on camera and Jacques looking like crap ala Dick Nixon in his 1960 debate against John F. Kennedy. He and Lesley shared some happy talk and then they sat down, the cameras started to roll and the claws came out. Within a few minutes, Stahl was pulling out documents and throwing them in Jacques' face, demanding comment. Nasser started to answer but then stopped and uttered two words that went right up my ass.

"Goddammit, Jason!"

"Rich, we had a deal," I said, "None of this ambush-interview-shit with documents we haven't seen. You agreed to that."

Bonin nodded.

I continued, "And I don't want anything that just transpired to air or this interview is over now. We'll look at those documents afterward and comment on them if they are actually real. Deal?"

Deal.

As was typical for this saga, the documents 60 Minutes had obtained were either out-of-context, incomplete or completely fraudulent; and we proved it. Stahl was unable to trip up Nasser, simply because he knew the subject matter like the back of his hand and stuck with the facts. Oh, and unlike Firestone, Ford had actually put the well-being and safety of the customer first throughout the crisis.

One more interview to go – Bill Ford Jr.

Earlier in the day, yet again, another bogus charge against the Explorer made its way into print. Our communications team of Ken Zino, Jon Harmon, Ann Doyle and Susan Krusel had gotten pretty good at knocking down what seemed like a daily scud missile of misinformation, usually arriving between 4:30 and 5:00 p.m., giving us little time to scramble before network news went live. News organizations across the country were still hoping to find the smoking gun of the disaster as Ford and Firestone were in open warfare by early October.

Firestone had hired "experts" who brought new "science" to the debate. They firmly planted the blame on Ford. Interestingly, these "experts" would make a big claim on Firestone's behalf and then magically go into what amounted to a sort of witness protection program, never to be heard from or challenged again.

Firestone had also developed a faulty chart they were going to use in the next U.S. House hearing. We got our hands on a copy. It was particularly damning of Ford. Only problem was: their numbers were laughable. I called Firestone's PR leader and took her through the bogus data they were preparing to share with Congress and the media. Literally, two minutes before the hearing started, the chart was yanked from the hearing room floor. This is the insanity and corruption we were dealing with.

On the day of Bill Ford's 60 Minutes interview with Tiger Stahl, unfortunately, a bogus scud made its way through and into a wire service report. Within 15 minutes, the story was retracted and we shared the data disproving the charge with a slew of media following the story. But right out of the gate, Lesley Stahl wanted to explore, no pun intended, the charge with Bill Ford.

"Time out," I shouted. "That was a bogus charge that has been retracted by the wire service that published it, and we have the data to prove it. What just happened, ain't happening if you want to go on."

Stahl and Bonin looked at our data and agreed. Stahl focused on Bill's role as the scion of family and the impact of the crisis on him personally, considering his familial roots with Firestone. He mentioned that it was sad, but to his credit, Bill put that aside and focused on what was most important to him – Ford's customers. During my brief tenure at Ford, considering the heat of the moment, it was his finest interview despite his nervousness going in.

Chapter Twenty: On with the Show

October 8, 2000 is a date that will live in my personal infamy. Earlier in the week, the Detroit papers had "above the fold" - page one stories reporting 60 Minutes had been embedded in Ford for more than a month during the tire crisis.

Steve Harris, my former boss at Chrysler, and now PR chief at General Motors, called my office.

"Are you crazy?" he said.

"Had to take our best shot, Steve."

"Gutsy call. I am surprised you convinced Bill Ford to do it. What are you expecting Jason?"

"I don't know Steve, I just don't know. I don't know what Firestone is saying."

"Good luck."

"Thanks."

My family had joined my brother-in-law, Chris Theodore, and his family at their home in rich and waspy Birmingham, Michigan. At 6:30 p.m., I was still at Ford headquarters working on more tire stuff. I ran to my car and headed there, but an accident slowed the Southfield Freeway. I knew I wouldn't make the 7 p.m. start of 60 Minutes, so I turned on WWJ-AM as 60 Minutes began their simulcast on the radio. When the time came to hear the famous tick-tick-tick of the stopwatch that opens the show, there was nothing but CBS News. The broadcast had been delayed by the San Francisco 49ers-Oakland Raiders NFL game that had gone into overtime.

I arrived at the Theodore's and ran in the house. With the game still on, I had the chance to relax. It was a chance, but I couldn't relax. I poured myself a glass of wine and sat on the floor in the middle of the room surrounded by family. With the game over, CBS immediately switched over to 60 Minutes. We were up first. My wife was pissed that one segment showed me in the office on a Sunday, on the phone, while my boys played with toy cars on my work table.

"This is Jason Vines, the head of communications for Ford globally. He hasn't had a day off for 10 weeks," Leslie Stahl voiced over.

"No shit!" said my wife.

The piece, although 14 minutes long, seemed to fly by as I waited for something bad to happen. It never arrived. When the stopwatch reappeared, I collapsed on my back.

"That was a puff piece," said Theodore.

"Thank God. I told Jacques if it was bad I would hand in my resignation," I replied.

"You what?" questioned my wife.

That night tens of thousands – perhaps millions – of couples had a conjugal moment. Betsy and I were not a part of that mix. A minute after the broadcast, my cell phone rang – it was John Rintamaki, general counsel and tire team leader. He failed to greet me with a "hello, hi or how you doing."

"That was a puff piece," he simply said." Good job, my friend. You calling Jacques?"

"Yes."

Chapter Twenty One: Gored and Bushed

We continued through the month of October and into November as one of the top – if not the top – news story in the country and in other parts of the world.

And then we got a gift.

Thanks to the inability of a bunch of citizens in Florida to successfully complete a voting ballot, suddenly the presidential race disaster between George W. Bush and Al Gore had sucked all the oxygen from the global room and the tire crisis was sent to the back of the bus.

In the many speeches outlining the tire crisis that I have given to university students and faculty, corporations and other interested organizations, I have always told them after that day, for weeks on end, I arose every morning and bowed to those "special idiots" in Florida for taking us out of the news cycle. I promised the heavens that should my wife and I be fortunate enough to make another male child, I would name him Chad as in "hanging chad".

We at Ford briefly reentered the news, thanks to new bogus charges by Firestone once the presidential race was decided, but only for a few days.

The rose was off the bloom in Auburn Hills as the problems at Chrysler, which were first starting to exhibit when I left to join Nissan, were becoming painfully obvious to their "Merger of Equals" partner Daimler. Chrysler was in a death march, their American CEO canned, now replaced by an affable German sent in to fix a very broken organization. All media eyes were on Chrysler's death march with tires and Explorers going to the back burner. Many journalists called me to express their joy as they were starting to experience "tire fatigue."

If they only knew.

Entering 2001, the relationship between Ford and Firestone was like a married couple that hated each other but didn't believe in divorce. For its part, Ford was focusing on the remaining Firestone tires still on Explorers but not included in the recall; therefore "good" tires. Or so we thought.

At the same time, Firestone was begrudgingly providing Ford researchers with more tire claims data, while NHTSA was continuing its investigation, now going into its eighth month. Then, Firestone made a mistake. One of the claims data dumps shared with Ford included claims information regarding Firestone tires purchased as replacement tires on non-Ford vehicles. Think of a Chevy Suburban owner going to a Firestone retail store and replacing their current tires with Firestones.

Ernie Grush and his team crunched the numbers and quickly found that the replacement tires were failing at an even faster rate on non-Ford vehicles, further exonerating the Ford Explorer. In addition to the Goodyear blimp smoking gun, the new claims data provided a one-two punch for clearing the vehicle as the problem.

Those same Firestone tires on the Explorer were failing on Chevys, Isuzus and Jeeps, oh my!

The news was shared with NHTSA and then USA Today, but only after alerting my counterparts at General Motors and Chrysler, Jeep's owner. I called my old boss Steve Harris, then head of GM PR, and talked with him and his number two, my dear friend Tony Cervone (now head of GM PR).

I explained that we would not be disparaging their vehicles in any way and would go out of our way to laud their safety records - again based on federal government accident data.

Both said simply: "You gotta do what you gotta do."

I had only met Chrysler PR chief Ken Levy once. Ironically, he had replaced Cervone as head of Chrysler PR when new CEO Dieter Zetsche cleaned house. Zetsche later told me he regretted firing Cervone, and once

I rejoined Chrysler, gave me permission to hire Tony if he was interested. Unfortunately, I couldn't pry Tony away from GM.

I called Chrysler's Levy, but he was traveling. His assistant told me to leave a message on his phone, which I did, with the same language I shared with General Motors. The next day I left another message. No return call. I had to go. USA Today was holding the story, but not for much longer.

The USA Today story was the first new news regarding the tire crisis for some time and Firestone was completely dismissive of the results of their own data. They were adamant: the Explorer was part of the problem. I guess you could then infer the Jeep Grand Cherokee and Chevy Suburban were equally a part of the problem. Firestone's arguments had evaporated.

That morning, Chrysler's Ken Levy finally called me back saying that he and his boss, Dieter Zetsche, were very angry and may be forced to retaliate.

"Ken, I called you three days ago to give you a head's up," I reminded him.

"I was travelling."

"What, you had no access to your voice mail?" Crickets until he went back to his "we may have to retaliate" over and over again.

"Ken, I have been telling the media covering this issue that the two highest rated SUVs in the FARS data are the Cherokee and Grand Cherokee and that the Explorer is third behind you. This is a tire issue, not a vehicle issue."

"If you continue, we may have to retaliate," he responded yet again.

Arguing at this point was… pointless. I kept thinking about that old line: Don't get into an argument with an idiot because people might not be able to tell the difference. So I ended the call with class.

"Go to hell, Ken."

Keep it classy San Diego.

Despite the latest win for the Explorer's and Ford's reputation, we would soon snatch defeat from the jaws of victory. In mid-March 2001 – around the 19th or so – Ken Zino burst into my office with a look of disbelief. He didn't need to knock. Without Ken, I would have probably gone insane. If he saw me going over the edge he was there to reel me in. Always. He knew vehicles far more intensively than I could ever dream. I could take a car apart with ease; I just couldn't put it back together.

"We've got a problem," he said, sighing and then giggling. Actually it was a cackle – a signature Ken Zino cackle that all who knew him had heard often.

A problem? Hell, all we had were problems since I had joined Ford a little more than a year prior.

"How bad?" I asked, as if Ken and I were suddenly playing a game show.

"The worst," he said, shaking his head.

"The new Explorer?" I said, although not completely in the form of a question.

We had launched the all-new Explorer in the midst of the old Explorer tire crisis. It was wider, more stable and better in all aspects than its predecessor. It was helping Ford retain the mantle of building the number one selling SUV on the planet despite the shit-storm.

"Yep, the new Explorer," he answered, again cackling. It wasn't a "ha-ha" cackle. It was clearly a "no shit Sherlock" cackle.

"How bad?" I asked again.

"The worst," he repeated.

"Tires?" I queried, thinking that in no way had I provided the correct answer.

"Correct," he shouted.

I know this sounds sick, but both of us burst into laughter. We had to or else we would be forced to cry.

The geniuses in manufacturing had somehow, someway – unbelievably – failed to widen the track the new, wider Explorer would travel as it made its journey on the assembly line. Virtually every tire on some 52,000 Explorers, many in customer hands, had been slashed – not enough to render them immediately dangerous, but yet serious enough to demand a recall.

NHTSA was notified immediately, and Ford's all-new Explorer customers were notified. No one was hurt, but it made people, especially the media, wonder whether Ford Motor Company was out of control. Thankfully, this stupidity vaporized in days. There were bigger fish to fry – like millions more Firestone tires.

Meanwhile, Ford's top engineer, Richard Parry-Jones, was leading a team of both engineers and scientists to determine if the Firestone tires on Explorers made at the two plants other than Decatur were actually much better. This testing went on for several months and the conclusion was depressing. While better than the Decatur-built Firestones, none-the-less, they were inferior to the Goodyear tires. Regrettably, both tires Ford placed on the vehicle were far inferior to a Michelin tire.

In fact, Parry-Jones and his team had determined that a brand new tire coming out of Decatur was in the same shape as a three-year old Goodyear tire; they were incredibly susceptible to heat. We all knew that heat was the tire's enemy and tires running at below their prescribed p.s.i. generated heat.

The other Firestone tires were better - but still not good. The Ford scientists and engineers estimated the un-recalled tires came out of the factory as "two year old tires", and a year had passed as we faced another hot summer. Their calculation: at least 8 people would die the summer of 2001 due to tread separation of Firestone tires equipped on Explorers.

Chapter Twenty Two: "Tired"

It was the evening of May 21, 2001. Nasser was mulling the Parry-Jones "estimated death report" in his office. He had cracked open a bottle of wine that probably topped my healthy monthly income. He shared with me the findings.

"Jason, at least eight people will die this summer unless we recall the rest of the Firestone tires," he deadpanned.

What do you say to that? I took a sip of wine, put down my glass and grabbed a few grapes. Nasser always had grapes in his office.

"Well, last year we were responding to a crisis. This time we can prevent one."

Nasser raised his glass in a toast. "Jason, it's the toughest yet easiest decision we will ever make."

We clinked our glasses and took a drink, when Nasser added, "You know we are both going to get fired for this."

I paused, thought about my wife and three kids and the absolute fatigue over the past year. "I wouldn't have it any other way, Jacques."

I left Nasser's office around 9 p.m. knowing the shit would soon be hitting the fan again.

The 2000 Firestone tire recall encompassed about 6.5 million tires. A new recall for the remaining 15-inch tires would include a whopping 13 million tires. The first recall was arduous. A new recall would be mind-boggling for Firestone and Ford.

Nasser told Bill Ford of his decision that night or early the next morning.

By late afternoon on the 24th, the New York Times Detroit Bureau Chief, Keith Bradsher, called my office saying he was hearing rumors of a new recall.

"Dammit," I thought. "This place is leaking like a sieve."

I called one of Ford's top security guys with whom I had become friends.

"Here are Keith Bradsher's phone numbers: office, cell and home. Can you find out if somebody from here called him today?"

He left my office and was back in about an hour. "Jason, like I told you in St. Paul, you don't want to know."

It was getting depressing; more self-inflicted wounds.

When the story hit the morning edition of the New York Times, Firestone's John Lampe went ape shit, trying to contact Nasser, who was in the air. I got a call from Carlos Mazzorin, Ford's executive vice president of procurement and supply. Carlos was famous for his command of buying stuff to keep the company running and infamous for his broken English. He had a 24-hour clock in his office. Like so many Ford execs, he spent most of his time at work.

"Jason, John Lampe is calling me and he is really pissed. Come to my office," Carlos said over the phone.

I was there in one minute, and Carlos told me to sit down as he dialed Lampe's number. Lampe was soon on the phone and was livid. Carlos was not so rude to put the phone on speaker, but regardless I could hear everything Lampe was saying. They agreed to a meeting the next Monday at Firestone's headquarters in Nashville.

Over the weekend the Ford team scrambled to gather the documentation needed to justify a new recall of a boatload of Firestone tires. The media was aflutter.

When the Ford team arrived early a.m. in Nashville, the room was icy. Sue Cischke, who Chris Theodore and I had recruited from our days at Chrysler to replace Helen Petrauskas as the safety chief, helped lead the meeting. Ford's team laid out the justification – the science – for a new recall to prevent a looming tragedy. Firestone wouldn't hear it.

Following Ford's presentation, Firestone officials excused themselves, returning a few minutes later. Firestone's Lampe handed Cischke and Mazzorin a letter ending the 100-year relationship between Firestone and Ford citing "significant concerns" about the safety of the Ford Explorer. Henry Ford and Harvey Firestone were spinning in their graves.

"You're trying to bring us down," Lampe told the Ford contingent.

Firestone, the supplier, had fired its biggest customer. The next day, Ford announced that it would pay to recall 13 million Firestone Wilderness tires.

Said Nasser: "We simply do not have enough confidence in the future performance of these tires keeping our customers safe."

Aha, guiding principle number one in the crisis rears its beautiful head! Nasser and I had five more months of employment.

The pissing match between Ford and Firestone over the next five months didn't matter. What mattered was that during the summer of 2001, not a single person died from an accident involving a Ford Explorer with a Firestone tire that experienced tread separation, despite the prediction. Ford had acted and had spent a fortune on the second recall of Firestone tires without Firestone's assistance.

Nasser was under an intensifying fire despite the fact that he had put millions of customer lives well ahead of his livelihood and that Ford Motor Company, with thousands of exceptional employees, had worked so diligently for more than two years to find answers to help its customers, and then paid billions to protect. I will always be proud and grateful we chose ethics over profits.

In August, Bill Ford decided to create an Office of the Chairman to give him greater control of the company. The last time that had been done, by his uncle Henry Ford II, it was an effort to push out Lee Iacocca. When I was told of the development while vacationing in northern Michigan, I knew it was over.

Chapter Twenty Three: "Fired"

The ugliness had been developing for months.

Previously, as Ford readied for its first annual shareholders meeting since the beginning of the tire crisis, all eyes were on St. Paul, Minnesota. The morning of the day we were to fly northwestward, John Rintamaki called me into his office.

Never frantic, John said, "Jacques is in the Emergency Room at Henry Ford (hospital) with stomach cramps and may not be able to go to St. Paul."

Stomach cramps through this shit seemed apropos. Within a minute, Bill Ford had slammed into Rintamaki's office.

"Jacques isn't doing the shareholder's meeting?" Ford asked.

Bill Ford was the proverbial deer in the headlights.

"We don't' know yet Bill," Rintamaki said.

A couple hours later, Nasser was out of emergency and on the corporate jet with me. As we arrived at the hotel, the New York Times' Keith Bradsher (again) was calling on my cell.

"I understand Mr. Nasser is not attending the shareholder's meeting," he said with a hint of indignation in his voice.

"Oh, I think he is. You want to talk with him?" I said as I handed my phone to Nasser.

"Hello, Jacques Nasser," Jacques answered.

Bradsher had a bad tip and hopefully felt like a complete asshole.

I grabbed our top security guy and asked him to find out who might have called Bradsher with the news that Nasser would not attend the shareholder's meeting. Two hours later he met me in the lobby.

"Jason, you don't want to know."

"Yes I do," I said, exasperated. "This shit has to stop."

He paused for few seconds. "His name is on the building."

WTF?

In mid-October, Automotive News had a front page story titled "Jac Nasser's 10 Biggest Mistakes." It was authored by Mary Connelly, an incredibly likeable reporter who was married to an automotive reporter for the Oakland Press. I didn't think Mary had a mean bone in her body, but the story was unusually "mean" for her. And, it seemed to be almost a plant; a plant from inside Ford intended to telegraph impending doom for Nasser. The media was now openly contemplating Nasser's imminent demise.

Several pro-Nasser executives cornered me and asked what we could do to show support for our boss. I suggested two things: first, those backing Jacques - put their money where their mouth was and buy an ad in Automotive News, signed and paid for by each of us, publicly proclaiming our full support of Jacques Nasser. As soon as the words left my mouth, testicles shriveled. Okay, Plan B: I'll write a letter to the editor in response to Mary Connelly's piece. Oh, they liked that.

Why not – it was only my ass.

I called Automotive News' editor Peter Brown and asked for equal time. He gleefully agreed. I went to work and within an hour penned a letter to the editor titled "Jacques Nasser's 10 greatest achievements." It would have been better if the letter would have come from Bill Ford, but I knew that was a dog that would never hunt.

The day before, I had written a statement for Bill that contained the line "rumors of Jacques' removal were untrue." When I met with Ford's chief of staff John Bozzella to discuss the statement, he handed me an edited copy with the word "untrue" scratched out and replaced by "unfortunate."

"Bill is okay with this statement," Bozzella said nervously.

We had become "sort of" friends, but the strain of the Nasser-Ford relationship, especially now, had taken its toll.

"Come on John, you know that this change means everything. Saying the rumors are 'unfortunate' does nothing to quell them," I said.

Right then and there, I knew the die had been cast.

I didn't share my letter to the editors of Automotive News defending Nasser with anyone but John Rintamaki, general counsel and my friend. I walked into his office and started to talk when he suddenly gave me the finger-to-the-mouth "sssssssh" sign. He went over to his big 'ol radio and turned on classical music – really loud. He then proceeded to whisper sweet horror into my ears.

"They're listening."

I had suspected it, but nevertheless it was chilling.

I handed him my letter to the editor and whispered in his ear, "You okay with this?"

Rintamaki took two minutes to read it thoroughly and then patted me on the back before giving me a thumbs up sign. The next Monday when Automotive News hit the "newsstands" it was the first and most prominent letter to the editor. Later that morning I had a scheduled meeting with Bozzella.

"Bill is pissed," he said. "But I'll try to smooth it over."

Yeah, right.

On October 5, 2001, the National Highway Traffic Safety Administration, after investigating the Firestone tire crisis for almost 17 months, finally ruled against Firestone. Their conclusion; Firestone tires were defective. Once again, the United States Government took 17 months to determine what a handful of Ford engineers had unequivocally determined in 17 hours. I was quoted in various media saying we had been "vindicated." Sue Cischke grabbed me in the hall the next day.

"NHTSA is pissed you used the term 'vindicated'."

"Really?" I said. "Tell them they can kiss my ass after 17 months."

Two weeks later I walked into my office after a press event at our Think! (stupid electric golf cart "car") plant in metro Detroit.

My assistant looked at me and said, "The big guy needs you ASAP."

I looked at her and said, "I'm not coming back."

As I walked up the spiral staircase between the 11th and 12th executive floors of the Glass House – passing photos of Henry Ford, Harvey Firestone and Thomas Edison – I passed by HR chief David Murphy's office just as he was exiting.

"Where you going?" he asked.

"Same place as you I think," I answered.

We walked into Nasser's office and he directed us to sit at his glass table. He sat down, solemn, and then slid us both a copy of the press release announcing his resignation.

"What d'ya think?" Jacques asked me.

"It's a board coup," I responded.

"You two guys are going with me," Nasser said.

I sat there for second. I hadn't been fired since I refused to detassle corn in 100-degree weather at 15 years old in the fields of Iowa.

"I wouldn't have it any other way Jacques," I said.

Murphy sat there stunned.

An hour later I was at Nasser's condo less than a mile away from Ford HQ on the TPC Golf Course. He had gathered the executive assistants, many in tears, and several of Ford's top executives and critically, a couple of the Ford security detail. The wine flowed, but I wasn't interested in wine. I was tired.

I grabbed a glass and asked my security buddy, "So, how long has my phone been bugged?"

"Oh, a few months," he responded dryly.

"How's my car?"

"Trade it," he said, laughing.

Geez.

I said adieu and headed home. When I arrived, my nine-year-old little princess Lane met me at the back door. It was 9 p.m. and her bedtime.

"Hi, Dad."

"Hi, Cutie. I got fired today."

"Does that mean you can drive me to school in the morning?"

"Yes, Cutie. Yes, it does."

While I was personally in pain – these words began the healing process.

I love my family for putting up with me.

Over the past dozen years, I have spoken numerous times about the Ford/Firestone tire crisis – Georgetown, The Wharton School, those buttheads in Ann Arbor (sorry, I'm a Michigan State Spartan) and conferences. And, to myself. The Firestone tires were defective and Firestone reacted very badly to the crisis: at best, sticking their head in the sand while people were injured or died; at worst, being deceptive. Ford Motor Company was not without blame.

As modern SUVs were "revolutionizing" the market in the early 1990s, led by the Explorer and the Jeep Grand Cherokee, sales and marketing of the vehicles got ahead – way ahead – of engineering prowess. A small pickup truck begot the Explorer. The Explorer was a truck. Period. But it was tuned – I heard many times in meetings – to drive more like a sports car; incredibly quick steering consumers expected in passenger cars; not trucks. The tire pressure specified by Ford for both Firestone and Goodyear – on the low-end among the SUVs at the time – was set to make the truck-based vehicle grip the road. At the time though, no one gave a crap about their tires or watching the tire pressure – nada.

Bottom line: the Ford Explorer was not designed for a really shitty tire that would produce great heat when under-pressurized...and potentially disintegrate. The resulting horrific tread separations freaked-out untrained, non-test drivers zooming down a Texas freeway at 75 MPH in a fully loaded vehicle. The drivers' overreacted and the quick steering – like a sports car – led them to quickly go out of control, and the high center of gravity of the, ahem, truck, led to disaster.

That may sound like an indictment of Ford Motor Company. It really isn't. The engineers were doing their best. They didn't want to kill their customers. Automakers, I have said many times, are greedy capitalists that want you to buy a car, then another one, and then keep on buying. We want you to be fruitful and multiply, and have your little shits buy cars and trucks. We drive our families in these vehicles.

You can debate which company was guiltier in the Ford/Firestone tire crisis.

But one fact is clear: only one company put customer safety and satisfaction first, time and time again – especially in an effort to avoid a potential second major, deadly crisis: the bastards that fired me. The Ford Motor Company.

Crisis Lesson Learned: A friend of mine told me that American organizational theorist and Professor Ian Mitroff a decade ago distinguished between crisis management and crisis leadership. Crisis management was fundamentally reactive in nature. Crisis leadership is proactive: identifying a potential crisis and preparing an organization "as a whole system" before a major crisis. The Ford team, as best they could, managed the first phase of the tire crisis, but "led" the second phase and successfully mitigated the crisis. Again, by putting the safety and satisfaction of its customers first. The company never let legal and financial considerations rise to the top. Toyota (2010) and then General Motors (2014) would later fail miserably in this area.

American Motors Corporation

J. Cappy   P. Semerena

Joe Cappy, the last CEO of American Motors, at the last press conference for the company before the purchase by Chrysler. Cappy, single-handedly, got me into PR. Hate, is too kind of a word. Just kidding. *Joe Wilssens Photography.*

For Lee Iacocca, it was "anybody but Bob (Lutz)" when it came to his successor. Bob Lutz is left, Iacocca right. As they say, a picture is worth a thousand words, unless of course you are on Twitter. *Joe Wilssens Photography.*

The real "oriental dude" – Mr. K. Nissan had created a silly campaign, "Dogs Love Trucks" featuring an Asian guy with a small mutt giving good deals. The real deal was Mr. K, the gentleman that had brought Nissan (Datsun) to America. We brought him back for a cameo as we revived Nissan's image and soon enough he was inducted into the Automotive Hall of Fame, where he belonged. *Joe Wilssens Photography.*

Please ignore the man behind the screen! Soon enough, Nissan's Carlos "le Cost Killer" Ghosn was reinventing business in Japan, quickly going from villain to mastermind. The Wizard of Ahs! *Joe Wilssens Photography.*

I found this on my chair in the middle of the Firestone tire crisis. It was a greeting card from my assistant, Lynn Quigley. Inside she wrote: "I just couldn't resist." What? Me worry?

60 MINUTES

524 WEST 57th STREET, NEW YORK, NEW YORK 10019-2965 (212)975-2006

OCT 23, 00

Dear Jason,

Rich, Jim and I have been on a marathon since we finished our story on Ford, working non-stop on a report about The U.S. Terrorism Czar. (Did you even know we had one!)

I'm just coming up for air. Otherwise, I'd have written sooner to thank you for all your help. As I told Jac, this was an act of real courage. Neither you nor Jac knew what we would say, what portions of the interviews we would edit in and edit out. My hat's off to you.

I was thrilled at your feeling the piece was fair. Did it have an impact? I'd love to know.

Say hi to those two good-looking kids of yours. Thanx to them too!

Til the next time!

Lesley

The tiger, CBS' 60 Minutes Lesley Stahl, thanked me for my efforts helping the news mag cover the biggest crisis in the history of the automobile industry.

CBS NEWS
2020 M. STREET, N.W.
WASHINGTON, D.C. 20036-3304
(202) 457-4321

1

Dear Jason,   October 25, 2000

Just a quick note to say how much I enjoyed meeting and working with you. In assessing the experience, I came away particularly impressed by:

1) Your power of persuasion. How you managed to get both Jacques Nasser and Bill Ford to sit down with "60 Minutes" was nothing short of inspired. A lot of people thought you were crazy. And they're right, of course, but for different reasons. You are The Master!

2) Your skill and tenacity in ducking my phone calls, especially when you were in Paris and the south of France yucking it up while I was in Dearborn fighting off the proponents of diminished access. No one has ever stiffed me as often and with such blatant glee as you did. It was both galling and brilliant on your part. Congratulations!

As for the "Wheel of Destiny," I thought you might find it as a useful guide in dealing with future crises. The next time one explodes on your watch, may I suggest choosing the category: "Go Back to Bed" or "Compromise Your Principles For Short-Term Gain."

Best regards,

Richard Bonin
"60 Minutes"

It was Lesley Stahl on the screen, but behind the scenes it was Rich Bonin, producing the Ford/Firestone tire crisis piece for 60 Minutes. Two weeks after the story aired, Bonin sent me this note; I laughed out loud.

Chrysler CEO Dieter Zetsche and COO Tom LaSorda were trying to help Detroit Mayor Kwame Kilpatrick save Detroit, but the mayor was too busy being a criminal, sadly. Dieter later grabbed the brass ring at Daimler and LaSorda got a king's ransom when Cerberus was "given" Chrysler in a "fire sale." Kilpatrick was awarded 28 years in the hoosegow. *Joe Wilssens Photography.*

"Brownie" and FEMA were late to the Gulf Coast after Hurricane Katrina, but Chrysler wasn't. Orchestrating a team led by my buddy Stephen Gordan, we provided trucks, food and water to folks in Louisiana, Alabama and Mississippi. *Joe Wilssens Photography.*

The Dogg days of summer, 2005. Lee Iacocca, Snoop Doggy Dogg and Chrysler marketing executive Vicki Carlini take a break from filming the "employee pricing" commercial, code- named 'Golfing Buddies'." *Joe Wilssens Photography.*

For the Detroit Motor Show launch of the Dodge Caliber, I was the straight man and foil for comedian David Spade, along with Chrysler marketing Chief Joe Eberhardt. Spade, my ClearBlue pals and I wrote the script the night before at Chrysler's auto show bar, the Firehouse. He called me "Larry" in the press conference. He was hilarious. *Joe Wilssens Photography.*

163

DaimlerChrysler Chairman Juergen Schrempp had one more month and Chrysler CEO Dieter Zetsche was only the same period away from taking Schrempp's job according to the hand gestures. *Joe Wilssens Photography*

I found this on my chair one morning with a note – "Having fun yet?" This is Cerberus, the three-headed devil dog that supposedly guards the gates to Hell. What idiots would name a company Cerberus, knowing this? The smartest guys in the "womb": private equity hot shots.

As the Price of Gasoline Takes Off, Oil and Auto Firms Trade Barbs

By JEFFREY BALL

With consumers again facing rising gasoline prices, the two industries most often blamed for the energy crunch—oil and auto companies—are trading potshots over who is at fault.

In an unusually public exchange, a senior official at DaimlerChrysler AG's U.S. unit has publicly slapped Exxon Mobil Corp., the world's most profitable company. The sniping frames a question fraught with economic implications at a time when the nation's heavy fuel use has become a bigger political football: Should either oil companies rolling in profits or car makers selling gas guzzlers be blamed for America's oil dependence?

Earlier this week, Jason Vines, vice president of communications for Daimler-Chrysler's U.S. arm, suggested that oil companies are contributing to high prices in a particularly blunt posting on a blog published by the company for reporters and financial analysts.

Auto makers "have spent billions developing cleaner, more efficient technologies," Mr. Vines wrote. "Big Oil would rather fill the pockets of its executives and shareholders, rather than spend sufficient amounts to reduce the price of fuel, letting consumers, during tough economic times, pick up the tab."

The posting was in part a response to a recent Exxon Mobil ad in several newspapers that put the onus for today's energy crunch on auto makers. Under a cartoon of a monster sport-utility-vehicle filling up at the pump, the ad hinted that blame lies with an auto industry that knows how to build more-fuel-efficient vehicles but isn't

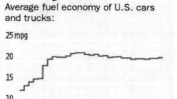

Steady Course

Average fuel economy of U.S. cars and trucks:

Source: Environmental Protection Agency

rolling them onto the market.

Noting that the average fuel economy of new U.S. autos hasn't improved in two decades, the ad argued that improvements in engine efficiency have been "largely offset" by the rising weight of vehicles, notably pickup trucks and sport-utility vehicles.

The squabbling comes as the Energy Department is predicting gasoline prices will be at least 25 cents higher per gallon than last summer. (See related article on page D1.)

It also marks only the latest outbreak of tension between the two industries, which have quarreled repeatedly in recent decades over how to address the nation's dependence on oil. The chicken-and-egg fights have common themes: The oil indus-

Please Turn to Page A9, Column 1

Day Two of the "Battle Royale" between Big Oil and the U.S. automakers over fuel economy standards. The Wall Street Journal was a day late to the news and my Chrysler friend Rob Liberatore thought I was stoking the fire the day after my blog got enormous coverage. I wasn't, but I couldn't put the genie back in the bottle. *Reprinted with permission from Dow Jones.*

Chapter Twenty Four: What Would Jesus Drive?

In the fall of 2002, out of the smoldering ashes of Ford Explorers rolling over in the deadly Firestone tire crisis, a new, supposedly "spontaneous" movement was gaining steam (which was, when you think about it, nothing more than very moist, hot air) to rid the American landscape of the hated Sport Utility Vehicle or SUV. It included few serious people, mostly consisting of a bunch of wackos, multiple hypocrites, a former New York Times journalist with an agenda (sorry for the redundancy) and a lethally dangerous eco-terrorist organization. The hypocrites included "environmentalists", earlier exposed by the conservative Washington Times in a hilarious story, packing their protest gear in a giant SUV.

There was one little problem for the SUV-haters: Americans absolutely loved their SUVs, and the fastest growing group of SUV drivers were women. So, how would they prevail in their quest? More often than not: by making shit up, convincing a sometimes gullible and lazy media their claims were factual, breaking the law and, pitifully, trying to recruit Jesus on their misguided team. Much of the movement – driven (pun intended) by a supposedly spontaneous group of like-minded thinkers - was being orchestrated by a liberal-minded PR firm. This same firm had earlier created havoc in the apple-growing industry by concocting the Alar scare – some call it a hoax – in the 1980s.

The Detroit News wrote: "The crowd decrying the gas-guzzling ways of America's vehicle of choice has expanded beyond traditional environmental groups and liberal lawmakers on Capitol Hill. A longtime Detroit journalist, national church groups, Hollywood power brokers and a radical group called the Earth Liberation Front have climbed on board. In the latest volley, conservative commentator Arianna Huffington just launched the 'Detroit Project,' an ad campaign that equates SUV ownership with supporting terrorism."

Carol Johnson, mother of three kids and two dogs, was supporting Osama bin Laden whenever she drove her kids to school in their Chevy Tahoe? Really? Huffington a "conservative?" Boy, that dog didn't hunt very long, did it?

Huffington, earlier in the fall of 2002, had penned a column equating SUVs with aiding and abetting terrorists; but soon the shoe would be on the other foot as she would be accused of aiding terrorists with her antics. Huffington was likely buoyed by the recently-released book, High and Mighty: The World's Most Dangerous Vehicles and How They Got That Way, by former New York Times' anti-SUV zealot Keith Bradsher. Yes, re-enter Keith Bradsher in my life, focusing this time on all SUVs, not just the Ford Explorer.

When Bradsher had been Detroit bureau chief of the Times, he got his hands on an internal GM marketing document characterizing the personalities of SUV owners. It's the sort of market research auto manufacturers do all the time: the companies want to know what sort of person buys this model or that, the better to produce cars to satisfy them and just as importantly, the better to reach the target segment with advertising and other marketing.

In the report, SUV owners were characterized as family people who bought the larger vehicles for practical reasons but were more self-absorbed. His newspaper account had been long on length, and short on analysis. But he used the report as the spine of his book, and ratcheted up his criticism of people who dared to buy SUVs, and the companies who dared to produce what their customers wanted.

The Detroit News had called Bradsher's offering "a book-length manifesto on environmental and social ills exacerbated by the SUV." The book made a huge splash with the liberal media; but here again, the

American consumer was not buying what he was selling and the publisher immediately discounted the book and pushed it into the remainder bin; a promised sales disaster. High and Mighty had become Low and Unread.

In November of 2002, the leaders of five religious denominations, led by the Rev. Jim Ball, launched a campaign asking "What Would Jesus Drive?" and travelled to Detroit to convince Big Three auto executives they were "sinning" by producing an ever-larger fleet of SUVs and other vehicles with less-fuel-efficiency than a Toyota Prius.

Within months, Huffington weighed in with her Detroit Project, despite the fact that the timing was suspect. Ford, GM and Toyota had just announced plans to roll out SUV models powered by more fuel efficient gasoline-electric hybrid powertrains. In fact, Ford was planning to sell a 40 miles-per-gallon gas/electric hybrid version of its popular Escape SUV later that same year. And the prior weekend, the eco-terrorist group Earth Liberation Front (ELF) had claimed responsibility for setting fire to a Ford, Lincoln and Mercury dealership in Pennsylvania "because they sold SUVs." Interestingly, the dealer victimized by the ELF arsonists told the press he had been deluged with calls and emails of support from across the country. Yep, America loved its SUVs and hated hypocrites and terrorists.

However, the Pennsylvania attack was not the first - nor the last - of ELF's handiwork. The group first surfaced years earlier, taking credit for putting spikes in trees that led to the dismemberment and sometimes deaths of loggers. ELF switched gears and decided to move onto SUV torching, first in March, 2001 when more than 30 Chevy Suburbans and Tahoes were scorched or destroyed in a $1 million fire in Oregon, followed by a Fourth of July fire in Michigan that destroyed eight Ford Expeditions. Talk about your rocket's red glare.

Following those "hits", Robert Kennedy, Jr., the senior attorney for the Natural Resources Defense Council (NRDC), joined the anti-SUV movement speaking out against the vehicles in a November 24, 2001 New

York Times op-ed. This would be the same Robert Kennedy, Jr., who would later protest "alternative energy" wind mills off the shore of "his" Cape Cod, designed to replace an aging coal-fired power plant, because of the aesthetics. Oh yes, the anti-SUV movement had hypocrisy coming out of all orifices.

Presumably, the words from the namesake of one of America's most-beloved political figures, served as an inspiration to ELF's terrorists. (Note: I dropped the eco-terrorist label. A terrorist is a terrorist. ELF's past actions had caused injury and deaths to innocent victims and its torching of dealerships with vehicles containing gasoline and other flammable liquids put firefighters and other first responders in harm's way every time a match was lit.) In July, 2002, ELF continued their campaign of terror, this time against SUV owners, by launching a wave of destruction in Richmond, Virginia.

Keith Bradsher's September 2002 High and Mighty, and Huffington's column a month later, plus her formation of Americans for Fuel Efficient Cars (AFEC), which linked SUVS with funding terrorists, no doubt added fuel to the ELF fires. A month later, Rev. Ball and his Evangelist Environmental Network had brought Jesus into the fray.

But Huffington was just getting started. In a November 25, 2002 column she wrote: "How nice it must feel for SUV owners, knowing that their swaggering imprudence is helping the world's anti-democratic oil sheiks sleep just a little better at night." (Almost a year later, she would tell the New York Times: "I have nothing against SUV owners.") Too late honey. In the wake of Huffington's comments and to round out the "Year of the Burning SUVs", ELF took credit for the destruction of 40 SUVs in Richmond, Virginia (dating back to earlier in the summer).

Then, on January 29, 2003, the junior Bobby Kennedy was back at it, this time bashing SUVs and the evil Big Three automakers on NBC's Today Show. While his rambling, stutter-filled diatribe was basically incoherent, nonetheless the automakers were taking note. SUVs made all automakers tons of money, while small cars typically lost a boatload of cash. In the prior year, three million SUVS were sold in the U.S., a near tripling of the 1.1 million sold a mere decade ago when the modern SUV, led by Ford Explorer and Jeep Grand Cherokee, took the market by storm. Soon every automaker had to have at least one SUV; some as many as a half dozen different models, from small "cute Utes" to the behemoths like the Ford Excursion.

The automakers were taking note, but no action; not one automaker wanted to take on the anti-SUV movement for fear of becoming a boycott target. They needed a junkyard dog to fight back against the false charges and fear mongering of Huffington, et al., before this nuisance turned into a full-blown crisis impacting their profits, and literally, the safety of the driving public. That's right, the safety of the driving public. More on that later.

Enter the dog; as in junk yard dog. Actually, it was 'dogs', plural.

After I "resigned" my PR chief job at Ford, along with my boss, CEO Jacques Nasser, I had joined Stratacomm, the Washington D.C. PR firm I had used at Chrysler, Nissan and Ford. In early 2003, a Wisconsin lobbyist named Bill Brouse contacted one of Stratacomm's partners, former NHTSA Administrator Diane Steed, with a proposal in mind. Brouse, sick and tired of the war on the SUV and its owners, had created the SUV Owners of America (SUVOA) four years prior. It was basically a one-man mission to fight the big bucks behind some knuckleheads in Congress, the "tree huggers", Huffington, Kennedy, "Jesus", Fenton Communications and ELF.

Brouse had attracted a few thousand members and had pumped $25,000 into running SUVOA, with admittedly little to show for it. He proposed that Stratacomm buy him out and take over the organization, knowing that the company had a stellar track record in working on automotive issues over the years. The company had been the lead agency in battling against unrealistic fuel economy standards and California's ridiculous and unattainable zero emissions vehicle mandate or ZEV (the latter, while enacted, failed miserably). The founders of Stratacomm mulled the deal. They weren't certain about how they could get the financial support to keep it running and it might be odd for a PR or ad firm to "create" its own client. However, what they did know was they had the chops to be effective and that the anti-SUV movement was based on shaky "facts", hyperbole and hypocrisy. And terrorism.

The deal was cut – founder Brouse was made "whole" with a check for $25,000 – and the company went to work to make the SUVOA as transparent as possible knowing the anti-SUV forces would attack it right out of the gate. It applied for non-profit status and was quickly approved (the IRS' Lois Lerner obviously wasn't paying attention). A board of directors was formed with representatives of naturally-aligned organizations, whose members appreciated the utility of SUVs – the boating, RV and trailer industries. Ever pull a 28-foot Beechcraft with a Nissan Sentra?

Didn't think so.

The funding would come from the most natural of sources: advertising. We began selling ad space on our website with the proviso that no advertiser would have any say in the stands our organization took or the statements we made. SUVOA would operate independently; just as any media outlet – ABC, NBC, and CNN – would deal with its advertisers. Yes, we would give them a "head's up" if something coming was controversial, but it was strictly "hands off". Ford Motor Company was a bit squirmy about that notion. Typical. Nonetheless, they accepted it. General Motors and Chrysler had no problem.

We announced the reformation of SUVOA in May of 2003 just days after Arianna Huffington's Detroit Project, along with the Natural

Resources Defense Council, released their newest television commercial claiming "Detroit" had the answer to increased fuel efficiency but was keeping it a "secret". The ad, as reported by USA Today, "had the glossy look of a traditional car commercial, depicting an apparently new model SUV parked in a desert with its outline barely visible under a billowing satin sheet.

'It is the first car built for the road and the world around it,' an announcer says. 'It can take America to work in the morning without sending it to war in the afternoon,' he adds, saying the vehicle's low fuel consumption can help break the U.S. dependence on foreign oil. As the sheet is pulled off, the dream car vanishes, however, and the chorus from the Talking Heads tune Once in a Lifetime rises in the background. 'The only problem is, Detroit won't build it,' the announcer says."

Ah, a conspiracy. That's the ticket! It was actually a consistent charge from liberals who almost always disregard capitalism and Economics 101. These folks would never consider that Ford and General Motors hate each other with such a passion that if one company had discovered the golden goose of a 50-miles-per-gallon SUV, they would put it in their showrooms in a heartbeat to corner the market. And of course, it was "Detroit" as the villain; no whacks at Toyota, Nissan, Mercedes and the others who were selling SUVs with no greater fuel economy or cleaner emissions than the evil, planet-hating bastards in Motown.

The anti-SUV movement was on full throttle and someone needed to put on the brakes. Ron DeFore and I were put in charge of the SUVOA project, and within weeks, I was named president. It was just in time, as the "What Would Jesus Drive?" knuckleheads were beginning a tour of the "Bible Belt" on May 28th. Repent and drive a Corolla! Their tour would continue for almost two months, concluding in Washington, D.C. on July 14; a day that would live in "Jesus" infamy.

Ron DeFore and I had been somewhat effective in pointing out the hypocrisy and falsehoods thrown out by the anti-SUV zealots. Keith Bradsher of the New York Times had claimed SUVs were killing drivers of small cars; but the numbers didn't add up. Worse yet for Bradsher's premise, SUVs were among the safest vehicles on the road when it came to federal government stats and those of the revered Insurance Highway Safety Institute. Robert Kennedy Jr., well, he was just too incoherent to make a difference. And, Arianna Huffington – this is pre-Huffington Post – was easily exposed as a wealthier-than-God hypocrite. In a debate on CNN Financial, she tried to character assassinate me for my past jobs in the auto industry and called SUVOA a phony front group. I quickly pointed out that Ms. Huffington travelled by private jet and had a mansion that consumed "five times the energy" of a typical California home, yet she was telling the average American "what he or she could or couldn't drive." I kicked her ass. Go to the videotape.

But what to do about the "What Would Jesus Drive?" people as they crisscrossed the nation spreading the gospel that the owners of Jeep vehicles, Suburbans and Explorers were right up there with child molesters, rapists and Hitler?

And then, I "found" Jesus.

Actually, a colleague, Katie, had found him. I had an idea on how to fight these idiots. As they say in Reader's Digest magazine, "Laughter is the Best Medicine." Why not find a Jesus, aka Hey-Zeus, who owned an SUV. Our staff went to work calling Jesuses in Miami and Houston. After about 20 calls, mostly to non-English speakers, Katie had the brilliant idea of looking in the metro-Detroit phone book. And that is where we found our SUV "savior."

Jesus Rivera went by Jesse. He was a retired General Motors employee. He was a grandfather. He was a Vietnam vet. He had two SUVs. Like the real Prince of Peace, he was perfect – for us. I drove out to his home and sat down with him. I explained the battle we were up against with the "What Would Jesus Drive?" people and the other loons. I told him we wanted to take a light-hearted approach to expose the ridiculousness of their crusade, but I added that there was a deadly side to this debate.

Prior to the start of the "What Would Jesus Drive?" campaign, eco-terrorists had three times hit dealerships or individual owners SUVs, damaging or destroying the vehicles, often times with potentially deadly fire. After the campaign was launched on November 20, 2002, ELF claimed credit for two more torchings of SUVs, one in Richmond, Virginia where 40 vehicles went up in smoke and the other at a dealership in Pennsylvania. "What Would Jesus Drive?", Arianna Huffington, Robert Kennedy Jr., Keith Bradsher – I argued – were "aiding and abetting" these jokers and it was putting firefighters in danger as they extinguished the blazes.

"How can I help?" asked Jesse.

"I want to take a picture of you alongside one of your SUVs and use it in an ad," I said. "I'll make sure you are happy with the ad before we place it. And, I'll give you 500 bucks for your time."

We shook hands and begin to chit-chat. I learned more about Jesse's family, including the upcoming birthday of his daughter on the Fourth of July.

"What a coincidence," I said. "My sister's birthday is also on the Fourth."

Then, and to this day I don't know why, I asked Jesse his birthdate.

"January 22nd," he said, smiling. "And yours, Jason?"

I paused and then reached into my back pocket and pulled out my wallet. I opened it and pulled out my driver's license and handed it to Jesse.

"January 22nd?" he said as his jaw dropped. "That's kind of eerie."

"Yeah," I said. "Almost biblical, huh?"

Days later, the full-page ad was completed and sent to USA Today for placement on July 14th, the day the "What Would Jesus Drive?" people were riding their "donkey" into our nation's capital.

When folks woke up in Washington, D.C., Detroit and Los Angeles and grabbed the paper, they saw the following headline: "What DOES Jesus drive? We asked him." There in all his glory was my buddy Jesse, aka Jesus Rivera, alongside his SUV, smiling and waving. The copy talked about why he drove an SUV – for its safety, utility and versatility. We also included a bit about Jesse – his service to our country in Vietnam - and his joy of being a retiree and grandfather.

The ad was like a nuclear weapon in the debate. The media coverage of an ad that cost us $25,000 to create and place was getting millions of dollars-worth of impressions around the world. The New York Times' Fara Warner would write a GINORMOUS piece for the next day's paper titled "S.U.V. Owners Fight Back". The "What Would Jesus Drive?" people refused Warner's request for comment. But the "What DOES Jesus Drive" people – me and Ron DeFore – had a field day commenting, doing more than 100 interviews that day.

In the New York Times:

"S.U.V. owners are sick of being demonized," said Jason H. Vines, the president of the owners' group, who is also a principal with Stratacomm, the media consulting firm that created the pro-S.U.V. ad. "We want S.U.V. drivers to have access to statistics so that when people yell at them for driving S.U.V.s, they can tell them their vehicles have lower tailpipe emissions than their small cars." Mr. Vines is also a former vice president for communications at Ford.

"Speaking of the critics' ads featuring the other Jesus," Mr. Vines said, "We think the campaign is a silly, stupid campaign, and we wanted to have some lighthearted fun with ours."

But the real fun, and perhaps the most effective hit we got was later in the day when the ad hit. The producers of "Hardball", MSNBC's live cat fight, were on the phone before I could gulp down my first cup of coffee.

"Can you come on the show tonight and debate the 'What Would Jesus Drive?' people?" they asked.

"I would love to," I responded.

It would not be my first time to participate in Chris Matthews' rodeo, as I had been on his show twice during the Firestone tire crisis. He had treated me fairly in the past, maybe because I was so damn good.

Ha! Actually it was because he was a good friend of my buddy and Chrysler colleague Rob Liberatore.

My Hardball television news debate foe was a formidable opponent, "What Would Jesus Drive" co-leader, the late-Reverend Bob Edgar. Edgar, a United Methodist minister and one-time leader of the National Council of Churches, who had also been a U.S. Congressman and later ran for the U.S. Senate, but lost.

Sitting alone in a studio just outside of the Detroit city limits, it was "lights, camera and character assassination." Edgar didn't want to talk as much about SUVs as he did about me. I, he pointed out, had worked for the auto industry. Egad! Therefore, I must be evil? Edgar went down this path for a while, until it was my turn.

With a smile, I responded. "You know Chris, as a Christian myself, I find it troubling that a man of the cloth gets on this show and instead of talking about the issue at-hand, resorts immediately to character assassination," I said. "And, by the way, I am proud of my work in the auto industry. It allowed me to learn a lot about cars so that I can talk intelligently about them. I won't apologize for my experience."

I had employed a Guiding Principle I had learned from my Dad: "Don't get in a pissing match with a skunk." Rev. Edgar then had a "hubbidee, hubbidee" moment, back on his heels, as Chris Matthews took him to task. Game, set, match.

Out of the studio and in my car, the call came from my comrade in this war, Ron DeFore.

"You kicked his ass," DeFore screamed into the phone.

The next night I was again paired with the Reverend on Alan Colmes radio program. It was a less personal attack this time, as he went down the "morality" path. Colmes, a celebrity liberal, had my back, so much so that I did very little debating.

"Do you really think this is a morality issue?" Colmes questioned Edgar, almost mocking him.

Edgar was toast.

The "What Would Jesus Drive?" campaign was mortally wounded, but not yet done. And, sadly, neither were the eco-terrorists led by ELF. On August 1st, ELF took credit for torching a huge apartment complex under construction in San Diego, California. Three weeks later ELFies destroyed 20 SUVs and a building in an arson fire at an auto dealership in West Covina, California.

We responded. On August 27th, we delivered a "cease and desist" petition, signed by more than 6,000 supporters, to Arianna Huffington, Robert Kennedy Jr., the Reverend Jim Ball and Fenton Communications. We included Fenton Communications because they were coordinating both the "What Would Jesus Drive?" and Arianna's Huffington's "Detroit Project", even though both groups initially denied it. Hypocritical to the max, if you remember that Huffington had slammed SUVOA as a "front group" for the automakers. And the media exposed them.

In USA Today, reporters James R. Healey and David Kiley wrote:

"Two small, but high-profile campaigns criticizing poor fuel economy, especially of sport-utility vehicles, involving a single public relations company that works for left-wing advocacy groups, has a history of dramatic and frightening ads and boasts a success rate good enough to scare car companies.

"...Both campaigns spent little and ran few ads but got worldwide notice because the ads were controversial.

"...The two (campaigns) say it's a coincidence they used Fenton.

"'There's absolutely no connection,' says the Rev. Jim Ball.

"....I think what is interesting about the different campaigns and efforts is that it is all spontaneous, says Huffington."

What a crock. But the good news was they couldn't hide anymore and had lost some credibility.

The petition demanded that Huffington, et al., "stop encouraging groups like the Earth Liberation Front in their jihad against SUVs, dealers and SUV owners."

"Last week's (eco-terrorist) events underscore a dangerous irony: Huffington's irresponsible efforts to link SUV owners with Mideast terrorists actually are giving aid and comfort to domestic terrorists like those who torched the West Covina dealership," said Ron DeFore, SUVOA communications director. "While Ms. Huffington and like-minded zealots have spent tens of thousands of dollars condemning SUV owners, they refuse to take any responsibility for providing moral cover for radical domestic terrorist groups that have been vandalizing SUVs, homes and apartment buildings."

The next week, vandals shot out windows, slashed tires and "keyed" 22 vehicles at a Houston dealership, and a few days later a Santa Fe Land Rover dealership was vandalized with the letters "ELF" spray-painted on SUVs. Huffington would go mostly silent after getting defensive in response to our "cease and desist" petition.

In an August 29th Ad Age magazine article by Gregory Solman, Huffington denounced the crimes: "What these people are doing isn't activism, its vandalism, and I strongly oppose it," she said in a statement released yesterday. "I have nothing against SUV owners. My problem is with Detroit."

Ah, yes. "Detroit." Not Mercedes Benz, or Bentley, or Jaguar, or Land Rover. Just Detroit.

And what did "Detroit" have to say? "I can't draw a direct correlation [between the crimes] to the ads," said Chris Preuss, staff director for government affairs and technology communications for General Motors (he told Ad Age). He noted that similar crimes predate the campaign. "But our polling suggested that no one thought the ads (linking SUV ownership with supporting terrorists) were anything but offensive."

In the article Preuss noted the irony of radical ecological groups causing pollution: "Even the Hummer is meeting stringent California [emission] standards," he said. "There is no question that the burning of SUVs and dealerships emits significantly more emissions than all those SUVs would have produced over their lifetimes."

With Huffington on her heels, the "What Would Jesus Drive?" people had one last gasp. On September 15, 2003, joining forces with the Michigan Interfaith Climate and Energy Campaign, the group started yet another round of silliness, this time called "What Should the Governor Drive?" campaign. It was targeted at Michigan Democratic Governor Jennifer Granholm. It came and went in hours.

The "What Would Jesus Drive?" campaign, along with their other cohorts-in-shame, that had chastised the American people for deciding that an SUV was the best choice for their business, family or leisure activities had finally, thankfully, run out of gas.

Crisis Lesson Learned: Stick to the facts and if your detractors are full of shit, hypocrites or just garden variety liars, call them on it.

Chapter Twenty Five: The Fall, Rise and Fall of DaimlerChrysler

"Hi Jason, it's Nancy Rae." The call came December 10, 2003. Rae was head of Chrysler Group human resources. She had worked her way up from a secretary in the early '80s at Chrysler to become one of the most powerful women in the "car guys" auto industry.

"We wanted to know if you would be interested in coming back home."

"Let's talk," I said, and we agreed to meet in a private room at the Hilton Suites just outside the Chrysler compound in one hour. I got on the phone with my wife.

"Guess who just called me?" I said. "DaimlerChrysler?" she immediately replied.

"Yep."

"It's about time," she responded.

"You okay with this?" I asked.

"Are you ready to go back into the frying pan?" was her rejoinder.

"Do I have to answer that?" I said.

"No, but get a long contract, honey."

Chrysler had been through a shit-storm over the past three years, first surfacing in December 2000 when much of its management team, including its president, were fired.

At the helm was Dieter Zetsche. Among the Germans who controlled DaimlerChrysler, Dieter was the rising star and potential heir to Chairman Juergen Schrempp's throne. We seemed to hit it off from the start. In my one interview for the top PR job, Dieter and Chrysler COO Wolfgang Bernhard, grilled me intensively. I was their second choice, as they had earlier approached Steve Harris, "Yoda", Chrysler's former PR chief who was leading the charge at General Motors.

"Steve Harris recommended you," Dieter said. "He said that 99 times out of 100 you were the best PR guy in the business. But, that for that one time, you were kind of out there."

Whoa boy. How do you answer that? I thought for a second.

"Dieter, do you know who John Candy is?" I asked.

"Ah, the big fat guy in the movies," he answered.

"Well, in the movie Planes, Trains and Automobiles, John has a line that best reflects my attitude: 'I like me. My wife likes me.' I'm not changing my stripes. You get what you get."

"Fair enough," Dieter responded, and the interview was over.

Nine days later I was back in the saddle. Giddy up.

Of course, there was a crisis at hand. At least Chrysler marketing thought it was a crisis. For the prior two weeks, Chrysler was getting creamed for sponsoring the inaugural "Lingerie Bowl," an event on Super Bowl Sunday that would feature babes in panties playing flag football.

I, for one, was looking forward to it, imagining that every other commercial would be for Viagra or some other boner-inducing drug. One of Chrysler's top marketing execs, Julie Roehm, who would later claim infamy in a brief stint as WalMart's marketing chief, had secured the sponsorship.

Chrysler's only defense of its gambit was that a chick was calling the shots, so that this "exploitation" of women was hunky-dory. But on the day I arrived, Chrysler announced that it was pulling out of the "Bowl." Many in the media assumed the two events were not a coincidence – as they were. Chrysler was somewhat lauded for the decision to bail. For me, it was a freebie.

The atmosphere between Chrysler PR and marketing was toxic. Marketing had been blaming PR for almost all of Chrysler's ills and had been treating my newly-acquired staff like shit. But, there was a new sheriff in town. Hopefully. My strength, the strength of my team, and the craft we had developed for exceptional PR would soon be tested. Another "crisis" was looming; one that convinced me these folks didn't know what a real crisis was.

Nobody was dying or getting injured, but Chrysler's use of diva Celine Dion, in its commercials, was being panned as a colossal marketing failure. Chrysler's marketing folks were looking for a way out. Unfortunately, there had been threats of a lawsuit from "Team Celine" if the company did anything to soil her reputation. After all, not only was she the "greatest" singer of all time, she was a newly-minted mother. Ah, the latter – that's the ticket.

I suggested a fix to Jeff Bell. Bell was one of the top marketing dogs who made this hyperactive PR guy look like I was on Quaaludes. Often one of the smartest guys in the room, Jeff believed he was ALWAYS the "smartest guy in the room." He had as many enemies as he had friends at the company.

The Celine fix? Have her "star" in a set of PSAs (public service announcements) with the Ad Council, talking about the proper way to transport our little ones. It was stage three of my earlier communications, first at Chrysler and then at Ford, to educate Americans on cars and kiddies. Bell liked it and, thankfully, so did Team Celine. She'd get her contractual money, could save face, and Chrysler could possibly initiate a commercial campaign that actually focused on the "cars" and not the "stars."

A few weeks later, with the PSAs in the can, we previewed them at a safety event in Washington, D.C. sponsored by the Governors Highway Safety Association.

The press reviews were, for the most part positive, but a couple of advertising publications still couldn't resist one final dig at Chrysler and Dion's failed marriage. Arriving the next day back in my office, on my chair was a press clip with a huge red circle around a nasty quote. Above the circle was a hand-written note in about 72 font.

"The honeymoon is over!!!!! -Jeff."

I grabbed the note, took a couple of quick breaths and walked down the stairway that connected PR's sixth floor with Marketing's fifth and made a bee-line for Bell's office. He was there. Alone.

"Hey buddy," he said.

He had just taken a crap on my desk and it's "hey buddy?" I slammed the press clip, with his love note, down onto his desk.

"I didn't get a honeymoon, pal. I am trying to clean up all the shit from someone else's ass. Don't you ever do anything like this again."

I walked out. Believe it or not, we would become friends.

Chapter Twenty Six: My "heart attack" will go on

With the "Lingerie Bowl" and "Celine Dion" crises – please, give me a break – behind us, it was time for the real thing. And it was only a few months away.

CEO Dieter Zetsche and I had bonded quickly. The German had come to Chrysler and took no prisoners, firing thousands. Yet, he was loved by those that remained. He was wicked smart, self-deprecating and had the heart of a lion. And, the mustache of a walrus. He embraced Detroit, spiritually and culturally. Everyone knew he was there to help. An engineer, he was car guy to the core, but even more so – a business maestro. We had an agreement from day one; nothing, absolutely nothing would be withheld from me, the top communications guy. I would have a seat at the table – crucial for the head of PR in ALL organizations.

My team and I would not be cleaning up after the elephants in the parade.

But then, one night in early May, 2004, I got a call from journalist Paul Leinert.

"What happened with Mitsubishi?" he asked.

"I don't know what you are talking about," I answered.

"Daimler announced that they are pulling out of Mitsubishi," he responded.

I was livid. Why didn't I know this? Off the phone with Leinert, I called the DCX corporate PR guy in New York, Han Tjan.

"What happened?" I begged.

"Oh, I am sorry I didn't get a chance to tell you earlier."

By now, I was fuming and I felt betrayed by my boss. Dieter and I had a deal. My anger lasted throughout the night and into the early morning. As I readied for a shower before going into work, I was still spewing to my wife. Then, she entered the bathroom, phone in hand. It was Dieter. I took the call as the shower ran.

"Jason. I need you to come and pick me up at my house," he said ominously. "How quick can you get here?"

"I'm in the shower. I'll be there in 30 minutes."

"OK, see you then."

"What is it?" my wife asked.

"I don't know. I've got to go to Dieter's house."

Arriving a half hour later, Dieter came out of his house in obvious pain. His neck, again. His security guard and chauffer, Jack, was dutifully standing next to Dieter's ride.

"Jack, you take Jason's car into the office and he will drive me," he politely ordered.

In Dieter's 300, I got behind the wheel and he gingerly climbed aboard.

"It's my neck. We've got to go to my doctor. I will tell you everything on the way."

Dieter's pain in the neck was induced by the palace intrigue he would share with me over the next half hour as we motored to the chiropractor's office.

As part of Juergen Schrempp's grand plan to be the global automotive industry grand master, DCX had acquired a controlling 34 percent stake in Japan's Mitsubishi Motors. The vision was that it would serve as a gateway to Asia that Daimler and Chrysler, prior to the merger, both had sought and failed to achieve. It would eventually be Schrempp's undoing, but at the time, he was riding high as it was before the collapse of his newly acquired Chrysler.

By May of 2004, Chrysler was showing signs of life while Mitsubishi was crumbling under a mountain of debt and a recent bout of hideous corporate scandal. DCX's Supervisory Board and its shareholders had had enough, and Schrempp was forced to announce DCX would divest its Mitsubishi share. But – big but – not before Schrempp's secret, failed solo mission to Japan to salvage a deal.

And then it got "uncomfortable." The DCX Board of Management, composed of the top ranking guys from all the divisions, met to discuss the options regarding Mitsubishi. Dieter Zetsche earlier had been assigned to make the business case to stay with the Japanese or fish-and-cut-bait. Of course, this was in addition to his duties required to save Chrysler. Talk about a work load from hell.

Zetsche presented his findings to his management colleagues wherein he argued the facts demanded a divestiture from Mitsubishi, not a further investment. DCX needed to cut its losses and move on.

Schrempp, the Chairman, would disagree. Forcefully. And his ally, Eckhard Cordes, the head of Daimler's commercial division and, more importantly, a potential heir to Schrempp's throne, eagerly supported the Chairman in his disagreement with Zetsche, his main rival for the top job.

"That's when Wolfgang went crazy," said Zetsche as we neared his doctor's office.

Wolfgang was Wolfgang Bernhard, the Germanic former Chrysler COO who had just a month before been named to "become" the head of Mercedes – the prime job in the auto world. Wolfgang was the new "Mr. Mercedes." At least in Germany, it is THE top of the world.

He had George Clooney good looks. Check that: he was prettier. And, he was smart as a whip and communicated with ease - although a tad bit hyper. The latter, of course, I appreciated, thanking God I wasn't the only human with ADHD.

"Wolfgang went crazy," Zetsche said. "I tried to protect him, but I am afraid he is gone soon."

The Management Board of German companies, made up of top executives, is supposed to argue decisions, but then are expected to come to an agreed-upon path moving forward. They then take that decision to the Supervisory Board, made up of outside directors and the head of the unions, and get it blessed without question.

Normally.

But this particular Management Board meeting was anything but normal. No agreement on Mitsubishi could be reached.

Zetsche told me, "Finally, Juergen stood up and pointed to two doors. If you agreed with him; follow him out this door. If you agreed with Zetsche, follow him out the other door."

Cordes, Dieter's fierce rival to replace Schrempp – and a stoic, stuck-up prick from my brief interactions – dutifully followed the Chairman. Wolfgang and most of the gang followed Dieter. Game on.

"Holy shit," was all I could say.

I understood Dieter's neck pain now. Wolfgang was toast and so, quite possibly was my new friend. My boss.

"So, what happened?" I asked, trying to not get us killed as we drove 80 miles-an-hour on M59 eastward just south of Chrysler headquarters on the way to Dieter's quack-quack.

"We went to the Supervisory Board completely split," Zetsche said. "It was horrible and wrong. After much back-and-forth, the Supervisory Board came down on my side. It was not the way I wanted to win. I was trying to be objective. I don't give a shit about me, but I fear Wolfgang is dead."

I pulled into the office complex where Dieter's doctor resided.

He got out of the car and said "This shouldn't take too long. Thanks for this."

As he walked away, I got my wife on the phone. "In the shitter again, honey," I said. "It's going to get ugly."

"Not again," she answered. "Can't you get a break?"

Apparently not.

Chapter Twenty Seven: Springtime for the Japanese in Germany (Sing along please)

Dieter Zetsche's proposal for DaimlerChrysler to walk away from Mitsubishi – the right decision – had sealed the fate of both Schrempp and Wolfgang Bernhard. Wolfgang "resigned" soon afterward. Schrempp's career was mortally wounded, but still on life support for the time being. The battle for his job between Zetsche and Cordes was in full-throttle mode and would be for the next 12 months – the best 12 months of my career.

The year was almost crisis-free, if you can believe it. I was living large: family was great, money was unbelievable, and Chrysler was the coolest car company on the planet. My incredible PR team was loving it. A poll taken later in 2005 of American and international automotive journalists said our team was the best in the industry. We received kudos for access to our executives, our press ride-and-drives and our auto show unveilings. The latter, our use of theatre to launch our vehicles, no one could touch; although they tried. And failed.

The summer of 2004 was my Beach Boys "Endless Summer." I couldn't screw up. "Wouldn't it be nice if we were older," yada, yada, yada. I had a fun-loving, down-to-earth, talented, and dedicated PR team of real people and the greatest assistant, Sandy, who would become a best friend; and the greatest, most affable German (WTF?) CEO on the planet who needed no media-training. We had the hottest car on the planet, the Chrysler 300, thanks to Chrysler's design genius Ralph Gilles; a half-black dude who was a PR dream and a full-black "mutha-fucker," Calvin Broadus, loving us.

Oh snap! Calvin had changed his name to Snoop Doggy Dogg. Fo-shizzle my Bizzle. I am down with that!

Mr. Dogg, who smoked more dope in a day than I had in my life –
which in my junior/senior years in college was quite substantial as I
listened constantly to Pink Floyd's "The Wall" (cut me some slack) – had
left a message for Dieter Zetsche on the office phone of Chrysler's West
Coast sales leader. He, the sales guy, not Snoop – called me the next day
and sent me the voicemail.

Saideth Mr. Dogg, in a phone message for my German boss: "What I
gotta' do to get that brand new 300 up outta you?" he said.

The email containing the phone mail message reeked of weed.
Professionally, Mr. Dogg outlined Dr. Zetsche's next steps:

"Get back in contact with my nephew so he can make it happen; then
it's official like a referee with a whistle."

Official like a referee with a whistle. God, I loved my job.

I brought my PR team into my office to witness this "gift." However,
we didn't parlay it into gold for several days.

Three days later, in early June, Dieter and I were in Chicago. He was
speaking to the Chicago Economic Club. It was a ginormous event – a
thousand-plus people - and Dieter was the keynote speaker. At the end of
his remarks, he opened the floor to questions and the "Gift of the Weed
Magi" was presented. One of the participants asked about the incredible
sales success of the new Chrysler 300C. Without pausing, Dieter got into a
groove.

"It is so popular that I got a call the other day from Snoopy Doggy
Dog and he wanted one."

Not Snoop Dogg. Not Mr. Dogg. Dieter had voiced the words
"Snoopy Doggy Dog." The crowd went nuts and Dieter was instantly
more loveable than Charles Shultz's absolute prick-of-a-dog. It was
accidental. It was genius. The reporters at my table were awe-struck.

"Is this real?" one asked.

"Yeah. I will send you the phone call. It's on my computer," I said.

The story exploded a few hours later. Mr. Dogg's manager threatened a lawsuit, claiming something stupid that I refuse to remember; meanwhile we gave "Snoopy" a couple of 300Cs and he put them in a video. In the end, it was a "rap" – that went around the world.

We, Chrysler, be smokin'.

A month later, Zetsche, with his wife Gisela, were backstage with Mr. Dogg at a concert at Pine Knob, the suburban Detroit outdoor concert venue. He had stopped by before leaving for Germany on the corporate jet out of Pontiac Airport, just a half hour away.

"The smoke was quite heavy," he would relate to me. "I actually don't remember taking off in our plane. However, I do remember that I was very hungry."

When Dieter Zetsche wasn't sharing second-hand dope smoke with Snoopy Doggy Dogg, or saving the livelihoods of Chrysler employees and their dealers, he was trying to help Detroit's "hip-hop" mayor try to save the city.

Ultimately, the city would file for bankruptcy in the biggest municipal debacle in U.S. history in 2013. But Dieter was trying to assist the city a decade before. Zetsche had sent in Chrysler financial pros – no, that is not an oxymoron – to help him develop a budget for the troubled municipality. It wasn't that the young mayor Kwame Kilpatrick was dumb; he just didn't have the training necessary. He was a lawyer by degree who had never practiced law; but, he was a politician with rock-star appeal. Kwame provided a "hope" for a city running on empty. Zetsche saw it, as did others, such as Peter Karmanos.

More on the latter later, Jose.

"As a favor, would you mind meeting with Mayor Kilpatrick and give him some PR advice," Dieter asked.

Kilpatrick needed all the help he could get as his administration seemed to bungle even the small things. Zetsche made the call, and the next day I was sitting down with the Mayor, mano-a-mano. I had brought with me a massaged version of the PR strategy we were employing at Chrysler; a version carefully crafted for Detroit. It was basically "Do This. Don't Do This. Absolutely Don't Do That." Mayor Kilpatrick was furiously taking notes.

"Mr. Mayor," I stopped him. "You don't need to take notes. I created this deck for you. I believe in what you are doing. You can call me anytime, day or night. My kids and my wife's future are riding on the strength of what you are trying to accomplish."

We went through the rest of my "presentation." In the span of two hours, we had become "friends". I was done presenting, when he asked me: "Any last words?" I had been a "Detroiter" – this former Iowa farm boy who had castrated little baby pigs – for almost twenty years. My wife, my family and my friends were Detroiters. Yeah, I gave a damn.

I looked Kwame Kilpatrick in the eyes and said, "Have your team stop lying. It's bullshit that everyone can see. It's embarrassing. And, Kwame, Mr. Mayor, never, ever play the race card. This region has had too much of that bullshit over the past twenty years. You are better than that."

We didn't shake hands. The Mayor gave me a hug. He was the Hip Hop Mayor; I was the Hip Hop PR Guy.

Less than a decade later, Kwame wouldn't play the "race card." He would play the whole damned deck in the process of ending up in the hoosegow for 28-plus years.

Chapter Twenty Eight: "On a Roll"

Dieter, Chrysler and I charged into 2005 with extreme momentum. The Chrysler 300 had basically swept up all the serious "Best of" awards and, by spring, we were operating on all cylinders. Unfortunately, the U.S. economy was beginning to cool down and car sales started to slow. Somehow, the Titanic woke up, and General Motors created one of the most brilliant marketing scams in the history of retailing. Not just automotive retailing. Retailing. Period. In the summer of 2005, someone inside GM Marketing or one of its ad agencies came up with a whopper of an idea: give normal folks the same deal GM employees received when they purchased a car. What could be better?

The American auto-buying public went nuts, scooping up supposed deals despite the fact that it meant less of a discount offered in previous rebates on many models of cars and trucks. Ford and my Chrysler were caught with their marketing pants down; we were the corporate equivalent of singer George Michael in a public restroom. GM's move was simply brilliant. And, we had to respond without seeming copy-cat.

Chrysler marketing and its agency, BBDO, were working on a campaign that would feature Chrysler CEO Dieter Zetsche. I was not a fan. Detroit and the automotive press loved Dieter; but to the great-unwashed, he was nobody.

"Why do we want this incredible engineer to be introduced to America as a car huckster?" I asked Marketing and Sales Chief Joe Eberhardt, the most un-German-German I had ever met.

Joe and I had bonded despite the past bad blood between Chrysler PR and Marketing. Joe had given PR about $15 million out of his marketing budget for us to spend on PR events that kept our products alive.

"We spill more in a day than you spend in six months," he told me.

Joe became my brother-in-arms, and secretly, my smoking buddy in the executive garage. I would later have a hand in him getting fired – while trying to save him. I know that sounds screwed up; but that is the way of business sometimes.

We met in Zetsche's conference room, just across from his secretary Cindy's gate-keeping desk. The boys and girls from BBDO started taking Dieter, Joe and me through their story boards of Dieter Zetsche selling Chrysler, Dodge and Jeep cars, trucks and SUVs.

Suddenly, Dieter stopped the proceedings. "Joe, Jason, I need you two to come outside for a minute."

We got up and joined Dieter in his office. Neither Joe nor I was prepared for what was next.

"I have no problem doing these ads," he began. "But do you think it would be appropriate if you knew that 25 days from now I would be named the new Chairman of DaimlerChrysler?"

Oh, my, goodness. Dieter had won despite all the bullshit.

One month previously, Henry Dormann, the publisher of Leaders Magazine, who had hounded me for months to "purchase" an interview of Dieter Zetsche for his miserable publication, told me he had learned "from the highest levels of DCX" that Juergen Schrempp's replacement would be "anybody but Dieter." Joe Eberhardt and I looked at each other and smiled. Our boss, our friend, had won. Good guys do finish first. How about that? Dieter ended our chat with an admonition.

"You two are the only ones that know this information here and only a few know in Stuttgart," he said. "Please do not tell anyone, not even your wives."

"No way are you doing these ads," I said, snapping out of my nirvana stupor.

"We'll take care of it," answered Joe.

Dieter stayed in his office as we returned to the meeting.

"Gentlemen, give us a few minutes and we will be back with you," Joe said.

Eberhardt and I needed a smoke in order to help digest the news we had just learned. It is truly amazing the medicinal qualities of tobacco. Really. As we stood in the executive garage, puffing on Marlboros, Joe asked me,

"Who are we going to get?"

I thought for a millisecond. "The ultimate car salesman," I shot back.

"Who?" Joe came back.

"Lee Iacocca. We'll get more in free press than you will ever spend."

"Oh, that is interesting," Joe responded. "How?"

"I think I know, Joe."

Four Marlboro dead soldiers later, Eberhardt and I were back with the BBDO creative team sans Zetsche.

"We need a Plan B. Dieter is out," said Joe. "Let's meet back here tomorrow afternoon. Jason and I have some work to do."

The BBDO team left, and Joe and I asked Cindy if we could talk with Dieter. We walked in.

"Considering the news, the wonderful news, you just shared with us, we have an idea," Joe told Dieter as he opened it up for me.

"Lee Iacocca," I said. "We bring him back and we give a whole bunch of money to charity for his services."

Dieter looked like he had just had one of those vomit burps. "Do you expect me to sell this to Juergen after Iacocca said so much shit about the merger?" he asked.

We all remained silent for a few seconds. I was itching to say something smart-assed like "that's why you make the big bucks".

Finally, Dieter broke the silence. "Let me handle this. This is why I get paid so well."

Like, I was thinking. Only Germanic.

An hour later, Joe and I were back in Zetsche's office. Juergen Schrempp wasn't exactly keen on the idea of bringing back the former Chrysler icon considering Iacocca's previous nasty quotes about the takeover of Chrysler. However, Schrempp was on the way out, and didn't want his legacy spoiled by the Chrysler he had bought in his grandiose global vision - crapping the bed in the most competitive market in the world. Getting Iacocca to come on board would be Zetsche's call. Getting Iacocca on board would be my job. It would be painful.

Chapter Twenty Nine: If you can find a better Italian

I made a bee-line for Vicki Carlini's office; she worked in marketing. Her late father, Hank, was Iacocca's "number two" – if you know what I mean, Dr. Evil. Vicki and I had been friends for twenty years. I sat down.

"I need to talk with Lido," I said matter-a-factly. "We want to use him in commercials. I need your help."

She couldn't talk for a moment. "Are you kidding me?" she finally said.

An hour later we were on the phone, thanks to Vicki, with Iacocca.

"What the hell do you want me to do now, Jason? The last time you wanted me to sell Japanese cars for you," came the voice from Los Angeles.

"I want you back selling Chrysler cars, Dodge trucks and Jeeps," I shot back. "We'll give your diabetes charity one million bucks to start, and then one dollar for every vehicle we sell during the campaign."

"What does Juergen Schrempp think about this idea?" he asked.

"My call, Mr. Iacocca," I said brazenly.

"My first response is yes, but I have to check with my girls, Jason. You know the drill."

Iacocca hung up.

I looked over at Vicki. She was crying. Lee Iacocca – Chrysler's savior in the 80s who had become a pariah after being suckered by billionaire Kirk Kerkorian in a failed attempt to take over the company in the mid-90s – was almost back home. And her dad was smiling in heaven.

Naturally, things got tricky. The negotiations over the deal started to bog down and time was of the essence. General Motors was creaming us with their Employee Pricing campaign and our dealers were screaming for a response. Two days later Dieter Zetsche called my cell at the same time I was talking with Iacocca. I switched lines and answered my boss.

"Do we have a deal or not?" Zetsche said, clearly agitated.

Zetsche was never a prick of a boss, but he also took no prisoners. In one top executive meeting he had told one of my colleagues to achieve a particular goal. My colleague responded, "I'll try." Zetsche quickly responded, "Don't try – do it."

"Dieter, I've got Lee on the other line. Give me a little more time," I begged.

"You have five minutes," he said.

Zetsche couldn't risk a stumble, after all, he was on the precipice of his career dream job.

Back on the line with Iacocca, he was busting my chops about whether or not somehow we would renege on the deal. In his failed takeover attempt with Kerkorian, we, Chrysler, and I brought out every piece of artillery we could assemble to kick the crap out of him and Kirk. And after the "merger of equals" with Daimler, Iacocca had some harsh words for the deal and the Germans. So, I was playing with fire. Finally, I had had enough of Lee's bitching.

"Listen Lido, let me cut to the chase. I have a pretty good gig here. The last thing I need to do is fuck it up by screwing you. Let me know if you are in or out in 24 hours. Enough talk. Sir."

I called Dieter back. "I gave him 24 hours."

Twenty hours later, we had the skeleton of a deal and we announced a press conference to tell the world. The Detroit area media was gathered at the posh Detroit Athletic Club for a 4 'o clock presser. Still no definitive deal, though. I had been working throughout the day with Dana Ball, who ran the Iacocca Foundation, whose sole purpose was to fund research to eradicate diabetes in our time. It was the disease that had taken Lido's wife, Mary, more than two decades earlier. Mary never got to see her Lido – the father of the Ford Mustang and the Chrysler minivan – become perhaps the most famous CEO of all-time.

Dana was on-board; he knew it meant millions for his 501c3. But, Iacocca – and his family – were nervous. When 4 o'clock came and went, I called Dana.

"What the hell is going on, Dana?" I asked.

"Lee's nervous about this," he said.

"Do you realize how much money is involved here?" I asked. "It's a windfall for you guys for crying out loud!"

"I know," he said. "I'm all in," he said, clearly frustrated. "Let me work on Lido."

I had to face the press with nada. Dave Sedgwick of Automotive News had been leaked the story several hours before, and I told him to please hold it until the deal was done. I would let him break the news. He grabbed me as I walked toward the entrance of the DAC.

"What the fuck is going on?" he screamed. "I've held this for two hours now!"

"Go with it," I said.

The press conference was bizarre. All I could say was we were talking with Lee Iacocca about doing some ads. One minute after it ended, Zetsche called my cell. He had watched the wacky presser.

"Why did you do that?" he said.

He was pissed. He never got pissed with me.

"I had no choice. Automotive News had the story," I said. "I promise you we will get a deal tonight."

We did. Whew. I looked up to Heaven and whispered "Thank you." We were about to answer GM and top the kids in Dearborn and I knew then and there that God hated Ford as much as I did.

The ads were, for the most part, okay. Not great. Not shitty. They were quickly written over the Fourth of July weekend by the team at BBDO led by Hugh Broder. But, where they scored was in the area they were designed to hit; they cut through the clutter of all the automotive ads in the fever pitch of GM's Employee Pricing.

How do I know? A month later, I was on the first tee at Pebble Beach, getting ready to sacrifice a few hundred golf balls into the Pacific. Dutch Mandel, publisher of Autoweek and a great friend, shared my golf cart. We shared a love for golf despite the fact we both pretty much sucked. A Pebble Beach honcho came up to Dutch and started chit-chatting.

"So, Dutch, you're the expert," he said, "What do you think about Chrysler's ads with Lee Iacocca?"

"Don't ask me," Dutch replied, "Ask the grand master, they were his idea," he said, pointing toward me.

"Let me just say this," I responded. "You're talking about them. That's all I wanted."

Several ad critics, mostly feckless buttheads, tore the ads apart. BBDO's creative team had quickly put them together. The first featured Seinfeld actor Jason Alexander in a complete rip-off of his George Costanza character, with Iacocca serving the role of New York Yankees owner George Steinbrenner. It was somewhat clever. The second ad featured Lido as a grandfather discussing employee pricing with his "granddaughter." During the shoot, Iacocca had called me from the outdoor set in full bitch-mode.

"I'm 80 years old and it's colder than hell out here," he yelled from the Nantucket set.

"Thanks for doing this," was all I could think to say and quickly hung up.

The final ad was, well, surreal. It featured Snoop Doggy Dogg as Lido's golfing buddy. Their unlikely "joint" venture was brilliantly chronicled by then-Detroit News reporter Bill Vlasic, who had asked to be a fly-on-the-wall as the commercial was shot. Wrote Vlasic:

"The grounds of the country club had been turned into a Hollywood set by 9 a.m., with camera crews and lighting technicians and makeup artists hustling to get ready for the day's shoot. Waiting nearby, behind the tinted glass of side-by-side luxury motor homes, were the two stars of the Chrysler Group's latest television commercial, 'Golf Buddies.'

"And when the cameras started rolling, the bright lights hit auto legend Lee Iacocca and platinum-selling rapper Snoop Dogg together in what has to be the most surreal pairing of spokesmen in automotive history.

"...At age 80, Iacocca is proving once again that the art of the deal never gets old – even when he's sharing the stage with the lanky, diamond-studded, "gangsta"-rapping Snoop Dogg. 'I don't know what the hell Snoop is saying,' Iacocca said with a smile. 'But he called me 'nephew,' so I guess that means I'm in.'

"...Despite being retired from Chrysler for a dozen years, Iacocca still commands the spotlight like no other celebrity CEO ever has. 'The goal of using Lee was to cut through the clutter,' said Jason Vines, Chrysler's head of communications. 'And our research shows that we cut through the clutter big-time.'

'So far, the Iacocca ads have hit the mark. Chrysler recently announced it would extend its employee discounts on vehicles for all consumers after sales jumped 27 percent in July.

'...My brother said this may be the biggest thing I've ever done," he (Snoop) said, "sitting side by side with the biggest boss of them all ... Mr. ...Lee...I-a-cocca!"

'...Resurrecting Iacocca as a spokesman had its risks. Was he too old, too identified with the Chrysler of the past, too Frank Sinatra-era to resonate in a hip-hop world?

'Yeah it was risky,' said Hugh Broder of Chrysler's ad agency BBDO Detroit. 'But this is Lee Iacocca we're talking about.

'...It was a unique moment even for Hollywood, the first meeting ever between Detroit's one-time Chairman of the Board and the self-proclaimed 'Doggfather' of rap music.

'An odder couple could hardly be imagined than Iacocca, the paragon of corporate power, and 33-year-old Snoop Dogg, the up-from-the-streets rap star with a criminal rap sheet and a language all his own.

'It's a big company and a big-time rapper doing big business together,' said Snoop. 'We are bringing the generations together and it's a beautiful thing.

'Last year, Snoop made headlines when he personally called Chrysler chief Dieter Zetsche to get one of the first available models of the sculpted new Chrysler 300C sedan.

'Snoop has already been identified with some of our recent products,' Vines said. 'And to pair him with Lee is just a 'holy cow' kind of thing.

'...When Snoop exclaimed that he's 'got the hook-up, nephew,' on a good deal for a Chrysler car, Iacocca feigned puzzlement.

'I'm not sure what you just said, but now anybody gets a great deal,' said Iacocca. Snoop, in his own words, agreed.

'Fo-shizzle, he said, 'Ica-zizzle.'

'...When it was over, Iacocca moved slowly through the crowd, shaking hands with the director and the assistant directors, the crew members and the caterers, the lighting guys and the wardrobe gals. And as he walked away toward the parking lot, he glanced over his shoulder one last time.

'Did I miss anybody?' he asked. 'You know, I don't want to leave without saying goodbye.'"

BBDO's Broder would later recount: "The funniest part of the whole shoot was listening to Iacocca and Snoop, still miked, talking off-camera. Iacocca says: 'I know your real name is Calvin, so that's what I am going to call you.' And Snoop very politely says, 'OK, Mr. Iacocca." Then Lee says, 'You know, my granddaughters are really excited about me doing this with you.' And Snoop answers, "Yeah, and my grandmother says she's excited I am doing this with you'."

Come on! If that isn't special, nothing is.

Chapter Thirty: "The Good Guy Wins"

The wheels of Dieter Zetsche's corporate jet touched down in Stuttgart in the early morning hours of July 27th, 2005. On-board, along for the ride were COO Tom LaSorda, EVP Eric Ridenour, Sales and Marketing Chief Joe Eberhardt and me. We were almost home free, as the news about Zetsche's rise to the top of the heap hadn't leaked.

That night, I was working solo with Daimler PR chief Hartmut Schick to get all of the communications in order – we were the only PR people who knew what was about to happen; the two top guys had to do all the work. At 10 p.m., we were done. Zetsche called a few minutes later. "I cannot believe the story didn't leak, can you?"

"No, quite frankly. I am happily flabbergasted that it didn't," I said.

"Listen," Dieter continued, "before things get crazy tomorrow, I just want to thank you for all the work you have done on my behalf and how you helped my family." I was on the verge of tears, but stopped just shy. I was so proud of my boss; my friend…and, to be honest, I was pretty damned proud of me.

"Thanks for the chance you gave me," I said. "I'm going to hit the sack Dieter. Oh, and when this is official, we need to talk. Good night Mr. Chairman, in a day."

The next morning's announcement took the industry by storm. Zetsche, for the miracle that he had pulled off saving Chrysler, was given the brass ring over his arch rival Eckhart Cordes to replace Schrempp, fatally damaged by his debacle with Mitsubishi the prior year. Hail to the Victors! (Shame on me for saying that; I am a Michigan State Spartan!)

Cordes was now gone. As the corporate jet lifted off a few hours later for the return flight to Michigan- we were on the top of the world - both figuratively and literally. A "Chrysler Guy" was going to run the DCX Empire. The champagne flowed. Zetsche joined in the frivolity for a while and then got all serious for a moment. "Let's go back there and continue our conversation from last night," he said, pointing to the table near the back of the plane.

"You said last night we need to talk."

"There have been some active forces against you that need to be dealt with," I said. An outside agency led by of a former Daimler PR leader, while getting paid more than one million Euros a year by DaimlerChrysler, had been trashing Zetsche in favor of Cordes behind the scenes during this power struggle; as had a current Mercedes PR mid-manager who reported to the PR chief Hartmut Schick. "They need to go now," I said. "These guys are real pieces of shit."

"I will handle it," he said, clicking champagne glasses. In short order, he did.

The rest of 2005 went pretty much without much incident with the exception of Hurricane Katrina. Responsively, Chrysler was one of the first companies to lend aid – more than one hundred trucks donated for emergency responders, food, water and money. I think we arrived a couple of months before FEMA and "Brownie". I was kind of the field marshal barking out orders. By "kind of" I mean that one of our contract employees, Stephen Gordan, was the "General Marshall" of Chrysler's efforts on the ground. By day, Steve helped plan our media events. In the wake of Katrina, he led an incredible effort on Chrysler's behalf down in the Bayou. He literally worked several days straight without sleep. He called after the third day, purely exhausted. He was melting down. He was almost delusional.

"Will anyone remember what we are doing here?" he begged.

"Yeah, I will," I said trying to calm him down. "You're doing God's work Stephen," I said. Easy for me to say; I hadn't "not" slept in a van the night before like Stephen. "You've got a place in heaven sewed up, buddy," I said. "You should be proud of what you have done leading this charge. I will never forget it, my friend."

As the crisis of Katrina was subsiding, a different kind of storm was just beginning to brew inside Chrysler. Before that storm could actually achieve gale-force winds, I had my own crisis to create. Maybe I didn't create it, but I surely stoked it. It would expose a gigantic fissure between two of the world's most powerful industries – autos and oil – and it would test my will and character. This tempest would prove even one of the cockiest, self-assured, highly-paid PR guys on the planet at the time could screw-up brilliantly. And survive. There were lessons to be learned that I would carry on to future PR storms.

Chapter Thirty One: Big Oil and Me

It all started with a November 30, 2005 memo from Rob Liberatore to the Chrysler Group Executive Committee and myself. The subject: Oil Industry CAFE ads. CAFE stands for Corporate Average Fuel Economy and the National Highway Transportation Administration (NHTSA), which controlled the fuel economy standard, was contemplating raising it for both passenger cars and trucks. Rob was (is) a dear friend and was running Government Affairs worldwide for DaimlerChrysler after a stellar career as Chrysler's top guy in D.C. prior to the "merger of equals." He was, by far, the best auto guy in the swamp of D.C.; he was revered by all who mattered. In the early 90's he had been embedded in the Chrysler PR department to "learn." He learned in about a week. That is how smart he was.

Fast forward to the days just past Thanksgiving 2005 when the NHTSA was being pressured from all sides – including the tree huggers and so-called consumer groups – to force automakers to make vehicles more fuel efficient in the wake of Hurricane Katrina. Katrina had "caused" gas prices to soar; along with, not so coincidently, gigantic Big Oil profits. Big Oil was in a public opinion blood bath.

Everyone assumed Big Auto and Big Oil were in bed together making mad love. Not!

I don't wish to bore you with all the gory details of Liberatore's memo regarding the Oil Industry ads, but, alas, I must; it sets the stage for a brief monster of a shit-storm in which I eventually found myself in the "eye."

Liberatore wrote: "In recent weeks ExxonMobil said in a full-page ad: 'The best available science suggests that a further 50 percent improvement in the efficiency of the internal combustion engine may be achievable – without limiting consumer choice.' Chevron's ad campaign says: '...if automakers improved fuel economy across the board by just 5 mpg, we'd save over 22 billion gallons a year.'

Obviously these ads are designed to move the attention from the oil companies' enormous profit to the auto industry. It risks propelling CAFE or mandates to build 'innovative technology vehicles.' Despite overwhelming CAFE victories in the Congress earlier this year, $3.00+ gasoline and threats of shortages this fall have created the most volatile atmosphere for 'doing something' about oil dependency and automotive fuel efficiency that we have seen in many years. Having the oil companies throwing their gasoline into this fire is very troublesome.

"GM, Ford, Toyota and DaimlerChrysler met with Exxon, Chevron and Phillips, along with our trade association heads today," Liberatore's memo continued. "We agreed to start a regular exchange between our policy people and our technical people on issues which concern us and where we disagree. (They really object to ethanol mandates and other subsidized alternative fuels.) The heads of the Washington offices (John Bozzella for DaimlerChrysler) will meet every six weeks to ensure ongoing dialogue.

"We are hopeful that they will pull these ads as a result of our meeting. If they continue to run, we need to be prepared to escalate our engagement. We might do our own ads, start supporting a windfall profits tax on their enormous recent surge in profitability, etc. Hopefully, we can start a cooperative dialogue because at the end of the day autos fighting oil is our enemies' wildest dream."

So endth the memo. But, then came a question. Eric Ridenour, Chrysler Group's COO scribbled on the memo and sent it back to Liberatore and me asking, "What are we going to do about this!!!" Despite Ridenour's lack of proper grammar – after all, it was a question and questions are not punctuated by triple exclamation points – it was clear the issue was beyond urgent.

Two big ugly industries on the brink of a civil war. The media would eat it up.

Liberatore was right: Big Oil was deflecting the criticism against its grotesque corporate and executive profits and pay. If you think about it, it made no sense. Higher fuel economy for America's cars and trucks meant the purchase of less gasoline. But, Big Oil, led by ExxonMobil and ChevronTexaco, were like the co-conspirators in a crime suddenly turning state's evidence and testifying against their accomplice to avoid the public's electric chair. "He shot the guy; I was just driving."

The ExxonMobil ad was especially offensive, because while not outright lying; their play-on-words was a Shell game (pun intended). "America has made progress since the 1970s 'energy shock'. The U.S. economy today is nearly 50 percent more energy efficient than 30 years ago. Every form of planes, trains and automobiles – now benefit from improved fuels and engine systems. So why is it that despite this overall progress, the average fuel economy of American cars in unchanged in two decades?"

The facts were that over the past "two decades" the average car fuel economy and the average pickup truck fuel economy had soared. The auto industry had made enormous gains in both fuel efficiency and emissions (pollution control). But, Big Oil, led by ExxonMobil, was trying to wear a white hat while shooting out the legs' of the auto industries' horse.

The ExxonMobil ad, throwing the auto industry under the bus, ended with the following lines: "Would a 50 percent improvement (in fuel efficiency) be worth the investment needed to achieve it? We think so. And through partnerships with manufacturers like Toyota and Caterpillar we're working on fuel and engine systems that could dramatically improve efficiency and reduce emissions – without restricting America's 'right to drive.'"

Sanctimonious assholes.

Two weeks later, Liberatore faxed a memo to Chrysler COO Eric Ridenour saying: "Eric, I don't think we will see any more of these (Big Oil) ads. Jo really ripped Exxon for putting Toyota in this ad."

Jo, was Josephine Cooper, head of Toyota's Washington office. ExxonMobil obviously thought they were being clever by sucking up to Toyota by saying in its ad that it had a "partnership" with the Japanese automaker to improve fuel economy, and thus, by implication, that Toyota supported a huge increase in the fuel economy standard.

In response to Cooper's "rip," ExxonMobil Washington chief sent a complete bullshit "don't worry, be happy" letter to Cooper that both Chrysler's Liberatore and Ridenour naively hoped was a Neville Chamberlain-like "peace in our time" appeasement statement. The threat of war was over.

Not!

When Ridenour had earlier asked Liberatore and me "what are we going to do about this" – the Big Oil attack ads -- my ADHD kicked in immediately. I was on the phone with Stratacomm's Jeff Conley and Ron DeFore within minutes. "Find out where all the oil money went. From what I read, there hasn't been a new refinery in decades and they fight improvements to their fuels and alternative fuels at every junction. Meanwhile, Americans are getting raped every time they fill up while these bastards live like kings," I said.

"How soon do you need this?" Conley asked.

"ASAP, but don't cut corners," I said. "Facts only." DeFore, who handled much of the money side of Stratacomm, chimed in: "What is the budget?" "Whatever it takes to get it right. The stakes are incredibly high," I said.

Twenty-two days later, Stratacomm would deliver its research on Big Oil under the title of the "Fuels Research Project." The firm had poured every bit of its expertise into the research. The 51-page report hit my desk on December 21, 2005. Christmas had come early. However, the contents could turn out to be a lump of coal if not handled properly.

The cover page of Stratacomm's report featured a recent editorial from the Washington Post, dated October 28, 2005:

"By most favorable comparisons, the $9.92 billion profit earned by ExxonMobil Corp. in just three months is almost unimaginable. It would cover all Social Security benefit payments for three months. It would pay for an Ivy League education for about 60,000 kids. It would pay the average list price for more than 160 Boeing 737s. It would fund the military operations in Iraq and Afghanistan for more than two months. Yet oil industry executives and ExxonMobil yesterday made a game effort to cast the record profit, earned during a quarter in which the Gulf Coast was shattered by hurricanes and gas prices rose well above $3 a gallon, as middling at best."

Understand now why Big Oil was deflecting and throwing the automakers under the bus?

The Fuels Research Project that I had commissioned resulted in a startling summary: "If one desired, one could make a strong case that ExxonMobil and ChevronTexaco continue to fight against cleaner fuels and are not investing enough in critically needed exploration and field development, despite the fact that they are the most profitable companies (and CEOs) in the world. While other industries are making long-term investments with an eye toward improving America's energy security and environmental standing in the world, ExxonMobil and ChevronTexaco continue to squander their unmatched profits for near-term gain. Their greed and inaction threaten our national security by perpetuating our vulnerable reliance on foreign oil. To provide added context, one could also make a strong case that these same companies price gouge Americans, perjure themselves before Congress, create devastating environmental damage, practice environmental racism and receive excessive corporate welfare."

Whoa, Free Willy! The detailed back-up data for the report was amazing and overwhelming.

I spent two weeks drilling through the report – over the Christmas holiday season and beyond – going back-and-forth with the researchers. It had to be rock solid; it was. Not sandstone. Not limestone. It was granite. But it would have to wait. We were in the midst of auto show season; first in Detroit, quickly to Chicago, then Geneva and finally New York. Meanwhile, Big Oil was playing "nice", so perhaps it was a moot point after all.

Enter the Ides of March, plus a day. The cease-fire was over. Another ExxonMobil ad in Washington D.C. publications targeted at the Hill and the federal bureaucrats, bitch-slapping the auto industry for inaction whilst the oil industry sported angel wings. The call came from Stratacomm's Ron DeFore. "They're at it again Jason."

I got off the phone and told my secretary, Sandy, to get Ed Garsten. Ed was in my cube in seconds; no great feat as his office was 15 feet away. I had given Ed the Fuels Research Report back in January after I was sure it was solid. But the question going forward back then was: "what do we do with this and how do we do it?" We, at Chrysler PR, had a blog called The Firehouse. For the media, the name made sense. For the past few years, Chrysler PR – thanks to our creative agency and now-defunct ClearBlue – took over an abandoned Detroit firehouse directly across the street from the Detroit Motor Show and turned it into a "Cheers-style" bar. Media members would enter for free and eat and drink until they stumbled their way back to their hotel rooms. It was THE place to be. CEOs of our competitors begged to be let in – of course, we did. It was the place to be seen. You grabbed a free Guinness and spewed uncensored insight. Unfettered brilliance was the intention of our blog site, aptly named The Firehouse.

However, we couldn't put out a 51-page report on a blog. Blogs, while still in their infancy, were quick, snappy and brief. Ed Garsten, a former CNN correspondent, and one of the brightest people I have ever worked with, created and ran The Firehouse for us. I had kept Ed apprised of the on-going fight with Big Oil, the supposed-cease fire and my cynicism that the gasoline guys would play fair; thus the research that would produce the Fuel Research Project, subtitled "ExxonMobil, ChevronTexaco and the Oil Industry 'Lowlights'."

"I'm a good writer," I told Garsten, "but you are better. Take this sucker and boil it down so that we can blog it when the time comes, if necessary. No hurry. Probably won't happen, but I want to be prepared."

Unfortunately, the time would come a few months later. Garsten grabbed a chair. "What's up," he asked. "Where's that blog about Big Oil?" "Are you kidding me," he said with a bewildered look on his face. "I put that on your chair a couple of months ago," he said in his not-finally-gone New Yawk accent. My office cubicle looked like al-Qaida had hit it. Married to a neat-freak, alas, I was an office slob. Garsten looked around. "Here it is," he said grabbing the document. "OK," I said, "I'm going to spend the rest of the day going through this and will get you changes. We gotta move."

Brief aside: For those wondering how was it that a corporate vice president had a "cubicle," it is the truth. When I arrived at Chrysler I found a demoralized PR team. After a month I gave up my glass enclosed officer office for a cubicle in the middle of our floor with two entrances but no doors. I wanted to show my team I was no better than them. All of my direct reports had real offices. In my mind, if I was asking my troops to go to war, I needed to be on the battlefield with them. Now, don't get me wrong; my cubicle was quite large and my compensation was swell. In fact, very swell, baby.

Back to the Big Oil blog. I spent the afternoon doing, honestly, only minor edits. Ed Garsten knew my writing style better than anyone else. As I read his prose, I was reading me, only better. When done, I called Garsten back into my office. "I'm going to send this to our Washington office for their approval," I said. "This sucker is an incendiary device. Factual, yes; but none-the-less white-hot. Trust me; Washington will turn it into a popcorn fart. I'll tell Bozzella (Chrysler's D.C. chief) to work through you, Ed."

Almost one month later, on April 10th, Ed Garsten stuck his head back in my cubicle with a simple request: "When do you want to post the Big Oil blog?"

"I thought you sent that out a couple of weeks ago," I said, perplexed. I assumed that the Washington office had completely neutered what Ed (mostly) and I had written. "Send it out now," I said nonchalant. It was about three in the afternoon.

At 4p.m., the call came in from Mark Truby of the Detroit News. "Jay," he said as I answered the phone. My friends call me Jace or Jay. Mark was and is a great friend.

"What's up," I replied.

"Is this fucking real?" he said, seemingly hyper-ventilating.

"Is what real?" I said, clueless.

"Your blog about the oil industry?" he came back.

"Yeah," I said matter-of-factly.

"Holy shit!" was all Truby could say, until he added, "You stand by this?"

"Of course I do," I said as I attempted to chit-chat with my friend.

"Hey, sorry, gotta go. This is too hot. Call you later, but I gotta go," he said, hanging up.

Holy shit. What had I done? I knew immediately. I, the head of
Chrysler public relations, the miraculous PR guy who had earlier been
named the best PR professional guy in the automotive business the year
before – a second time (but who's counting) – had committed a cardinal
sin. I had issued a communique – this one with my name on it – that I had
not fully reviewed. Frantically I went to The Firehouse to see what had
been posted after it had purportedly gone through the sterilization process
in the Washington office.

Ahhhh!!!!!!!

It was all I could say as I read my blog. Not only had Washington not
neutered it; they had actually – slightly really – made it even hotter.

"Ed!" I shouted. In a second, Garsten was in my cube. "Washington
didn't shit-can this?"

"No," he replied with a smile. "They made it a tad-bit juicer."

Then my phone rang and rang and rang. First up was Bernard Simon
of the Financial Times. "Jason, do you stand by this? He queried. That's
what Brits do; they query. I didn't hesitate; mainly because I did stand by
it although I was still pissed at myself for not paying attention to the
important act I had just committed. I was more than careless; I was sloppy.

"Yes, Bernard," I said. "I stand by every word."

For the first time in my now-17-year PR career, I had no idea whether
I was safe or totally screwed. I had always been outspoken and brutally
frank. It made me… me. But this time, I was in unchartered waters. I
called Mark Truby at the Detroit News.

"This is a thing of beauty," he said after sharing hellos.

"Ah Mark, where is it going?" I asked.

"Are you shittin' me? Page one, above the fold, banner headline," he
triumphantly proclaimed.

I packed up my stuff, grabbed my airline tickets for the flight to New
York and headed home. I had a beautiful wife, three great kids, a

ginormous house, a dog and a vacation home in northern Michigan; and I had just put all of them in jeopardy because I had blown through every principle of proper communications strategy and tactics that I had been taught and had preached to my teams at Nissan, Ford and now Chrysler.

Critically, I had made this mistake while going "full commando", alone, taking on the most powerful and profitable industry in the world. As Slim Pickins' character lamented in the movie Blazing Saddles: "I am depressed." But, I told my wife Betsy nothing.

She went to bed. I would be a few minutes behind her. I needed to call my boss Tom LaSorda, in Stuttgart for meetings, and tell him about the radioactivity that was coming in the morning. The call went to voice mail. "Tom, the shit is going to hit the fan in the morning. Please call me ASAP," was the message I left. As I climbed under the sheets, Betsy was already out and I just stared at the ceiling, my mind racing. I had set my alarm for 3:30 a.m. in order to shower and get to Metro Detroit Airport for a 6 a.m. flight to LaGuardia. But, I didn't need an alarm clock. At 3:25 a.m., my wife awoke and found me sitting up in the bed. "What's wrong, honey," she asked, half asleep. "I did perhaps the dumbest or greatest thing I have ever done in my career," I lamented. "And, it might get me fired."

Again.

"Oh, get over it," was her response as she laid her head back on the pillow. "Dieter loves you."

I got up, showered and headed to the airport. On the way I called my buddy, Mike Rosenau, one of the principals of our creative agency that put on our auto shows. He also was on the way to the airport, 15 minutes ahead of me. "Hey, buddy, stop and get a copy of the Detroit News and let me know what you think," I said.

Rosey, as we call him, had no idea what I was talking about. He called about 10 minutes later from a 7-11 off of Telegraph Road. "Oh my

God!!!!!" he said as I answered his call. "Can you buy all the copies?" I said, working on absolutely no sleep. "Together, we can remove at least one percent of the papers from the newsstands." Even in this time of extremely tight-sphincter anxiety, I could see the humor. "See you on the plane," I said.

As I boarded, many more eyes than normal were on me. Why? The plane was largely loaded with automotive people. Many, eerily, looked at me, whispered to their next-seat cohort and then pointed at me. It was as if O.J. Simpson was boarding carrying a duffle bag with a knife protruding out of its side. I was suddenly THE most famous – or was that, infamous – executive in the auto industry. Hell, maybe of all industries – at least for that day in April 2006. Luckily, I had a bazillion Northworst miles so I was automatically in first class and didn't have to walk the gauntlet through economy class seats, where Rosey was sitting. But within seconds, Rosey made his way up to first class as the plane was boarding (a completely white-trash move). When he got to my seat – 3B – he had the biggest shit-eating grin I had ever seen. He handed me that morning's Detroit News. The humongous banner headline took my breath away: "Chrysler Slams Big Oil."

As I started to read the article, I quickly noticed that Rosey had drawn a quote balloon coming out of the mouth of my picture. It read: "These oil fuckers are going to put me in the Hudson River." I looked at him and all he could do was laugh. "Hi de ho, Kyle," he said, going back to his seat. (For those that don't get it; we were both South Park fans and I was quite possibly Mr. Hanke, the Christmas poo – a piece of shit - about to be flushed.)

We landed in New York. As I walked up the jet way, I turned on my cell phone. It almost melted; 29 missed calls. I went through the list. Two from Germany. Damn! That's either LaSorda or Dieter firing me. The bulk, however, were from Detroit's most popular radio host, Paul W.

216

Smith – on his personal cell – or from his producer Ann Thomas. The two accounted for a dozen of the calls. Paul W., as he is still known, talked to a million Detroiters a day and he apparently had been begging me, on the air, to "call him." So I did and was interviewed for 10 minutes in the back of a New York taxi headed to the NY auto show. We ended the interview with Paul W. saying, "You're either going to be a hero or goat for this. Right now, based on our callers, you are a huge hero Jason Vines."

I was magically pumped. I was on no sleep. It was pure adrenalin. And, as I said being ADHD, it was good. Endorphins were streaming through my veins – the rush gave me the courage to call the Germans next. Well, not actually; I needed to call my boss, Canadian Tom Lasorda, our CEO.

"Hey, buddy, how's it going," he said as if I was calling my brother to check on our mom.

"Um," I was tongue-tied momentarily. "Did you see the headlines?" I asked.

"Yes I did," he responded. "And I want you to know that Dieter and I are behind you 100 percent."

My heart almost exploded.

A few minutes later, Rob Liberatore was calling me. I had not even gotten into Manhattan.

"The oil guys are going ape-shit," he said. "You've got to retract this!" (Remember, Rob and I were - and are - friends. He was the reason I had turned down an offer to join Carlson Companies in Minneapolis back in 1993 and instead opted to stay with Chrysler and be loaned to the Big Three's trade association in Washington, D.C. – AAMA.) "Why didn't you send this blog to us before you sent it out?" he asked.

He was pissed.

"Dammit Rob, I did," I said. "Bozzella got it and actually made it stronger. Besides, everything in it is factual. These Big Oil assholes lied to you; they lied to the entire auto industry. I won't retract shit."

Rob was exasperated, but he was one of the smartest, savviest and most decent people I had ever known. Again, he was a friend.

"I've got to get on the phone with the oil guys and try to put out the fire," he said. "I'll let you know how it goes."

"Hey," I said ending our call. "Sorry to put you on the spot. I promise not to add any more fuel to the fire."

A few minutes later, Rob would have his ass handed to him. When he asked DCX Chairman Dieter Zetsche to compel me to make a retraction, Dieter – according to Tom LaSorda – told him something like "You guys in D.C. didn't do your job; so Jason had to."

Ouch.

Soon Liberatore was on the phone with Red Cavaney, the president of the American Petroleum Institute, and Dan Nelson, VP of government and industry relations for ExxonMobil. He reiterated Chrysler's – hell, the industry's – objection to Exxon Mobil's ad which had run on March 16th and said it was the company's plan to voice the company's objection to ExxonMobil directly and not in the public sphere. "Jason's comments are his own," he told Cavaney. I was apparently a lone gunslinger.

Bullshit.

By noon Liberatore would tell DCX senior management of his talk with Big Oil and their lobbyists: "They want to put this issue behind us. I suggested that either Dieter or Tom should talk with Rex Tillerson, the Chairman of ExxonMobil. Both Cavaney and Nelson agreed that this the best way to keep this issue from escalating into an oil industry vs. auto industry battle which will only help extremists who would like to see both industries put out of business."

For ExxonMobil, if they could magically wipe away this controversy, they would have probably paid a king's ransom; which was pocket change for them. But all the money in their corporate coffers couldn't overcome an even bigger coming shit-storm that had been severely exacerbated by my blog. The company was just three days away from being forced, as a publicly traded company, to announce their former Chairman Lee Raymond had retired with a $356 million golden parachute. Make that a diamond parachute. The April 15th headline of the New York Daily News would say it all: "Oil Vey!" Timing, a chief tenet in the world of PR, was everything.

Finally inside the NY auto show, I was surrounded by inquiring media. It went on all day. I learned from my PR friends at Ford and GM that the very first questions posed to GM CEO Rick Wagoner and Ford's executives in their press interviews were their reaction to my Big Oil blog. The next morning, the Wall Street Journal had a front-page story about the cat fight. "Earlier this week, Jason Vines, vice president of communications for Daimler-Chrysler's U.S. arm, suggested that oil companies are contributing to high prices in a particularly blunt posting on a blog published by the company for reporters and financial analysts. Auto makers 'have spent billions developing cleaner, more efficient technologies,' Mr. Vines wrote. 'Big Oil would rather fill the pockets of its executives and shareholders, rather than spend sufficient amounts to reduce the price of fuel, letting consumers, during tough economic times, pick up the tab.'"

Rob Liberatore, back in Washington D.C. from Stuttgart, was on the phone and livid.

"I thought you said you were going to stand down!" he exclaimed.

"Rob, I did. The Journal is just a day late to the story. Do you see any 'new' quote from me in the story? No, you don't. I cannot control it from here on out. The genie is out of the bottle. Good bye." I hung up. I didn't want to get into a pissing match with my friend.

Then Liberatore checked his Blackberry and saw a message from DCX Chairman Dieter Zetsche and quickly fired off a note to ExxonMobil Washington chief Dan Nelson: "I traveled back from Germany today and returned to a message from Dieter Zetsche saying he had talked with Gerry Kohlenberger (ExxonMobil big wig) and that they had agreed that the ads would stop, as would the commentary, and we would all get back to work."

Finally.

I left New York the next morning and flew to Las Vegas to meet up with my family for some R&R. I had not talked with Dieter Zetsche since the Big Oil blog had hit. Standing outside of the Vegas airport waiting for a taxi, the call came in from his office.

"Dr. Zetsche would like to speak to you," his assistant Melke said.

I waited a few seconds for my friend to come on the line.

"Hello Jason," he said, somewhat ominously.

What the hell was about to happen, I thought?

"I got a call a few minutes ago from the Chairman of ExxonMobil," he said.

To me, Dieter was speaking in slow-motion.

"He apologized for the ads and promised they will stop."

"Good," I said. What else could I say?

Dieter continued in classic Dieter style. "I probably wouldn't have done it the way you did it; but I like the results. Good job. See you."

Whew. Victory! No. More like survival, despite a perhaps, career-ending stupid mistake.

Chapter Thirty Two: The Beginning of the Fall

By the fall of 2006, Chrysler was bleeding cash. The gas spikes that began after Hurricane Katrina and continued through the summer of 2006 were killing the truck-heavy Chrysler; sales were plummeting. Money-losing Chrysler was beginning to look like a drag on the magnificent DaimlerChrysler conglomerate. Automotive News' publisher Keith Crain quipped that the "C" was silent in the DCX abbreviation for the company. German shareholders were starting to squawk; dump the Americans! Dieter Zetsche, now 10 months into his reign as Chairman, was on the hot seat.

Chrysler had fallen fast. Earlier in the year, Zetsche had praised Chrysler as the most solid part of the DCX Empire as Chrysler had continued to outperform GM and Ford. Both, as USA Today said, "are reeling from increased competition from Asian rivals, spiraling health care costs and labor woes."

"The Chrysler Group is the only member of the former Big Three that has avoided this fate," Zetsche said. "Thanks to its enhanced efficiency and, above all, its successful new models, it has increased its market share to significantly more than 13 percent and further improved earnings."

But, the missiles of October had arrived. DCX's Finance Chief Bodo Uebber decided to hold a call with analysts at Chrysler's Auburn Hills, Michigan headquarters. He was holding court in a massive conference room, surrounded by his finance minions in their tight European suits. The question came, obviously a plant from a German analyst: Is Daimler thinking of selling Chrysler?

Bodo got giddy. I am not making this up. "All options are on the table." And, then he repeated it. "All options are on the table." I was expecting the diminutive CFO was next going to jump off his booster seat, climb on the conference table, shout "ja wohl" and click his jack boots. What an ass.

As he continued to repeat his line the U.S. analysts on the phone started to hyper-ventilate, and Bodo would peek over at his staff of henchman who were gleefully giving him thumbs ups. We Americans, including CEO Tom LaSorda, were being treated as if we weren't even in the room. I stared at LaSorda. I think my eyes were on fire.

I got up and walked around the table and whispered in LaSorda's ear: "I've gotta go. This is a shit-storm." It took me two minutes to run back to my office.

"I tried your cell," my assistant Sandy said as I got to my cubicle. "Your phone is ringing off the frickin' hook man," handing me a stack of 20 messages.

"Get Hartmut (Schick) on the phone," I barked. Sandy had become a great friend to both me and my wife, so at this point, she didn't take my barking personally.

"Bobo," I said, knowing his real name was Bodo; but I was livid. "Bobo, just announced that Chrysler is potentially for sale, Hartmut. Is this true?"

I don't know what was at the time the most popular dance in Germany, but Hartmut started dancing. I couldn't get anything close to a straight answer. That was too bad. I considered Hartmut a friend. A few weeks after the announcement that Zetsche would replace Schrempp, I had had dinner at his house.

"I assume that Dieter will put you in charge of Communications soon and that I will work for you," he said. "Actually Jason, I look forward to it. We're friends."

That WAS the way it was going. Earlier when I asked Dieter if I should take German language lessons he said: "That would be wise." Actually, he said, "That would be vise."

I would not accept Hartmut's dance steps.

"If we are potentially for sale, say so. If not, get a statement out right away that 'Chrysler is Not for Sale!" I demanded.

Four hours later, Hartmut issued a statement: "Chrysler was not for sale."

Four hours later. Four-fricking hours later. "Bobo" Uebber followed the Yellow Brick Road back to his corporate jet at the Pontiac airport and took off for ze Fatherland. The damage was done, just like with Sleeping Beauty; by a "little prick."

All options were NOT on the table. Once "Bobo" had made the statement, the only "option" was Chrysler WAS for sale. Period. We waded through the next few months, the Grim Reaper seemingly waving down the employees at the exit off the I-75 to Chrysler HQ. If he had a sign, it would be: "Willing to Work for Non-Germans."

On April fourth, DCX held its very first shareholders' annual meeting in Auburn Hills. It had been planned almost a year before when Chrysler was the shining light of DCX, not the anchor dragging it down. I met Dieter in an office on the top floor. He pushed his speech my way on the desk. I read it. "All options are open," regarding Chrysler. "Once you make this statement," I said, "there are no options. You know it." I was pissed, but understood Dieter's position. "Nice working with you, my friend. Hell of a ride," I said.

"How is your son?" he asked.

"Not good yet," I answered. Dieter cared. "Still working on it." (Next book: Spoiler alert)

I asked Dieter, "How's Gisela?" (Dieter's wife, my friend, suffering from breast cancer. It would end sadly.)

"Not good," he responded.

"Despite this shit, keep me up to speed on her. I have friends. OK?" I said, referring to Compuware co-founder Peter Karmanos, who had created one the world's most magnificent cancer centers following the death of his first wife, Barbara.

"OK," he said. "I will."

Dieter had the greatest job in the automotive world, he was dealing with throwing off Schrempp's purchase of Chrysler (a company he had Iacocca-like saved), and his wife, the mother of his three exceptional kids, was dying. I thought I had it tough. Loved this man like a brother.

Within a few weeks, Chrysler was on the chopping block and the vultures were swirling over the complex in the outskirts of Detroit. Magna International, the giant Canadian automotive supplier, wanted Chrysler badly. Stephen Girsky, former auto analyst and then-principal at Centerbridge Partners was foaming at the mouth, calling me almost daily once the company was on the block. The third suitor was Cerberus Capital Management. "Cerberus" was the three-headed devil dog that guarded the gates to Hades.

Swell.

Chapter Thirty Three: Private Equity – The smartest guys in the womb

Cerberus was the creation of Stephen Feinberg, who had more money than God. His firm was clearly the front runner from the get-go and we scrambled to produce a power point presentation for Chrysler's potential buyers. For a week, suitors came in for day-long presentations as we put on our best face. It was a corporate garage sale. Nothing less.

A few weeks later, the winner was about to be announced.

Tim Higgins, a young reporter at the Detroit Free Press, called me the night before the announcement. He had a scoop. The winner was Magna International. He had planted himself at Magna's HQ just outside of Toronto. I could not, by law, share what I knew. But, I tried to make Higgins look a bit "less stupid." The Free Press (known as the Freep) didn't like me, collectively. The Freep was the liberal rival to the much smaller, and hungrier, Detroit News. Thanks to crack auto reporters Bill Vlasic and Mark Truby, the News had rendered the "Free Press" the junior varsity in their coverage of the industry - always a day late and a dollar short.

"Tim," I said, "your editors don't like me, I know that. But, let me give you some really good advice." Geez Louise! How could I more telegraph my punch? "You need to come home Tim." Higgins wasn't buying what I was selling.

The next morning he, and the Detroit Free Press, shit the bed. With a banner headline announcing Chrysler's sell to Magna, the Free Press had committed a "Dewey Wins" colossal screw up.

"I told you in no uncertain terms Tim," I said, calling Higgins. An hour later, we announced a hook-up with Stephen Feinberg's Cerberus Capital Management. It was the beginning of Chrysler's final road to hell before a bankruptcy and Italian ownership would finally set them straight.

A few days later, Feinberg and his top aides were in town to talk with Chrysler's shell-shocked management team, many who had been through the ringer multiple times – the early 80s bailout, the near-collapse in the early 90s and then the "merger of equals" with Daimler. They had more tread marks on their backs than most dead possums lying on the road.

The meeting featured an all-star team of automotive talent: Dieter Zetsche from Daimler and newly-hired Wolfgang Bernhard for Cerberus, along with Feinberg. The latter spoke eloquently about his desire to rescue an "American icon." A quirky little dude, he was, none-the-less, magnificent. He won over, I believe, everyone in the crowd.

The next weeks involved Cerberus's due diligence, designed to end on August 6th, 2006, with Cerberus taking full control. Everything was peachy. Until August 4th. The call came on a Saturday from Chrysler CEO Tom LaSorda. "Hey buddy," he said. "For Monday's press conference I need a backdrop that reads 'The New Team.'"

"What do you mean by the new team," I asked. "I can't tell you," he came back. "Bullshit, that's not the way we work Tom," I said, pissed.

"Trust, me. It's all good. Just do it, OK?"

At 2 o' clock the next day, I was at a graduation party for the kid of one of my friends. It was LaSorda on the phone again. "Hurry and get to my office."

I tossed down my glass of wine and drove to headquarters. In LaSorda's office was Nancy Rae, the head of HR who had recruited me back to Chrysler almost four years earlier. I sat down. "What's up?" I asked.

"I'm no longer CEO. Eric Ridenour is gone. I am the new COO and we have a new CEO," LaSorda said, grinning. (I guess I would have grinned too at a demotion if I had the guaranteed financial package LaSorda had been given.)

I stood up and walked around his office for a few seconds. "This is bullshit."

Tom tried to calm me down. "Buddy, it's OK," he begged. "We've got a great new CEO."

"Who?" I asked.

"His name is Bob Nardelli,"

I thought for a second. "Bob Nardelli. Bob Nardelli. Wait, Bob Nardelli? The Home Depot guy?"

"Yes, I met him a month ago (major lie) and he's great," LaSorda beamed, his nose now at six feet long. "He'll be here in five minutes."

Within in few minutes Nardelli arrived and we quickly got down to business. The next morning was the first day of Cerberus' ownership of Chrysler and we were planning a massive press conference to celebrate the new Chrysler: Day One. Nardelli seemed affable enough. We talked for 20 minutes until I told them I needed to go to my office and write him a speech. As I was leaving what would be his new CEO office, I said I would return in about two hours with a draft. "Thanks, Jace," he said.

It was akin to flashing a crucifix at a vampire. All Jasons know, they know, that only dear friends and family members call any Jason by the nickname "Jace." Something wasn't right – and I knew it.

In my office, I quickly "Googled" Bob Nardelli. Oh, the horror. The media coverage of his departure from Home Depot was startling. I was certain that Hitler had gotten better coverage after his suicide in the bunker but I didn't have time to search and I was pretty certain that Google wasn't that good. Anyway, I had a speech to write.

Two hours later I was back in "Bob's" office and handed him the script. He went over it as I sat at his table. "This is good," he said. "I'm going to take it back to the hotel and practice so that I don't screw it up tomorrow." An executive that actually wants to practice his remarks? Maybe he's not as bad as I had read. Hmmm.

The next morning, Bob Nardelli was on the big stage at Chrysler's Cerberus coming out party. He was, honestly, fantastic. He knew his speech like the back of his hand. We had tele-prompters for him, but he didn't need them. So far, so good. When the event was done, I returned to my office; there was Sandy, my assistant.

"This guy's a dickhead," she said.

Sandy wasn't my "secretary" anymore. She was my sister-from-another-mister.

"He got a 200-million-dollar golden parachute, for crissake," she said.

Sandy was a single mother, just shy of her college degree, but real close. Her son Alex had become my quasi-son. He called me "J-Dog." I called him A-hole.

"Come on Sandy, cut Bob some slack. He's treating me okay."

That, would change quickly. Within two weeks, I organized a lunch at the Detroit Athletic Club in front of the Automotive Press Association (APA). Nardelli had fared well on Day One of the new Chrysler, but this time he decided to fall back on G.E.-speak, as in his old employer, General Electric. Nardelli was one of three guys destined to replace G.E. legend Jack Welch, but he lost out and jumped to Home Depot. (He "resigned" with a king's treasure from Home Depot after his well-documented "leadership style" – presumably borrowed from a book – almost single-handedly destroyed the culture of a remarkable company steeped in a rich tradition of excellence.)

Nardelli's off-the-cuff remarks at the automotive press event included lines like "a laser-like focus" and "I prefer a quick yes or no rather than a slow maybe." And, then, out of the blue, he invented his own term, referring to a car's – "optionality."

After the lunch, Autoweek editor Dutch Mandel grabbed me. "What in the fuck is 'optionality'?" "Dutch, I have no idea whatsoever. Help me, brother."

Within a month, Chrysler had hired Deborah Meyer away from Lexus. She immediately melded with Nardelli, who I was by then referring to as "Shallow Bob," first to Sandy and then generally to my staff (yes, it was unprofessional, I admit it). Between the two of them and me, it was turning into open warfare. All bets were off.

I was told to get on an 8 a.m. phone call with Nardelli by HR's Nancy Rae. Am I getting fired with a huge package? God in heaven, you have heard my prayers? Thank Jesus!

No, it was that we were in discussions to hire away Jim Press from Toyota. Holy Fricking Moly! Mr. Toyota - the highest ranking American exec in Toyota history. He wanted to join us? Later there were rumors that Press was selling his wares to GM and Ford with no takers. In reality, Cerberus had been "feeling out" Jim Press under the guise of downloading his industry knowledge in several lunch meetings that summer. Rumors or facts, it didn't matter. Jim Press coming to Chrysler? Huge! The issue languished for a couple weeks, with no resolve.

Opinion, mine: Nardelli wanted no part of Jim Press. He would represent the "Second Coming of Christ", which I had told Nardelli, and Bob wanted no part of "someone" getting in the way of his resurrection from corporate hell.

Nardelli was going to get back at that bastard Jack Welch for passing over him for Jeff Immelt as well as those simpletons at Home Depot who wouldn't accept his brilliance and his "laser-like focus" or his "a quick yes or no versus a slow maybe." Maybe they thought his "optionality" simply blew. Whatever the case, they won the management lottery when he left; Chrysler would not be so lucky.

However, Jim Press was coming -- like it or not. I got on the phone with him.

"Hell, I have spent my whole career, I think, fighting against you...What a privilege to work alongside you," I said, completely sucking up.

But, I meant it.

"Jason, you are my favorite PR guy. Always have been. Let's have some fun."

The mutual respect society meeting ended. What a hoot this would be. I knew "Jim Press" meant "great press."

The next day I was in Nardelli's office. "So, when do you want to do a press conference announcing Jim Press?" he asked.

"No press conference," I said. "We can only lose. This announcement is so over-the-top good, all we need is a press release with comments by you, Press and LaSorda. We let the media run with that. We need absolutely nothing else."

Nardelli looked at me like I was retarded. "Are you sure," he asked.

"Absolutely."

Nardelli wasn't happy; I sensed he "wanted" the press conference to make it clear Press was "his" catch; which it clearly wasn't.

"Well," he sourly said, "you're the expert."

Why was he being such a dick?

Chapter Thirty Four: The "Second" Coming

The next day, the press release announcing Jim Press' arrival landed and it was, well, magical. Jesus, Himself, would have blushed at the coverage – Jim Press Superstar! It was everything I had promised Bob Nardelli, and he wasn't pleased.

He scheduled a one-on-one Saturday morning meeting in his office; actually his conference room. Like I hadn't been busting my ass enough, Bob wanted a Saturday meeting with his PR guy. (With Dieter Zetsche, Tom LaSorda, Jacques Nasser or Carlos Ghosn, it would have been at their house; not in the office on a Saturday.) I sat down and we started to discuss the Chrysler Museum, just on the edge of Chrysler's HQ compound. It was a financial disaster that I was trying to fix. We had thousands of worthless vehicles tucked away in warehouses; few people visited the actual museum. It was a bad idea conceived when Chrysler was fat and sassy. I wanted to sell off or trash all the crap and make it, at least, sustainable.

"The problem with the Museum is the same problem with the Automotive Hall of Fame (for which I had served as Chairman for two years)," I said. "They are testaments to dead white guys and both aren't very appealing. You come once and you don't come again. We need to fix the model."

I thought I was being particularly harsh until Nardelli opened his mouth to grace me with his particular words of wisdom.

"That's the problem with this city (I think he meant the Metro Detroit area). It has a car cancer," he said.

I was stunned and could not react for seconds.

"What does that mean, a car cancer?" I asked, and then began to roll. "You know, the baseball players have a Hall of Fame, and that's a kid's game. Same for hockey and basketball. This industry, the auto industry, created the middle class in this country. This town turned itself into the Arsenal of Democracy in World War II and saved the world. It deserves a Hall of Fame. And a Chrysler museum."

It went in one of Nardelli's ears and out the other. He was the master of his own universe. We were all just plebes.

A month later, after one of Nardelli's staff luncheons, he pulled me aside. "Listen, I got a call from Cerberus this morning and they want you to slow down on the Jim Press interviews," he said. By then, honestly, I wore my indignation of him on my sleeve.

"Cerberus called about that?" I asked, wanting him to know I thought he was totally full of shit.

"Yeah, they did," he said.

"Well, does Cerberus know that every interview with Jim Press leads to a great article about Chrysler at a time that Cerberus is on the street trying to raise money for our company?"

"Yes," Nardelli answered, "They and I just believe Jim needs to go to work."

"OK Bob, I'll tell Mike."

Mike was Mike Aberlich, one of my top guys who was Jim Press's handler. I made a bee-line for his office, closed the door, and shared Nardelli's message coming on-high from "Cerberus." We both started laughing. Jim Press was getting in the way of Bob's personal redemption plan; and he was pissed. We were getting 50-100 interview requests a week. "Slow it down Mike," I laughed as I left his office.

An hour later, Aberlich sent out an email to Press, me and Nardelli outlining an upcoming Businessweek interview for Press.

Nardelli immediately sent me an angry email: "I guess Mike (Aberlich) didn't get your message," he slammed. I composed myself and put in a chew before responding. "Bob," I wrote. "You asked me to slow down the Jim Press interviews. We get 50 to 100 interview requests a week. We are slowing it down to just one this week. Did you really mean for me to STOP?"

No response from the bully.

November, the next month, was no better. After Thanksgiving dinner, I was sitting at our kitchen island going over media reports. I obviously looked depressed.

"What's wrong Honey," my wife asked.

"This," I responded.

I showed her the media analysis that disclosed Bob Nardelli's image was lower than whale dung in the days immediately following his firing from Home Depot versus current ratings that were near the top of the automotive executive pile.

"You've done a good job, Jace," she said. She had the right to call me Jace.

"Yeah," I said dejectedly. "But, I feel like I am making Hitler look good. I can't do that anymore."

"Then quit," she said. "I'm going to bed."

Two weeks later, Chrysler PR was kicking off its Freedom Call program. It had been in the works long before Bob Nardelli arrived. The premise was simple: use our communications system to connect Chrysler parents with their kids serving in the military in Iraq. We'd use our satellite system to provide some quality family time with our men and women on the front lines.

We were kicking off the program on December 7th, 2007. How apropos. Bob Nardelli was all-military-all-the-time in his "service" as the head of Home Depot, despite the fact that he had never served. No commentary here: supporting our military with or without personal service is noble and needed. So, it was all good.

Except my day had been spoiled earlier by Nardelli's latest attempt to manipulate and diminish our well-oiled and respected communications machine.

Following the Nardelli staff lunch, Deborah Meyer, the former Lexus executive now head of Marketing, wanted to talk with me. Sitting in her office, she announced that Nardelli had "commissioned" her to "evaluate" my "PR Operation." She didn't want to do it, she said, but "Bob" had forced her. (This, of course, was complete bullshit. I have seen many organizations, unsuccessful by the way, where the marketing folks like to run herd over the PR people. That was in fact happening when I had arrived at Chrysler in 2003.)

Then Meyer got started. I remained calm. "You spend more than twice what Toyota does at the Detroit Auto Show," she charged.

"Well," I answered, "you were there; Toyota has one, maybe two press conferences at the Detroit Show. We have at least three or four unveilings, plus the Firehouse that alone costs us a million bucks."

Deborah went down her list of other "transgressions" with me protesting along the way. Actually not protesting, but pointing out where she was wrong. I asked her if she talked with anyone on my team in compiling her "facts."

She said she had not. The truth was she had gone behind my back and asked one of my team members for all the negative press clips over the past few months. Not ALL the press clips, mind you; just the negative ones. Finally done sharing her findings, she offered to edit her memo to Bob Nardelli based on our conversation.

I took a breath and thought about the Thanksgiving conservation I had with my smarter-than-me wife, Betsy.

"Actually, don't change a fucking word," I said. "Send this piece of shit just like it is to Nardelli," I said, out of my mind. "Deb, if I may call you that; when I got here four years ago, marketing was shit- and still is. I took a demoralized group of great PR people and we created the best PR team in the industry. Send your report just the way it is. You and Nardelli are destroying a great company with your incompetence! I am quitting. I don't give a damn!"

At 4 o'clock, I was in the executive conference room on the top floor of Chrysler's HQ with a Chrysler "family" whose son was serving in Iraq. Assembled were the soldier's young wife, sisters, mom and dad and grandma and grandpa. It was, magical, especially when their soldier and his comrades came on the video screen. I tried to do the "housekeeping" about how this would all transpire, but it was, fantastically, out of control. A young wife from suburban Detroit, probably not a pot to piss in, was for the first time seeing her husband who any day could get his limbs blown off with a roadside bomb. This was mom and dad's kid protecting Iraqis, not Americans. Here was nana's and papa's little grandson on the screen. The tears flowed. I tried to keep it together, but was struggling mightily.

"I will be back in a minute," I said leaving. "I have to bring in my boss to kick this off."

I walked the 75 feet to Nardelli's office and entered. "They are ready for you," I said. "It's really kind of magical. The soldier is already on the screen." I had given Nardelli talking points. "So," I said, "introduce what we are doing and why – just a couple minutes – and then we get out of the room and let the soldier spend time with his family."

Nardelli and I entered the room. The self-absorbed putz proceeded to speak for 10 straight minutes. Unbelievably, he asked the soldier and his men and women comrades if they had any questions "for Bob". Narcissistic Nardelli had hijacked this family's sacred moment.

I looked over at my "Number Two," Dave Barnas. I had been preparing him to replace me should I eventually get hit by a bus. Today, the bus would be "The Nardelli Express." As I stared at Barnas, my eyes had to be bleeding. Nardelli was holding a Q&A with soldiers putting their ass on the line while he was living in the most exclusive hotel in metro Detroit and had a driver and a corporate jet at his family's disposal.

Not surprisingly, Bob Nardelli, Chrysler CEO, jumped the shark. Ending the video conversation with these brave American soldiers, "Shallow Bob" voiced the following: "From one patriot to another; thank you for what you do." I almost passed out. He had called himself a "patriot." I looked at Barnas. He looked like he had just wet himself. We walked out of the room. Nancy Rae, head of HR, was there. "In your office in ten minutes with my resignation letter."

"No way; stop it," she said.

I wrote my resignation letter, printed it out and gave it to Sandy. Then, I headed up to Bob's office.

My automotive career was dead in minutes.

As I left the Chrysler complex, Mark Truby, former Detroit News reporter and now a top gun at Ford PR, was on the phone.

"Did you just quit?"

"How do you possibly know that, Mark?" I asked.

"I was just told that Nardelli called Alan Mulally (Ford CEO) and said you had a non-compete."

Unbelievable. Nardelli was a piece of work. I said a prayer for him, hoping he enjoyed his money, knowing that I had something more priceless: friends.

Hi-de-ho Kyle, you smell a lot like flowers.

Crisis Lesson Leaned: If your communications organization is kept in the dark, is manipulated, is minimalized or is solely being used to clean up after the elephants in the parade, your organization will step in it eventually.

Chapter Thirty Five: Sex, Lies and a Stubborn Greek Billionaire

It had been roughly two weeks since I had walked out of Bob Nardelli's office and said farewell to my friends at Chrysler. I was headed to the Capitol Grille in Troy, Michigan for a leisurely lunch with my old friend Tom McDonald, the PR guy victimized by the bogus Audi 5000 sudden unintended acceleration scam decades before. On the way, my cell phone rang; it was Compuware co-founder and CEO Peter Karmanos.

Karmanos and I had become friends over the past few years. Whenever I needed money for one of the charities I was working with, Pete would gladly open his own wallet and give lots of money. Years before, he built the Barbara Karmanos Cancer Institute in Detroit in tribute to his late first wife who sadly waited too long to address her battle with the dreaded disease. Pete didn't want others to follow that path.

He had built his fortune from the ground up. The ultimate American success story; the son of Greek immigrants, Pete was gregarious, loved to laugh, had a quick temper and was stubborn as hell. The latter goes without saying - as he was a Greek, self-made billionaire. I'm married to a Greek, go to a Greek church and know Greek men. Their mothers and fathers spoil them rotten.

"Jason, I want to apologize for not calling you sooner," he said. "When I read that you had left Chrysler I wanted to call you immediately, but I was traveling. Listen Tiger, I think you are extraordinarily talented and I want to work with you."

"Thanks, Pete," I said, thrilled by the call.

"Listen, Danialle (his new wife) and I are having a Christmas party tomorrow night," he continued. "Why don't you and your wife join us?"

"That'd be great, but we can't stay long," I said. "We're flying down to Cabo the next morning, real early."

"That's fine…We can have a serious discussion right after the New Year. I think we can do some fabulous things together."

Cabo was great. Caught a 125-pound tuna, laid by the ocean and thought about what Karmanos had in mind. Compuware was a main frame service and software computer company Karmanos had turned into a billion-dollar business with offices around the world. I, of course, was a computer expert when it came to turning on a computer, turning it off and swearing at it or smashing it with my fist when it wasn't working fast enough. After all, "why can't I get on the fucking Internet" is actually a very complex programming command.

Upon return from paradise, I met Pete at the Caucus Club restaurant in downtown Detroit for lunch. Pete laid out his plan. He needed my help with three things: rebranding his 30-year-old company Compuware, getting its subsidiary Covisint ready for an IPO, and finally, helping him revamp the image of the City of Detroit. Pete proudly called Detroit his home. He had previously relocated his business headquarters there as a sign of goodwill for a city on "life-support".

"I know how much you care about this city," Pete said.

I did, but whoa. "Why don't you add into the proposal 'achieving Middle East peace' - and I think we've got a deal."

We both started laughing. Pete's smile could light up a room. Pete picked up the tab and we headed to his office where he introduced me to my new boss, COO Bob Paul, a Brit by birth but without the accent (most of the time). The three of us talked about moving forward. "What title you want?" Pete asked. "I don't know," I said bewildered. "Well, you could be an Executive VP?" Pete said. "How many of those are there here?" I asked. "Oh, just a hand-full," he said.

"How about Senior VP?" I said. "Let's not go too big, too fast."

My title: Senior Vice President, Compuware 2.0, whatever that really meant.

On January 11th, 2008 Compuware made the announcement:

"We are absolutely thrilled that Jason is bringing his reputation, enthusiasm, creativity and communication skills to Compuware," said Karmanos. "This is both a riveting and pivotal time for Compuware, its subsidiaries and our headquarters' home in the city of Detroit. I am counting on Jason to be an integral part in moving forward in these areas."

"This job is a dream come true for me," I added in the announcement, "as I can apply what I have learned over the past quarter century in business, communications, marketing and government affairs to help both a proud company revitalize itself and a great city on the verge of a major renaissance."

Or not.

The "you-know-what" was about to hit the fan.

Again.

Oh, brother. It would result in lots of Detroit officials going to jail and would permanently, and somewhat unfairly, taint the legacy of Peter Karmanos for his un-wavering support of Detroit's hip-hop mayor Kwame Kilpatrick, who would eventually betray Pete and all of Motown.

I was walking around the Detroit Auto Show when my appointment was announced. A journalist friend grabbed me to offer congratulations.

"Hey, I think my kid bought a computer from Compuware," he said.

"No," I answered, "that would be CompUSA."

"What does Compuware do?" he asked.

I paused. "Actually, I am not sure," I said, "but I'll know when I start on the 21st."

January 21 and January 22, 2008 were both fun days: starting a new, challenging job one day and my birthday the next. It went downhill from there, warp speed.

On January 23rd, the Detroit Free Press blew the lid off a "text messaging scandal" involving the mayor of Detroit and his chief of staff (or was that "chief of his staff"), Christine Beatty. Mayor Kilpatrick would soon replace his fine tailored suits and monogrammed dress shirts for "prison orange." But not before he would reach of the height of indignation and take Peter Karmanos, my new employer, along for a very bumpy ride.

You want some fries with those sex and lies?

There had been a "party," allegedly, at Mayor Kilpatrick's official residence, the Manoogian Mansion, during the Labor Day weekend of 2002. It had "allegedly" involved strippers, including one who went by the name of Strawberry. Sometime during the "alleged" party and the "alleged" stripping, the mayor's wife Carlita showed up and "allegedly" went bat-shit and "allegedly" beat the snot out of the "alleged" Strawberry. Seven months later Strawberry was murdered while sitting in a car, hit-style. Nothing alleged about her death. She was shot multiple times.

Two Detroit cops, Gary Brown and Harold Nelthrope, had been snooping into the behavior of Mayor Kilpatrick and his security detail, including the "alleged" party and rumors that the mayor was "doing the dirty" with his chief of staff, Beatty. Beatty was infamous for an earlier traffic incident in which she shouted at a police officer: "Do you know who the fuck I am?" Brown and Nelthrope were on to something. Subsequently, they were both fired on May 9, 2003.

Days later, Brown would issue a memo outlining their investigation. Mayor Kilpatrick denied all the allegations. Brown and Nelthrope filed a lawsuit against Kilpatrick and the City of Detroit citing "whistleblower" protection.

A year and a month after the officers were fired, Michigan Attorney General Mike Cox and the Michigan State Police issued a "report" saying they could find "no evidence" of the "alleged" party. "Rumors" began to swirl that Cox was "allegedly" AT the party… along with my new boss Peter Karmanos.

In late August 2007, the Brown/Nelthrope whistleblower trial began and it was salacious. Under oath, both Mayor Kilpatrick and the chief of his staff, Christine Beatty, testified that they had not had any kind of romantic or sexual relations and there was no retaliation involved when they fired the two cops. But the jury wasn't buying what the two "alleged" love birds were selling and awarded Brown and Nelthrope $6.5 million.

Ever defiant, Kilpatrick promised an appeal. It was September 11, 2007. It was the start of the mayor's own 9-11. Why? Because the officers' lawyer, Michael Stefani, wasn't quite finished on behalf of his clients and subpoenaed the Mayor and Ms. Beatty's text messages; they were city property, not personal property. After reviewing them, he went back for more money; and got it. $1.9 million more. And then, the Detroit Free Press went to work and would win a Pulitzer Prize.

Its reporters, Jim Schaefer and M.L. Emrick, "somehow" got their hands on the text messages; a total of 14,000 between Kilpatrick and Beatty. What they found was almost pornographic. Check that: what they found WAS over-the-top pornographic and on January 23rd, just two days after I joined Compuware to help revitalize the image of the City of Detroit, all bets were off. Two days later, Wayne County Attorney Kim Worthy opened an investigation. Not an investigation about Kwame cheating on his wife and not an investigation about the "alleged" party. No, this was bigger. Had Mayor Kilpatrick and Christine Beatty perjured themselves in the whistleblower trial five months prior?

"He didn't do anything illegal," Peter Karmanos shouted, his arm flailing in the air.

"He cheated on his wife," I said.

"That's not illegal," he shot back. "It may have been wrong. It may have been stupid. But it's not illegal," he continued, getting angrier by the second. Karmanos was, in effect, excusing the mayor's actions. He had to; or he would have to, quite possibly, indict himself.

I walked into Lisa Elkin's office. She reported to me and was head of communications. Sharp and funny, Lisa was a trusted advisor for Pete, but told me she had witnessed Karmanos' rage often in her tenure; but rarely, if ever, directed at her.

Everybody at Compuware, rightfully so, loved Lisa. She was a soldier for the company and Pete. I told her about my conversation just minutes prior in his office. "I've gotta show you something," she said, rolling her eyes. She reached down into the bowels of her desk and pulled out a folder. In it was a July 4th, 1998 Businessweek article headlined "Compuware: No Way to Treat a Crisis: How the company mishandled its explosive sexual-harassment case."

"What the hell is this?" I asked.

"Just read it."

Businessweek reported:

"It was spring of 1998, and Peter Karmanos Jr. was sitting on top of the world. A fireplug of a man with a piercing gaze and iron handshake, the then-55-year-old co-founder, chairman, and chief executive of Compuware Corp. had built it into a $1.1 billion purveyor of computer software and services. Sales were soaring, earnings were fat, and Wall Street loved him."

"Moreover, the hometown boy was revered around Detroit for his community involvement and philanthropy. Thanks to his 12% stake in Compuware--now worth $656 million--Karmanos had given millions to cancer research. And, realizing a lifetime dream, he even owned a National Hockey League team, the Carolina Hurricanes."

"But things soon started to sour. On May 20, at Compuware's regularly scheduled quarterly meeting, the usually convivial Karmanos turned somber, according to several directors present. Karmanos sadly told his board members that one of the company's highest-ranking officers had complained he had sexually harassed her. Sheila McKinnon, the company's senior vice-president for human resources, the board was about to learn, had told other executives that Karmanos twice suggested she engage in an extramarital affair with him, that Karmanos allegedly rubbed her leg at a social event and on a company plane, and that he later turned hostile and abusive when she spurned his advances."

Yikes. It all made sense now. As the heat intensified around Kilpatrick, Karmanos – that stubborn, self-made, Greek billionaire – dug in his heels. He was very openly and publicly throwing his support behind the mayor despite calls from all corners for Kilpatrick to step down for the "sake of the City" – Pete's beloved city. And we were becoming at-odds over the issue. It seemed like a week didn't go by where Pete wasn't being quoted saying the mayor had not broken any laws.

In a particular rage in his office he told me, "What the Mayor should have done is call those two cops and tell them they weren't doing the jobs they were supposed to do and that is why I am firing you!" And then, Pete jumped the shark when he publicly delivered the knock-out quote: "He's the best mayor in 25 years!"

Karmanos' support seemed to be unwavering. As the waves were crashing on Team Kilpatrick, Karmanos made it a point to attend the mayor's televised State of the City address. Kilpatrick talked boldly and confidently about what HE had done for Detroit; and then he got angry, whipping up his supporter's. He used the "N-word" to describe threats against him and his family and said he was up against a "lynch mob mentality."

Kwame wasn't just playing the race card; he was using the whole deck. The white folks in the suburbs responded with a collective "not again." Two mayors ago, Coleman Young played the race card like a fiddle for more than a decade and it had severely divided the region. Now Kwame was doing it with full gusto to save his sorry, criminal ass.

And there would be financial support. One day, Lisa Elkin came into my office in a panic. "Laura is really upset!" Laura was Laura Fournier, Compuware's CFO. "Pete wants her to cut a check to the mayor and she doesn't want to."

"Let's go see her," I said.

Seconds later in Laura's office she was visibly upset. Karmanos had demanded, on the spot, a $75,000 check for one of the mayor's "funds."

"I don't think we should do this," she said.

"Do you want me to talk with him?" I asked.

"No. He'll just bite off your head like he just bit off mine."

Moments later the check was cut and delivered to the mayor.

More famously – and after I had departed – Pete would convince three other Detroit business giants – Roger Penske, Dan Gilbert and Jim Nicholson - to each chip-in $60,000 for a $240,000 loan "plus interest" as an incentive for Kwame to get the hell out of Dodge, er Detroit, and let the city begin to heal. All pillars of the community, nonetheless these three gentlemen would have their names temporarily soiled when the secret deal was exposed in subsequent court proceedings that had the same basic theme – Kwame was lying, hiding funds and lying some more.

The public was not nearly as forgiving, though, when it came to Karmanos. In the comment sections of the hundreds of stories about the scandal you would often find a sarcastic rant from a reader wondering "what does Kwame have on Karmanos?"

The answer was, nothing. There were accusations Kwame gave Karmanos a "sweetheart deal" to move the Compuware HQ from the suburbs to downtown Detroit. The truth was Kwame's predecessor, Mayor Dennis Archer, cut the deal with Pete and was placed on the Compuware board once out of office.

Finally, on September 4th, in my 10th month at Compuware – with not a smidgeon to show for my task of helping Karmanos improve Detroit's tattered image – Mayor Kwame Kilpatrick copped a deal, pleading guilty to obstruction of justice and "no contest" to assault on a police officer – oh, he did that too! He would (fail to) pay $1 million in restitution to the city – chump-change compared to the $8.4 million the city had forked out to the cops. Da Mayor was sentenced to serve 120 days in jail.

Pete Karmanos wasn't going to take this "loss" sitting down. As we headed toward the close of October, rumors were swirling that once out of jail, Pete was going to hire Kilpatrick. My phone started ringing off the hook.

Within a half hour I had talked to seven print, radio and TV reporters all asking if the rumor was true. The typical answer in this situation is for the PR guy not to respond to rumors with that pithy line: "We don't respond to rumors." But this situation was far from typical. COO Bob Paul hurried across the hall and into my office.

"Hey, our sales guys are saying customers are asking if it's true about the mayor coming here," he said. "This is not good. You gotta talk Pete out of this. I'll go with you."

We marched down to Pete's palatial office and walked right in, as we always did. I will say that Pete was one of the most approachable CEOs I had ever met or worked for. Despite his riches, he had not forgotten his humble roots. Perhaps the reason he also was one of the most generous philanthropists in Detroit history.

"Pete," I said, "I've gotten seven calls from journalists asking me to confirm or deny that we are hiring Kwame."

His face got beet red and he wagged his finger at me. "You tell them to go fuck themselves!" he shouted.

"No, I am not telling the media to go fuck themselves," I charged back.

Pete was beside himself. "Pete, can I give you some advice, and then I will shut up."

"What?" He semi-screamed.

"If this is true," I said calmly, "people are going to be very angry, but they're not going to take it out on you. They're going to take it out on Danialle in next month's election."

Pete stopped in his tracks. Danialle was his wife, 30 years his junior, and was running as a Republican for a slot on the Wayne State University Board of Governors. Being a Republican in Detroit meant an up-hill slog to start with. Add to that your billionaire "sugar daddy" is going to flip-off the city by hiring a philandering convict when so many people out there were hurting? Dead duck, for sure.

"OK," Pete said, calming down. "I won't do anything rash. Tell the media we're not hiring him."

Bob Paul and I walked briskly back to his office. Once inside, he gave me a bear hug. "Good job buddy," he said. "Hiring Kwame would really hurt our business. For once you earned your pay check," he said, laughing.

I left Compuware on December 7th, just 11 months after joining. My relationship with Pete, sadly, had deteriorated, thanks primarily to the Kwame Kilpatrick saga. On February 3, 2009, Kwame was out of jail and the next day got the first $150,000 of his "get-outta-town" loan. A week later, Compuware announced the lay-off of 250 employees as its business was slowing down. Unbelievably, just three days later, Peter Karmanos hired ex-con, ex-Mayor Kwame Kilpatrick and assigned him to Compuware's Covisint subsidiary. The outrage was palpable. Kilpatrick packed his bags, grabbed his loaned-loot and moved into a mansion in a swank Dallas suburb. It was his final "fuck you" to the City of Detroit and its citizens. But Kwame's time away from Detroit would be rather brief, as he made multiple court appearances as the Feds focused on growing evidence that Kwame, his father, a thug of a business friend and several top aides had been running a criminal racket that would later be dubbed the "Kilpatrick Enterprise."

On October 10, 2013, the Hip Hop mayor was sentenced to 28 years in a federal penitentiary. Perhaps Peter Karmanos was right all along: cheating on your wife "wasn't illegal"; but racketeering and extortion were and Kwame had been convicted on two dozen charges.

Don't drop the soap, Mr. Hip Hop Mayor.

Crisis Lesson Learned: If you finally discover you were wrong after all, fess up. Don't dig in your heels. Again, an old cliché: if you are in a ditch, stop digging.

Chapter Thirty Six: On a Mission from God: A New Bible

I was on the way to the annual summit of the political and business movers and shakers on Michigan's majestic Mackinac Island when my cell phone rang; it was a 616 area code number – western Michigan. "Hello - Jason Vines," I answered.

"Jason Vines, a voice from your past; Steve Sammons."

Sammons and I had worked together at Nissan; he was one of the marketers in the screwed up Infiniti luxury division, but smart.

"Where are you calling me from Steve; Grand Rapids?" I asked.

"Exactly. I'm the CMO (chief marketing officer) at Zondervan."

"The Bible people?" I said, while being dazed and confused.

Steve and I had had a great working relationship at Nissan, and one thing I remembered going back a decade was that Steve shared an affinity with me for salty language. And now he was in charge of marketing for the one of the biggest Bible companies on the planet? What the hell?

Steve, I would learn afterward, had remembered that although far from perfect, I was and still am, a devout Christian. In one of our previous conversations - which seemed so long ago - we talked about how lonely it must be to be an atheist. Years later, in a Detroit News column, I would chastise the American Atheists organization for their ad campaign, "Atheist? You are not alone." If you are an atheist and you go tits up- you are necessarily alone; except for the worms crawling up your butt as you lie there in the casket.

Without pause, Sammons told me why he had called. Zondervan, a few years earlier, had stepped in it; big time. They had launched an updated version of the world's best-selling Bible, the New International Version or NIV, and renamed it Today's New International Version or TNIV. Same Bat Time, Same Bat Channel; but with a few tweaks. (For you young college people hopefully reading this book, that last sentence was in reference to the "original" Batman; not the Christian Bale one - and certainly not the Michael Keaton quote, quote, quote, Batman. Not Kanye West, but Adam West.) With the new translation of the Bible, ironically, all hell broke loose in the evangelical Christian world.

Ahem. Not to get mired in the ins-and-outs of Bible translation; but, let me give you a brief layman's biblical tutorial so that you can set your "outrage" compass. If you don't believe in Jesus Christ, or even the "often-used" higher being; just play along for shits and giggles to get to the next chapter if you are still reading.

Howard Long was a Seattle-based engineer with General Electric and an extremely devout Christian who wanted to spread the Gospel of Jesus Christ to his friends and anyone who would listen. But, he was using a Bible laying out God's words in "proper" English that was nearing Noah's formative years – around 380 years old. It was the 1950s; we had Elvis and the birth of rock 'n roll, and no one, no one used the terms "thy" or "thine" or "thoust". Long envisioned a translation of the Bible that would be true to its original meaning, yet in contemporary English. After all, what good was God's word if you couldn't understand it?

Long was a Christian Reformed Church member. (Remember the "offies" who went to the private Christian school in my home town of Pella, Iowa? Long was an "offie.") More important, all jabs aside, he was a just and determined man of exceptional faith. Not only did he convince the muckety-muck leaders of his denomination to join him in his quest, he eventually garnered the support of the National Association of Evangelicals for a new translation. Over the next decade Long would maintain his mission. Heck, Long truly believed he was on a mission from God. There, at a small Christian school about an hour outside of Chicago, Trinity Christian College, a multi-denominational group of evangelical scholars met and kicked-off their arduous work on what they would eventually call the New International Version, or NIV of the Bible.

Arduous may be an understatement. This group of scholars and translators weren't simply taking the current version of the world's first translation into English, the King James Version, and making it modern. Rather, they were going back to the original texts – Aramaic, Hebrew and Greek – and starting from scratch (or Genesis). Yowza! Think about it in terms of completely renovating your home (HGTV kind of thing). Sand the wood floor and restain in today's cool colors. Refigure rooms. Take out that in-door hot tub. You have a wonderful "fixer-upper" - the bones of the house are still so, so solid. It is standing on the firmest of ground. You have a great view of the water; of the entire world. And, maybe even a boat slip with access to one of God's most beautiful waterways...all for Christians around the globe to enjoy.

A Bible? No. The Bible.

A year after the decision to move forward was made, a large group of evangelical leaders and scholars would convene and create The Committee on Bible Translation, a dozen or so Bible scholars that would be responsible to translate "The Word" into modern, mid-20th Century English. Heavy. Their painstaking handy-work would take more than a decade to finish with a NIV New Testament completed in 1978 and the full text, including the Old Testament, completed two years later. Christian denominations around the U.S. and the globe went, well, biblical, and soon the NIV was the standard translation, selling tens of millions of copies. Yes, even more than Harry Potter could ever amass.

"And God saw that it was good."

Fast forward to post 9-11, and Grand Rapids, Michigan-based Zondervan. They would now lead the charge for a new update, a new re-translation of the fabulously successful NIV completed just a quarter of a century earlier. Had the English language really changed all that much since 1978? Sure - we had new words and phrases entering our lexicon over the past 25 years: the "Internet" was not something inside a "net" and "rap" was not something bad you hoped you didn't get. "Fag" was a homophobic slur and not an English cigarette and "I'm down with that" actually meant "good" in urban communities. "Getting stoned" meant being back stage at a Snoop Dogg concert. Like any for-profit business, now owned by HarperCollins (a division of Rupert Murdoch's FOX News empire), Zondervan had to keep the cash registers ringing.

Working through The Committee on Bible Translation, the scholars behind the original NIV, it was announced that the current scholars wanted to create a new version of the NIV based on its roots; namely bringing contemporary English to God's words. Like the NIV, the TNIV would be in the sweet-spot between the literal translation of the Bible that only a handful could comprehend and the "new age" Bibles that came about in the 1960s that were more novel than Bible: think of a Bible you can still comprehend when you are completely stoned. "Wow, this Jesus dude is heavy, man. And, holy smokes, isn't his picture on the cover of my reefer papers?"

The only problem was America was beginning to become, in my opinion, a bit too-politically correct (PC) for the leaders of the evangelical community. Yet, Zondervan and The Committee on Bible Translation weren't paying attention. The TNIV made some incredibly defensible re-translations of Bible text. "Mary was with child" became "Mary was pregnant." No one in 2002 would have said, "My wife is with child." "Where is your wife with a child? At a mall? At home?" The Bible scholars made hundreds, perhaps thousands of such common-sense changes in order for the Word to be easily understood.

Then, unexpectedly, The Committee for Bible Translation "jumped the shark." Actually, it was the Tilapia. Tilapia were the fish that Jesus helped his disciples net in the Sea of Galilee (I would learn on a trip to the

251

Holy Land). Whatever. The group of some of the greatest Bible scholars jumped something and waded into gender-neutrality. Not just gender neutrality, but what some considered gender-neutering.

"He-him-man" references, so prevalent in the King James Bible and the 1978 NIV, were changed to "them-they-we-us"; and the dumbfounding worst example of all: "mankind" was changed to "human kind." Think about it. What would have been the reaction if Neal Armstrong climbed down that last rung of the Apollo 11 lunar lander in June 1969 and said, "This is one giant step for us; one giant leap for human kind?" Second on the moon, Buzz Aldrin, would have pulled out his Remington 1100 and promptly shot Mr. Armstrong before his foot hit the surface of the moon.

While The Committee on Bible Translation's intention was undoubtedly pure – as I believe God was and is talking to them and all of us, not just us dudes – the Committee had created PC words like "human-fricking-kind." The new, fresh TNIV had taken 13 years to create and when it launched, it was an unmitigated disaster. Despite, and again with truly holy intentions I believe with all my heart, the Committee's goal of using "inclusive language" in the new Bible had rendered it toxic to many leaders in the Christian community.

Despite support from the Christian Reformed Church, the Evangelical Covenant Church and the Free Methodist Church of North America, the Zondervan TNIV Bible was indeed, dead on arrival. In June 2002, some of the nation's most prominent evangelical leaders signed a "Statement of Concern" regarding the TNIV. The Presbyterian Church in America and the Southern Baptist Convention had put out what amounted to a "fatwa" on the TNIV. The names taking a giant dump on the re-translation were legendary: Colorado Spring's James "Focus on the Family" Dobson; Jerry "I was mocked in a George Burns/John Denver classic Oh! God! as a shill preacher" Farwell; Pat "500 Club" Robertson and Dr. R. Albert Mohler, the president of The Southern Baptist Theological Seminary – the self-described flagship school of the Southern Baptist Convention and one of the largest seminaries in the world. It was like the Miami Heat playing a high school basketball team. Their efforts forced Lifeway, a gigantic Christian bookstore chain, to follow suit and quickly ban the TNIV from its stores. Think Ford dealers banning sales of the Explorer SUV.

Zondervan was reeling and jumping through hoops to salvage this dead, on-ward Christian soldier. In 2006, Zondervan produced an audio version of the TNIV voiced by an unbelievably strong line-up of top-shelf African-American Hollywood stars from Angela Bassett to Cuba Gooding Jr. to Denzel Washington. It sold well initially, but not well enough to mitigate the damage. In fact, protests against the new re-translation became so vile, a TNIV Bible was delivered to Zondervan headquarters with a bullet hole clean through its middle. The Fab Five – Matthew, Mark, Luke, John, and Jesus, had been the victims of a drive-by shooting.

Sadly, while so many people around the world seemed to be at war with Christianity and a Christian nation, Christianity was now at war with itself. What would Jesus do? He must have been crying through all of this garbage. Maybe that's why my little brother's hometown of Des Moines was constantly flooding. Jesus' tears were flowing through the heart of America.

So endth the tutorial. Or is it "thine" tutorial?

Okay, back to my call with Steve Sammons, the former Nissan marketing man who was Zondervan's marketing chief. Zondervan, despite its misstep with the TNIV was getting ready for a do-over as it prepared to move forward with a re-translation of the original NIV, almost 29 years since its creation. If their efforts failed, Zondervan was dead meat. Bible revenues represented more than 65 percent of profits.

"We need to avoid this crisis and I need someone to help me navigate through a potential storm," Sammons said.

"Why does it matter Steve?" I said, sarcastically. "Hell, I think I read a couple of weeks ago in Newsweek magazine that Christianity is, in fact, dead. Didn't you get the memo," I laughed.

"Exactly," he said joining in the laughter. "That's the shit we're up against."

"How about I help you?"

"I was hoping you would say that," he answered. "That's why I called."

"Let me get on Mackinac Island and I will call you back," I promised. "Give me a couple hours. The ferry to the island takes like a day."

By now I was less than 30 minutes from the ferry that takes passengers to the island made famous in the Christopher Reeves movie "Somewhere in Time." I was travelling through one of the most beautiful stretches of roads in the world. And, I was thinking about going to work for, well, Jesus. Holy shit! Oops, I thought. Holy cow. Ah, that's better.

I checked into my room in one of the island's oldest hotels. I had grabbed a quick lunch with former Compuware execs who were up on the island rubbing elbows. I went back to my room and called Sammons.

"So, what's really going on?" I asked.

"This team here in Grand Rapids is completely unprepared for all the garbage you and I have faced."

"How did you end up there?" I asked. I had to know.

"A cancer scare," he said bluntly. "I survived and knew God was giving me another chance."

Wow.

"Can you come to Grand Rapids next week and meet the CEO?" he said. "This hire is my call but I want to make sure you and she are okay with this. This isn't selling cars. It's a helluva lot bigger than anything you and I will ever do my brother."

Whew.

Within days I arrived in Grand Rapids and checked into my hotel. My dinner meeting with Steve Sammons was a couple hours away. I called my sister-in-law, Becky, in Texas.

Becky, and her (my brother) husband Thom, were devout Christians. My brother had been somewhat late to the party. Not atheist, but certainly closer to agnostic in his early parenting years. Only problem was, his twin daughter Kelsey was an "over-the-top" Christian with "Verses" she had personally painted on her walls. She was a Christian's Christian. She wore it on her sleeve. And then God took her home. Why? I don't know. Traveling home with her twin sister in the normal two-mile trek between Lubbock Cooper High School and home at the beginning of her senior year, a 70-year-old dump truck driver lost control of his truck, crossed the median and killed Kelsey on impact. My worst fear as an auto industry exec had been realized; somebody I was close to would be killed in a car crash.

I had bitched and moaned constantly about all the "crises" I had faced in my career while getting paid large sums of money. Here was a real crisis. A personal crisis. Losing your child at 18. Kelsey's death and funeral sucked the life out of me and almost killed my big brother. But someone would save him; it wasn't his wife Becky, the other twin Kayla or their first child: Jeremy. It was Jesus Christ.

Thom was on the way to accepting Jesus as his personal Savior, but the death of his daughter had put him at a crossroad. No pun intended. He chose to embrace the Messiah, knowing Kelsey was in a far, far better place. The eulogy offered at her funeral were the words taken from her diary, espousing her unconditional love for and dedication to Jesus Christ. My big brother would later tell that story in his book, Tragedy and Trust. Read it. It's won several awards and is damn good.

On the phone with Becky, still just a year since losing her daughter, I told her I was in Grand Rapids to talk with Zondervan. All she could say was "the Lord works in mysterious ways" and handed the phone to Thom. I explained my situation to my big brother. "This may sound a bit eerie, but just before you called, I was reading Zondervan's Study Bible," he said. After a brief chit-chat, I hung up.

"What's the dealeo?" I thought.

Chapter Thirty Seven: "Keep your enemies closer" is not a cliché

The next morning I was at Zondervan headquarters in the middle of cornfields about two miles from Grand Rapids' tiny, but great, airport. The HQ was one-quarter offices, one-quarter cafeteria and one-half warehouse. From the outside, it looked more like a nail manufacturer than a major publishing house.

The interviews were not typical interviews; it was apparent I had the job if I was willing. It was as if I was kicking the tires of the company; not the other way around.

Returning home that night, it seemed like a no brainer and a great new challenge. The offer came two days later. It was far, far below what I had been bringing home to the family. "This is not about money, honey," my wife said when I presented her with the offer. A week later I was living in a little apartment in Ada, Michigan just outside of Amway's headquarters, to be separated from Betsy except on the weekends.

Day one, my boss Steve Sammons introduced me to Neil Martin. Neil was a stereotypical Brit who looked like a cross between Elvis Costello and Carrot Top. Sporting spiked, bright red hair and speaking at warp speed, I couldn't understand the first 300 words he said to me. It was like letting your American ears adapt to a Monty Python movie.

Neil was a designer – as in publications, websites and the like. He was planning to go to seminary in Florida when Zondervan plucked him to help design all things Bibles as well as their other Christian publications; his knowledge of Scripture and all things Christianity were quickly evident. That distinct advantage gave him the propensity to overwhelm me in this setting. He possessed something else that would make us instant, great friends: a wicked, wicked sense of humor without the healthy dose of profanity (with which I liked to pepper my humor). Soon, we would discover we were completely polar opposites when it came to politics. Neil was a moronic, bleeding-heart liberal, where I was an intelligent, reasoned and rational conservative. (Oh, sorry vicar!)

Neil quickly cut to the chase. "Here you go," he said handing me an eight-inch stack of documents. "These are the emails, letters and press reports identifying how this company was literally slayed when it launched the TNIV. It will shock you beyond belief. Read them. It will be a fascinating tutorial. I think you will agree."

The next few nights, the Detroit Tigers were on the West Coast; the games didn't start until 10 p.m. so I had lots of free time to delve into Neil's stack. Three days later, I went to his cubicle and tossed the stack on his desk.

"Pardon my French, you Englishman, but these are some pretty shitty Christians." Neil started to laugh.

"That's the half of it," he countered.

Emails, letters and articles in supposed-Christian publications and from various leaders were over-the-top ugly. Zondervan, through its earlier re-translation of the Bible, had been accused of everything short of rape. Check that: I think one letter stated that Zondervan "had" raped the Bible.

Then Neil got all sentimental on me. We had known each other a total of three or four days. We had jockeyed with each other over politics and global warming and all kinds of things over a couple of lunches.

"I did a lot of research on you and I know Steve Sammons is a big fan," he said.

My mind was racing: is this Brit going to give me a sanctimonious smack down?

"You are here for a reason, my friend. I firmly believe that in my heart. We need you. You are not here accidentally."

Wow. Kind of heavy. Maybe, too heavy. I walked out of the building and jumped in my car and lit a Marlboro, driving through the barren roads of the southwest region of Grand Rapids and wondering if God made me go through all the crises I had faced over the past 15 years – including the horrific Ford/Firestone tire crisis – to prepare me for the real "Big Thing."

I drove all the way to Lake Michigan, about an hour away, and sat on the beach and contemplated life as I gave lip service to my buddies from Phillip Morris. I had to call my friend; my priest and the more-liberal-than-Neil-Martin, Father Nick Pathenos.

"Hello, my brother," he said answering the phone.

We were on speed dial. I explained the situation of re-launching the NIV Bible and the past tribulations despite the fact that the Greek Orthodox Church, of which I was a member and Father Nick served, had no skin in the evangelical Bible game.

"Am I a good enough Christian to pull this off?" I asked.

"Jason, you are as good a Christian as I have ever known. My problem is your stupid politics," he quickly responded.

"Kiss my ass," I slashed back.

"No, kiss my ass, you Republican moron," he countered.

That was, and is, the relationship we have. We laughed. It was cathartic.

My priest and new friend Neil, along with my boss Steve Sammons, were certain why I had been brought into the fray as a soldier for the new Bible; but many of my friends were scratching their heads.

"I want to do a story about your move from the rough-and-tumble auto industry to printing Bibles," said Detroit Free Press columnist Tom Walsh on a phone call. "It doesn't exactly seem, well, natural."

Tom and I talked for a few minutes, mostly about the auto industry, still mostly in the crapper from the implosion of 2008 and the bankruptcy proceedings of 2009, just months before.

"So, back to joining Zondervan?" he queried.

"It's simple: a friend asked me for help. I'm a Christian. And," I said with a smile, "Bibles don't leak oil."

Tom used that last part in his column a few days later. What he didn't know was that one particular Bible had been used for target practice.

It was mid-July 2009, only a few weeks at Zondervan, and it was time to get down to brass tacks. Although lead Bible translator Doug Moo had indicated that a thorough re-translation of the NIV would take at least a year and a half, we all knew we had to get out the word that a re-translation was underway. We had to control the message and we knew the news would leak. We didn't want to appear sneaky in the wake of the TNIV re-translation disaster a few years earlier. Soon I would be engrossed in the most intense communications strategic planning process and rollout of my career, where one wrong word, here-or-there, could literally sink our effort. I am not exaggerating.

It was clear we needed to adhere to the cliché "keep your friends close and your 'enemies' (of the TNIV) closer" – James Dobson, et al. Luckily, we had two weapons - two weapons that could help ensure we could at least be heard before any missiles were sent our way. One was the new Zondervan CEO, Maureen (Moe) Girkins, who was a charmer; the other was a legend in the study and application of true Christian living, Stan Gundry. Thankfully (for me), Stan loved cars.

Gundry was an evangelical theologian, seminary professor and prolific author. We became friends in our first meeting and he was my prime go-to source when I needed to bounce-off an idea. A few days after our first meeting, he popped into my office, grinning ear-to-ear.

"You got a minute," he said.

"Sure." I got up and started to head to his office.

"No," he said. "We're going outside."

A few steps from the front of the building was his pride and joy; a mostly intact Avanti. The Avanti, born out of the demise of Studebaker and built in South Bend, Indiana, were the pugs of the auto industry – rare, ugly and so loveable. I think five were built. (Actually, just a few more.) They died a necessarily premature death but remained a novelty – kind of like a Veg-o-Matic at a flea market.

Stan loved his.

We, the Brit Neil Martin and I, had developed the communications strategy for Gerkins and Gundry to share with those most voraciously against previous re-translations of the Bible that led to the TNIV's failure. It was simple, as we knew it would have to be: too many players would be involved and we knew in order to keep everyone seemingly on the same page, the "page" had to be short and sweet. Our theme: We were going back to the roots of the original NIV, the one the G.E. layman had crusaded for in 1955 until he hit pay dirt in 1978 and flooded the Bible world, this time in a "good" way. Gerkins and Gundry would call, and as a last resort sometimes actually fly into "enemy territory" to share the intentions of the Committee on Bible Translation. They would acknowledge mistakes had been made in the past; they would ask input from the evangelical leaders and would give them a transparent platform to offer their suggestions. Critically, yet with subtlety and finesse, they would ask these dudes to hold their fire. There were enough enemies of Christianity in the world. We didn't need any friendly fire.

The Committee on Bible Translation was committed to a process where they would literally go back to square one – the original biblical texts, including those unearthed far after King James – like the Dead Sea Scrolls – and apply their most unbiased scholarship. They would reconsider the "gender neutrality" or "inclusive language" issues that had doomed the TNIV. They would listen with open ears to others in the evangelical community. But, and I saw this in the spirited fire of their lead translator Doug Moo, they would not be compromised or pushed around.

We needed a theme that everyone could agree on as we entered the process. I sat down with Neil Martin. Sometimes the best work a P.R. person can do is not actually coming up with clever catch phrases or one-liners, but rather coaxing those words out of the folks who are actually the experts in the field. "Sum up the Bible we are trying to, ah, ah," I struggled to find my own fricking words, and I was the "lauded" wordsmith.

"Jesus!" I said to myself. (Oops, there I go again).

"Neil, sum up the two or three top words surrounding the Bible we are trying to develop," I finally uttered.

Neil loved mixing it up with me; he learned from me as I learned from him. "First of all," he started, revving his engines, "we are looking for accuracy or we are dead. Secondly, we need to take this supreme accuracy and provide the greatest clarity so that people can understand the Word of God. They cannot exist without each other. If it is true to the Word but the words cannot be understood, we have failed."

I had been taking notes, underlining the words "accuracy" and "clarity". "If we said our mission with this new NIV was simply 'accuracy and clarity' and then said no more, would you have a problem, Neil?" I asked.

"No," he said with a smile. I looked around the enormous conference room Neil and I had holed ourselves up in. It was barely big enough to fit a card table. But, then again, it was just the two of us with laptops and note pads. We quickly developed our messaging to share with the team.

We met with lead translator Doug Moo in Grand Rapids to set out our communications strategy. We needed to get Doug on board before we talked with the rest of the translation team. That team was scattered across

262

the country and the world and they would soon begin their incredibly intensive and highly – perhaps grossly - scrutinized work on the most important book of all time.

"Only you can be the spokesperson on the translation, Doug," I said. "The media, our enemies -- known and unknown -- will try to get to the other members of the Committee and try and trip them up." I said. "And then we lose. I don't want to accuse your fellow Bible scholars of not being able to handle a press interview, but I need them to send all media calls to me and I will coordinate how we handle interviews and media inquiries."

An hour later, in a somewhat bigger Zondervan conference room – think the size of a studio apartment bathroom, it was Neil Martin, Doug Moo and myself with some of the greatest Bible scholars on a speaker phone.

"Please don't swear! Please don't swear!" I begged myself.

Introduced by Doug Moo, Neil Martin and I laid out the strategy. Moo would be the spokesman. All media calls, I mean all, would be directed to me. We would announce any news regarding the NIV Bible on September 1, 2009. There would be no other, absolutely no other news in the prior days.

I hesitated to share our two key themes for the new NIV – accuracy and clarity. We had told the Bible translators to basically shut up - but they deserved to know beforehand, as we say these days, the "talking points." I teed up our message and Neil Martin drove it home. He then ended our call with a typically polite admonishment an Iowan-turned-Detroiter might have fumbled: "Gentlemen, you all are scholars of the world's greatest book. We must be most cautious and please count on us to assist you in any way we can."

Again. Wow.

As we prepared for the September 1st announcement at the original NIV's "home" of Trinity Christian College in Palos Heights, just outside of Chicago, Zondervan and the Committee on Bible Translation were, well, all atwitter.

I told Neil Martin we had to "beat the shit out of Moe (our CEO Maureen Gerkins) and Doug Moo" two days prior to the press conference.

"What exactly do you mean by 'beating the shit out' of them?" Neal said.

"The day before the press conference, you and I have to be the vilest bastards. We must make their lives miserable in order to prepare them for the pressure of the press," I said. "Forget who you work for. Bludgeon them. Make them sweat. Let them know what is at stake."

This was, as we call in the craft, "media training." Neil had never been even close to it. Minutes prior to our session with the Zondervan CEO and the head of the Committee on Bible Translation, he was nervous. As Gerkins and Moo were sitting at their "mock" press settings, I sat outside with Neil. "Take my lead on the tone and aggressiveness of my questions. I plan to pummel both of them so tomorrow the press conference feels like a cake walk."

I paused for a second, always the ugly American, wondering if a Brit would understand the term "cake walk."

"You know what a cake walk is?" I asked.

Neil looked at me and rolled his eyes, "Every term you Americans use, you stole from us in one shape-or-form. Get over it."

The media training was hot and wild. We had one break, but in total the "training" went on for two hours. When we concluded, Doug Moo was visibly upset with me. Yes, we had become friends over the past two months, but even more so we didn't agree – just like I didn't agree with Neil Martin – on politics. And, we had talked about it openly. No folks, not all evangelical Christians are conservatives. Neil and Doug were liberals. Period. And great new friends. It can happen people!

"Sorry to beat you up a bit there," I said to one of the leading biblical scholars in the world.

"I wanted to get up and punch you out," the six-foot-seven Moo said.

"Good...Then maybe, just maybe, you are ready."

I went over to Zondervan CEO Moe Girkens. Both Neil Martin and I had been more kind to her in our inquisition. Not because she was a woman; but because we knew Doug Moo, the head guy in charge of translating the Bible, would be the one on trial.

"Sorry to beat you up," I said.

She quietly moved up and kissed me on the cheek. "You did well."

The next day it was high anxiety as the press conference at Trinity Christian College was beginning to start. Because of our location in the boonies outside Chicago we expected only a few members of the media to attend, but we had a slew of Christian-focused press and our "enemies" dialing in to the conference call or on-line. Unbelievably, the press conference was, almost, eventless – a new high. Really. For once in my life, I wanted no news. I wanted the Bible translators to get on with their "business" and go to work without controversy.

As we left Trinity Christian College, I could only wait. I drove to downtown Chicago to meet my wife and daughter. I checked my email. No bad news. No negative quotes from our "enemies." Just plain, "New Bible Coming" stories. When was the shit going to hit the fan?

My wife, my daughter and I needed to go out with each other. We had spent far too little time together over the past few months.

I showered and called Steve Sammons.

"It couldn't have gone better," he said. "Go out and have an extremely expensive dinner on the company."

We did. I think about $300 for sushi for three.

That night, unable to sleep while my beautiful wife was zonked out in the cushy bed, Conan O'Brien was just into his monologue. He started talking about Zondervan changing the Bible.

I stood up in bed. I didn't just "rise." I stood on the mattress in my boxers awaiting the comedian's words. I can't remember it all as I was trying to wake up my wife, but it went something like this: "They are changing the Bible to make it match the language of today. Here's an example of the changes. On the seventh day, God 'chillaxed'." I jumped in the bed like Mary Lou Retton. We had become a part of the lexicon without negativity.

Two days later I was back in my lonely existence, away from my family in Grand Rapids. We had examined all of the early press reports. It was neutral to extremely positive. Pretty sweet.

In the car, while driving the short ride to my apartment, I called the lead translator, Doug Moo. We congratulated each other. Then, as usual, I pushed the needle. "Doug, could you do me a favor?" I asked. He thought it was a serious request.

"What? Name it," he replied.

"Is there any way you could slide my name in the new Bible. It would really impress my Mom," I said, as I immediately wondered if this smart-ass kid from Iowa had gone one-inch too far.

Without pausing, Moo replied, "What are you talking about? I can assure you that "vines" is in there at least 19 times."

So let it be written; so let it be done. Crisis averted. The new NIV launched without controversy.

Thank the Lord. It was time to get back to crises in the auto industry.

Crisis Lesson Learned: Consider that your "enemies" may be making some valid points that if incorporated in your strategy and tactics just may help you avoid or mitigate a crisis. It's especially important to consider your "enemies" arguments when they are, in fact, your customers.

And, whether you're in a crisis, are launching a product, promoting a cause or rewriting the Bible, solid communications folks serve their organizations best by following three character attributes a friend shared with me: be faithful, be truthful and be decisive. Good organizations will appreciate it; organizations that don't will die sooner or later.

Chapter Thirty Eight: "Government Motors" on Fire

General Motors had forgotten, ignored or didn't give a damn about the first guiding principle of surviving a crisis – protecting the safety and or/satisfaction of your customers – when it came to the "Ignition Switch" debacle that began in early 2014. Was it a single engineer going rogue, covering his ass, or was it due to GM's culture? The latter didn't make sense to me considering how I had personally seen GM react in my dealings with them.

In early fall 2011, my colleague at FleishmanHillard, Tom Pyden, called me. Pyden was formerly a high-ranking GM PR flack who joined the PR agency and then became embedded back in GM to steer the account – a huge one for FleishmanHillard. "I want you to meet with Selim," he said. "You can help him." Selim was Selim Bingol, GM's PR chief who had been brought in by CEO Ed Whitacre to serve as his consigliore; a role Bingol had served while Whitacre was CEO of AT&T.

I met Bingol at a Starbucks in his new hometown of Grosse Pointe, the "old rich" village north of Detroit. The meeting came off like a bad blind date. Selim was sitting next to me and conversing, but his mind was elsewhere. "How'd it go," Pyden asked in a phone call minutes after we parted company. "Awful," I said. "I think he thinks I want his job."

I did; two years earlier my mentor, Steve Harris – back out of retirement as GM's PR chief again in an effort to save GM's image – was talking with me about the possibility of replacing him. It would have been a great fit as GM CEO Rick Wagoner and I were friends. Hell, the day before I quit Nardelli's Chrysler, GM co-chair Bob Lutz had called me and asked if I wanted to work for a company that "appreciated" me. Alas, the possibility of joining GM was toast when the Obama Administration fired Wagoner and replaced him with Ed Whitacre.

"I told Selim I want GM to win," I told Pyden. It was true. I bled for Ford Motor Company – helping them navigate through the biggest crisis in automotive history – and they cast me aside when they fired Jacques Nasser. My beloved Chrysler was now owned by the Italians – Fiat. I had lots of friends at GM and the company was the heart of Detroit. GM loses; Detroit and Michigan lose.

"Oh shit, Jay," Pyden said. Pyden, one of the finest gentlemen I had ever met, had the right to call me by a nickname. He was (and is) a friend. "Let me work on this."

Two weeks later we had a do-over, this time with Pyden present. We sat down in a booth at McCormick and Schmick's. I wasted little time. "Selim, let me make this clear," I said, just warming up. "I wanted your job before you got it, but it just didn't work out. I don't want your job now. I just want to help you guys win. You've got to understand something: every morning, those bastards in Dearborn (Ford) wake up and say 'what can we do to fuck GM today'."

Two days later, the Detroit News ran an excerpt from Bill Vlasic's then-up-coming book Once Upon a Car in which the New York Times reporter quoted Ford marketing chief Jim Farley, in a media scrum, saying "Fuck GM." Selim called. "You weren't kidding, were you?" "Nope," I replied. From that moment on, Selim and I were partners and friends. And the shit would soon hit the fan.

Friday, November 25, Selim called me on my cell. "I need your help," he said. "And, it probably means working over the weekend."

Earlier that day, NHTSA had opened a formal investigation into potential fires involving the battery pack of the Chevy Volt. It was, for the most part, a completely bogus ploy by the safety agency. NHTSA had crash-tested a Volt in the spring and then treated the vehicle like a kabob. It took the crushed vehicle and turned it on its side for a while, then on its roof and finally on its other side. Test and BBQ complete, the totaled Volt was delivered to a NHTSA holding area. Three weeks later the vehicle caught on fire. Had this been a gasoline-only vehicle, NHTSA would have rightfully drained the gas tank, much as junkyards do with totaled vehicles, i.e. get rid of the fuel source. Stupidly, NHTSA did not remove the Volt's primary fuel source; its battery. Again, three weeks later it started to burn. Flash forward to November – a full five months later – NHTSA decided where there is fire…we all need to smoke something. Curiously, they decided to "crash" just the Volt batteries separate from the vehicle (yes, you read that correctly); think smacking a football player on his noggin with two-by-four, but without his helmet. That'll leave a mark. It took three attempts, but finally NHTSA succeeded in getting the last battery pack to spark. No shit, Sherlock. Transportation Secretary Ray LaHood, a former Congressman, ordered an investigation of the Chevy Volt despite the fact that not one Volt in real-world service had experienced this "problem." In the world of politics we would say, Secretary LaHood had a solution just looking for a problem – and he viewed himself as the solution.

Perhaps LaHood was worried that if he did nothing and a real problem presented itself down the road he would be blamed for "protecting" GM – which at that time had the unfortunate nickname of "Government Motors" as the U.S. Government still had a large stake in the automaker from the 2009 "taxpayer" bailout. LaHood couldn't be seen playing favorites with GM after he had stepped in a pile of cow doo-doo in early 2010 when he rushed to the microphone, inserted his head up his ass and told a boatload of Toyota owners to stop driving their vehicles because of alleged "unintended sudden acceleration". That old chestnut. Days later LaHood removed his head from the southern hemisphere of his body and claimed he had "misspoke." He merely wanted Toyota owners to take heed and get to a dealership as soon as possible.

"Here's what we are thinking, Jason," Selim continued. "We're going to offer all Volt owners a free loaner while we develop a 'belts and suspenders' fix for the problem, even though there is no problem. And, if a customer wants his money back, we won't argue. And, we're going to close the plant until we have the fix."

"Wow," was all I could say. GM was following the primary guiding principle of a crisis – customer safety is paramount – and then some. Over the weekend the communications plan was fully crafted and on Monday, GM honchos Mark Reuss and Mary Barra were on the phone announcing GM's plan. At Bingol's request, I had flown into Detroit the previous day to be on-hand as the announcement was being rolled out. When I walked into GM's Corporate Communications department to meet with Selim, the GM PR team looked at me. Staffer Alan Adler, whom I had known since his days as a reporter, said it all: "Oh boy, Jason's here. I guess we do have a crisis." And then the stupidity began.

But not on GM's part. The announcement was clear and powerful. Volt owners were getting the "white glove" treatment. As Mark Reuss, the heir-apparent CEO, and Mary Barra, head of product development, outlined GM's plans and then took reporters' questions, I realized instantly: this Barra is really, really good.

Transportation's LaHood was immediately under the gun for "waiting" so long to investigate the Volt. The "safety-expert-trial-attorney-shills" of course were activated. On December 6th LaHood officially announced that the Volt was "safe to drive" as the investigation continued and GM looked for "answers." It would be an answer to a question that should have never been asked. The "fix" they developed a few months later was akin to putting a third coat of paint on a wall – the first two coats did the trick, and the third just wasted paint.

The stupidity parade had former Speaker Newt Gingrich as its Grand Marshall. Republicans – my party – gleefully had another reason to sucker punch GM in the wake of the bailout; the certainty that the "taxpayer" would lose billions in the end, the fact the unions got a sweetheart deal while creditors and GM dealers got screwed, and the fact that Chevy Volt customers – typically blue-blood liberals – received a $7,500 "taxpayer" rebate when they bought the vehicle. The Volt fires were another broom stick to shove up Joe "bin Laden is dead and General Motors is alive" Biden's ass. Interviewed on the Sean Hannity Show, Gingrich was bitch-slapping the Volt, cleverly – in his fat mind – saying, "You can't put a gun rack in a Volt."

Stop it, Newt, my sides are hurting. I was listening to the radio show driving into D.C. with my wife. "What an asshole," I told her. "What moron puts a gun rack in ANY sedan?"

That night I penned a statement for Selim Bingol to use the next day to shut up Gingrich. In my office the next morning, Selim was on the line to me. "Hey, we're starting a new blog by me later today and I wanted to get your opinion on the opening salvo. It's in your email." I opened the document, read it and barfed. It was extremely well-written and factual. However, it was defensive and stale. It explained just who "owned" GM; that it wasn't the unions as GM's detractors – again, mostly Republicans – were claiming time and time again.

I called Selim. "No offense," I said, offensively, "you can't kick-off your blog on a defensive note. It will kill it."

"Yeah," he said, "I was a little bit worried about that. Any suggestions."

"Kick Newt Gingrich in the balls," I said. "He said something really stupid about the Volt on Hannity yesterday. I wrote a statement for you last night and was going to call you, but you called first. You can do your 'who owns GM' later when you've got some street cred. I sent my "Selim" statement to Bingol. Ten minutes later he was back on the line. "I like it," he said. "I'm going to tweak it a bit to make it my style. Back to you in a few minutes.

With Selim's edits – few, but good – GM fired off the blog and Newt must have felt a pang in his ample sphincter as dozens of media outlets scooped up Selim's gem. An hour after hitting the web, a young (surprisingly Republican) Volt owner placed a video on YouTube showing his Volt with a gun rack made out of PVC tubing. He had obviously heard Gingrich's stupidity on Hannity and ran with it. The one-two punch of the Selim blog and the video were shoved in Newt's pie hole, shutting him up.

GM and its Volt came out pretty much unscathed. They had put their customers' safety and satisfaction on the front burner. Few of the tremendously loyal Volt owners actually took advantage of GM's offer of free loaner cars. Even fewer asked for GM to buy-back their Volt. In the end, where there was fire, it was a joke.

And then, GM shit the bed as it was revealed that it had put the safety and satisfaction of millions of customers dead last and at least 21 of its owners were just plain dead. In February 2014, GM announced the recall of Saturn Ions and Chevy Cobalts dating back more than a decade for replacement of the ignition switch that "at least" one engineer at GM and more than a dozen engineers at switch manufacturer Delphi knew was "not up to spec" for some eight years.

As the news exploded, the game was on, and GM was caught with its pants down. Actually its skirt. Newly-minted CEO Mary Barra, the first female to grab the brass ring in the history of the automobile industry was thrown into a blast furnace. The stupid conspiracy theorists had their "aha" moment: "Oh, I see. GM saw this coming and put a woman in charge so people would go easy on her."

Bullshit. Barra deserved to be CEO. She was smart and savvy as hell. I had seen it earlier.

As the crisis evolved from bad to potentially the worst in automotive history (more on that in a bit), I refused to comment on questions from dozens of reporters – all of which were relating GM's crisis to the Ford/Firestone tire crisis – for two reasons: one, Selim was asking me for advice; and two, I absolutely abhor PR "experts" on the outside commenting on a company's crisis when they don't know shit-from-Shinnola. In the Chevy Volt "quasi-crisis," I knew the "shit" and the "Shinnola." With this ignition switch issue, I only knew the "shit." And, it was hitting GM like a tsunami of dung.

During our tire crisis at Ford, I would wince when I saw comments from supposed PR experts grading us on our response; who was guilty, who wasn't, who sucked the most. They didn't know what we were facing on a daily basis: bogus documents, lies and innuendo. One particularly active "PR expert" on the tire situation was Jeff Caponigro, who owned his own boutique PR firm in the Detroit area. I had never met him, or at the very least, I don't remember ever meeting him. He was constantly being quoted, usually taking a dump on what we, Ford, and I were doing. Finally, I had had enough. I called his office and got his voicemail.

"Jeff," I said, "this is Jason Vines at Ford. I see you quoted all the time regarding our situation. I would like to sit down with you at your convenience and give you a behind the scenes look at what we are facing daily so that you are completely informed the next time you comment. I will move my schedule to accommodate you."

Crickets. No return call. Just more commentary from the "expert."

Fast-forward two-plus years. I am the new head of Chrysler PR. The PR agency-of-record for Chrysler is Caponigro. "What you going to do about Caponigro," my lieutenant Mike Aberlich said. "Wait," I said. I was waiting for a return call from a couple of years back. Chrysler was Caponigro's biggest account by far. I was not going to be an asshole. I had been through too much crap and I wanted to be happy, not vindictive. Just a simple "Hey, Jason, we look forward to continue working with your team." No "get down on his knees and beg forgiveness" for his comments while I was at Ford. Again, crickets. For two weeks. "Fire him," I told Mike, meaning I was firing his firm that included some talented young PR people embedded in the Chrysler PR staff. "And then, hire those people back."

Back to GM.

Two weeks before GM's first Congressional hearing regarding the ignition switch debacle, Selim was on the phone. "Any advice," he said. "You've been through this shit." Up to now, GM had been vigorously putting out CEO Mary Barra in every form of communications thinkable, apologizing profusely for the past transgressions of the "Old GM" and the humanity of the "New" post-bankruptcy GM, including a hideous video in which Barra looked like she was a prisoner at the Hanoi Hilton in 'Nam.

"Yeah," I said. "First, it has to be Mary (Barra) in the hearing. Period. Not necessarily because she's a woman, but because she's the CEO. I learned that lesson when the D.C. office idiots at Ford tried to give the House lesser executives. Speaking of being a woman, do in fact use that gem; they'll beat her up less. And please, dear God, have her dress like a woman. Not like a FOX news contributor showing her hooters; but do put her in a dress. I mean, where in the hell did she find that 'Chairman Mao' outfit she was wearing on the video you guys put out?"

Selim laughed. I wasn't done. "Before the hearing, which will probably be a joke, beat the ever-loving shit out of her. We did that to Nasser to get him ready. Make sure she only talks with facts. If she doesn't know the answer, don't make it up. And, don't let her offer any cute answer, or you're dead.

"Finally," I said, "Whatever you do, do not let GM Legal or Government Affairs run the show. They obviously need to be part of the team, but if either is making the decisions that don't put the customer first, you will be dead."

Selim listened. But he obviously couldn't convince the folks running the traps for the Congressional hearing. Mary Barra had her ass handed to her. It was so bad that the next Saturday, she and GM were parodied in the opening skit of Saturday Night Live. It's one thing to be the butt of a joke by Leno or Conan, but if you open SNL, it is never good. Within days, my friend Selim Bingol would get the same "thank you" I had received from Ford.

Will this be the worst scandal, crisis, debacle or whatever you want to call it in U.S. automotive history? Will it top the Ford/Firestone tire crisis? It might. Defective Firestone tires equipped on Ford vehicles attributed to the deaths of 271 people and countless injuries. GM's ignition switch crisis has taken only, damn, only 80 lives, and counting.

I think of my late niece Kelsey as I write these words. It only takes the snuffing of one life to destroy or at the very least, impact a family and force the surviving members to create a "new normal". The men and women of Ford Motor Company tried to find the problem for years, only to be thwarted in their efforts by Firestone. And, when they finally discovered the problem, they worked tirelessly (no pun intended) to help their customers at great treasure. In the second round of the tire crisis, they acted alone and avoided another potential crisis without a smidgeon of help from Firestone. We communicated honestly and openly at all times, always putting the safety of our customers first above all other concerns.

General Motors' engineer(s) knew from the get-go their ignition switch was not, as we say, up-to-spec. Its supplier Delphi had produced the part as specified, but the GM guys didn't like the "feel" of the switch. So they asked Delphi to change the part. GM's initial claim that Delphi had delivered a part not up to GM specifications was complete bullshit and a pitiful attempt to throw Delphi under the bus. If GM tells you to adjust something to their liking, that is the de facto "new spec." But Delphi should have known better, as well.

Was a crime committed as some have suggested? The U.S. Justice Department began a criminal investigation in the Spring of 2014. Currently, the investigation is focused on the concealment of evidence from safety regulators linked to the legal department at GM. The criminality of their actions will be determined by the courts. However, GM's ethical lapses are crystal clear. I suspect, over time, they will be costly.

By 2006, GM engineers knew they had a turd of an ignition switch. They ordered Delphi to go back to the original spec for use in vehicles going forward so that the vehicles wouldn't suddenly lose power, rendering the car's power steering, brake assist and air bags useless. And here's where the "crimes" may have occurred; two-fold. Apparently nothing was "officially" done for the potentially faulty vehicles on road prior to the change. Until February 2014. Then, GM did not change the part number in 2006 for the new switch going forward – standard practice in the industry in order to track parts. The former was a sign that GM – at least an individual or individuals – were putting their careers ahead of public safety. And it would prove deadly. Not changing the part number was the sign of a cover-up.

I didn't realize how much the failure to change the part number was so heinous until a buddy of mine, Bob Kittle, and I were shooting the shit just days before GM's second round of public flogging in D.C.; this time the Senate on July 17. Bob had been a senior executive for many years at Takata, the Japanese seat belt and air bag supplier. A comment he made jolted me. My friend, who spent 19 years on the supplier side of the business, was dumbfounded by the lack of a part number change on the switch. "Those guys (GM) were the Gestapo with part number changes," Kittle told me. "They changed part numbers all the time. If it wasn't an engineering discipline, which I felt it was, it was a purchasing trick to slip in some new term in their purchasing provisions. Every time a new part number was issued, a new purchase order was issued. And every time a new purchase order was issued, we had to go through the terms with a nit-comb because lo-and-behold, some new escape clause, warranty provision or some other 'out' that benefited GM, and not the supplier, was added."

Somebody is going to jail. Or, at least should.

Crisis Lesson Learned: You shouldn't get to pick which customers you want to protect and which ones you don't give a damn about. No one will remember the former and the latter ones can help kill your image instantly. The TREAD Act, spawned out of the Ford/Firestone tire debacle, demanded the most stringent vehicle defect reporting requirements in U.S. history. Everybody in the auto industry who monitored these defects knew exactly what was required of them. Someone, or some people at GM decided to live by their own set of rules. And people died.

Epilogue: So What Did Jesus Drive?

The truth.

Whether or not you believe that Jesus was the Christ, a prophet, an idea or complete B.S., what He stood and stands for is undeniable: the truth.

It's been the truth that has been so hard to grasp and keep ahold of for thousands of years. And today, we see individuals, organizations and governments that seem to play fast and loose with the truth and then attempt to cover up their folly.

Again, not to go all biblical on you, but lies, and equally important cover-ups, are a part of our human existence, as they say, "from the beginning." Adam and Eve lied, tried to cover it up and then God "covered them up" in a delicious irony. I guess we were set to fail as we have all worked with snakes.

How do modern organizations and their communication efforts cope with this problem that has only been magnified in our digital age where news, lies, innuendo and silliness spread around the globe in mere milliseconds?

For one, realize the importance of honest and open communications. I have said this for years: I absolutely deplore the term "spin doctor" for my craft. It says bad things about what some in PR do, and, what some expect us to do. PR people out to "spin" are nothing but liars. Period. And, just as important, leaders that leave their PR people in the dark and then expect them to clean up after the elephants by "spinning," are no better.

It all seems pretty simple: tell the truth. If you screw up, admit it. We humans are incredible beings in our ability to forgive unless you are criminal in your intent (Bernie Madoff). And think about it, we even forgive criminals if the crime is not too heinous.

From Richard Nixon to Bill Clinton to Lance Armstrong to Tiger Woods to the IRS to Brian Williams to Bill Cosby and the NFL; why is it so painfully difficult to tell the truth?

Jason H. Vines
Bio

Jason Vines, 54, is an independent communications and government affairs consultant specializing in crisis management, reputation management, brand rehabilitation, product launch and automotive issues. Vines has counseled General Motors on issues surrounding the Chevy Volt, the U.S. Government divestiture of GM stock, the revival of  GM's European operations and other corporate and product issues, including the recent recall conundrum regarding the ignition switch issue. In addition, Vines has been involved with public policy issues regarding the electrification of the nation's automobile fleet. He has also counseled a chemical client in reputational restoration, a major Native American tribe currently under attack by various agencies inside the federal U.S. Government and the U.S. auto dealers' national association (NADA) on protection of the current, independent state-based dealer franchise system.

Vines served as the top communications professional for three automakers – Nissan, Ford and Chrysler -- between 1998 and 2008. He was named "Top PR Professional" in the automotive industry in 1999, 2005 and 2006 by Automotive News, the industry's lead trade publication.
He is credited with leading some of the most memorable product launches in the automotive industry including the Chrysler 300, Jeep Grand Cherokee, Dodge Viper, Dodge Ram and the reborn Nissan 350Z.

At Chrysler, Vines successfully led the company against allegations of sudden acceleration with the Jeep Grand Cherokee. The vehicle was exonerated by the National Highway Safety Administration (NHTSA). Then, in 1997, amid some regulators and media predicting huge injury and fatality numbers among children coming in contact with deployed air bags, Vines help conceive and instituted "The Back is Where It's At," a nationwide elementary education program encouraging children 13 and under to ride safely in the back seat. The predicted crisis never materialized as 95 percent of all schools in the country used the curriculum. It is still considered one of the most impactful passenger safety programs in U.S. history.

Vines joined Nissan in 1998 as the company was on the brink of bankruptcy and in short order helped restore their image, becoming the industry comeback story just two years later. His work resulted in his first honor from Automotive News as the best in the business.

He was recruited by Ford Motor Company in early 2000 as head of global communications. Just weeks after his arrival, the Ford/Firestone tire crisis began to simmer before turning into the biggest automotive crisis in history, pitting two 100-year-old companies in a struggle for survival. Ford was eventually exonerated by NHTSA after spending more than $4B replacing Firestone tires on its customers' vehicles after Firestone refused to replace their defective tires. Vines is a Director-Emeritus of the Automotive Hall of Fame.

Mr. Vines received a Master's Degree in Labor and Industrial Relations from Michigan State University in 1984 and a B.A. with a double major in Economics and Communications/Theater from Central College in Pella, Iowa in 1982. He has been married to his wife Betsy for more than 28 years and has three children: all college graduates without college loans thanks to their parents.

Acknowledgments

A non-fiction book about the crises I faced in my career over more than 25 years – still counting, trust me – in various industries doesn't get completed and presented factually without the help of a lot of people with me in the trenches.

The first is my ultimate editor: best friend and partner for life Betsy who has gone through a tsunami with me for almost 30 years – smarter than me by 50 percent, but too stupid to leave me.

Kudos to my fabulous past executive assistants, Bonnie Ruivivar, Lynn Quigley, and especially my crisis sidekick and friend from Chrysler, Sandy Fraser.

Add to the list former Lee Iacocca speech writer Mike Morrison, former Chrysler engineering genius Mike Donoughe, Autoweek publisher Dutch Mandel, columnist Doron Levin and the amazingly creative Larry Dietz. I am blessed to have a boatload of really cool friends, many in this book, including the engineering maestro Chris Theodore.

I want to thank my publisher Barbara Terry for her faith in me and her encouragement and enthusiasm along the way. My big brother Thom, a prolific writer, gave me the courage to write this book...while asking repeatedly for a loan. (Just kidding. That's what I do. Get over it.) Marc Winston Isaac for his graphic design skills, I thank you.

Oh, and thanks to Sammy my dog who laid on my feet, keeping them warm, when I wrote sometimes past 3 o'clock in the morning.

What did Jesus drive? He drove me to tell the truth.

Index